Sam Goundar
J. Avanija
K. Reddy Madhavi
Editors

The Future of Mobile Computing

nova
science publishers
www.novapublishers.com

DOI: https://doi.org/10.52305/NQYN7463

NOTICE TO THE READER

Library of Congress Cataloging-in-Publication Data

ISBN: 979-8-89113-715-8 (hardcover)
ISBN: 979-8-89113-758-5 (e-book)

Published by Nova Science Publishers, Inc. † New York

Contents

Preface

The book "The Future of Mobile Computing," comprises 15 chapters that collectively illuminate the evolving landscape of mobile technology. Chapter 1, delves into a Systematic Literature Review of Edge Computing, and lays the groundwork for understanding the cutting-edge concepts shaping the future. Chapter 2 introduces a Taxonomy of Edge Computing, providing readers with a structured framework to navigate this transformative field. Chapter 3, deals with Edge Computing's impact on enterprises and personal tech applications. Chapter 4 explores Smart Agriculture, mobile solutions for sustainable farming practices and contributing to a greener future. Shifting the focus to hardware and design trends, Chapter 5 focuses on Emerging Trends that will shape the devices of tomorrow. Chapter 6 brings the forefront to the symbiotic connection between Artificial Intelligence and Mobile Computing, highlighting how AI significantly transforms and enhances the capabilities of mobile applications. Chapters 7 and 8 delve into Intelligent Mobile Assistants and Edge Computing Technology, respectively, exploring the power of machine learning and navigating opportunities, issues, and future trends in edge computing. Chapter 9 focuses on Sustainable Mobile Technologies, unveiling eco-friendly innovations for a more environmentally conscious mobile future. Chapter 10 examines The Application of Mobile Computing in a Smart City, where technology converges with urban planning. Privacy and security concerns are addressed in Chapter 11, offering strategies for safeguarding user data in the realm of mobile computing. Chapter 12 explores augmented and virtual reality, shaping perspectives in modern mobile computing environments. Chapters 13 and 14 delve into innovative approaches at the intersection of technology and well-being, exploring AI-embedded blockchain security for smart student monitoring and enhanced computational analysis of anxiety and sadness in the context of mobile computing and mental health. Finally, Chapter 15 navigates the Innovation Frontier, providing a comprehensive exploration of transformative technologies and their integration with mobile computing. As editors and contributors, we are excited to present this collection, hopeful that it imparts valuable insights into the dynamic future of mobile computing.

Chapter 1

A Systematic Literature Review of Edge Computing

K. G. Suma[1]
Gurram Sunitha[2,*]
Sam Goundar[3]
J. Avanija[2]
and K. Reddy Madhavi[2]
[1]School of CSE, VIT-AP, Amaravati, A.P., India
[2]Department of AI and ML, School of Computing, Mohan Babu University, Tirupati, A.P., India
[3]RMIT University, Hanoi, Vietnam

Abstract

Edge computing refers to a distributed computing paradigm that brings computational power and data storage closer to the source of data generation, enabling real-time data processing and analysis at the network edge. This chapter provides an overview of various aspects of edge computing, including its importance in the content, evolution, challenges and opportunities, performance evaluation and metrics, applications, and future directions. Each section delves into the relevant concepts, discusses significant research findings, and highlights emerging trends in the field. By understanding these different facets of edge computing, researchers and practitioners can gain valuable insights into the current state of the field and identify potential avenues for further exploration and innovation. By embracing the future directions,

---

* Corresponding Author's Email: gurramsunitha@gmail.com.

In: The Future of Mobile Computing
Editors: Sam Goundar, J. Avanija and K. Reddy Madhavi
ISBN: 979-8-89113-715-8

researchers and practitioners can contribute to the ongoing advancement of edge computing, overcome the existing challenges, and unlock its full potential. With continued research and innovation, edge computing will revolutionize industries and empower the development of transformative technologies for a connected and intelligent world.

Keywords: edge computing, literature review, challenges and opportunities, research trends, applications, future directions

Introduction: Edge Computing in Context

Edge computing is a distributed computing model that extends cloud computing capabilities to the edge of the network. It takes cloud computing abilities closer to edge. Edge devices refer to the computing devices located close to the edge of a network. These devices include smartphones, sensors, IoT, gadgets, routers, gateways, and other hardware that gather, process, and transmit data. They often play a role in collecting and managing data before sending it to be centralized systems for further analysis and storage. Edge computing distributes tasks like data collection, storage, processing, and decision-making nearer to devices that create and utilize data (Shi and Dustdar, 2016). It leverages a decentralized infrastructure composed of edge nodes, which can be devices, gateways, or micro-data centers, located in proximity to data source. These edge nodes handle data processing and storage tasks. Thereby reducing the need for transmitting data to a centralized location.

Here, edge devices play a vital role in locally processing and analyzing data. They are equipped with computational capabilities, storage, networking capabilities to execute tasks such as data filtering, preprocessing, analytics, real-time decision-making etc.

Edge computing leverages the proximity of these devices to the data source to achieve low-latency processing, reduce network traffic, and enhance overall system performance. It enables data to be processed, at the location where it is generated. Localized processing not only enhances performance but also reduces network congestion and bandwidth consumption. Moreover, it allows for offline or disconnected operation, ensuring uninterrupted service availability even in scenarios where connectivity may be limited or intermittent.

According to Gartner's report, out of the total enterprise-generated data, 75% will be processed at edge; not in a centralized location (Panetta 2020). This prediction underscores the increasing significance of edge computing in digital landscape. Edge computing applications include industrial automation, healthcare, transportation, smart cities, agriculture etc. Processing at edge devices enable faster response times, improved reliability, reduced network congestion, and enhanced data privacy, making it a fundamental technology for supporting the growing demands of edge-centric and data-intensive applications.

The concept of edge computing encompasses a wide range of technologies. These components work together to create a distributed computing environment that can handle diverse workloads and applications. It leverages the proximity of resources to the network edge. Thereby enabling real-time processing, low-latency interactions, improved efficiency, and enhanced privacy. Its adoption is driven by the growing demands of IoT, data-intensive applications, and the need for distributed computing capabilities. Further this book chapter provides deeper insights into the concepts, challenges, and potential applications of edge computing. The objective is to provide a comprehensive understanding of this transformative technology.

Edge computing can be seen as a natural evolution in response to the growing demands of modern applications and services. The concept of edge computing emerged in response to the increasing volume of technologies generating real-time data. The idea is to process data at or near the edge of the network. By doing so the limitations of cloud-centric architectures like high latency, network congestion, bandwidth constraints etc can be addressed.

Evolution of Edge Computing

It first emerged in the early years of computing, when central mainframe systems were prevalent. As technology improved and computing power became more reasonably priced, the emphasis changed to distributed computing models (Satyanarayanan 2017).

The advent of the IoT marked a significant milestone in the progression of edge computing. The volume and velocity of data generated at the network edge increased exponentially. This is due to the proliferation of interconnected devices and sensors. Traditional online computing architectures faced challenges in terms of latency, bandwidth, and scalability when dealing with this massive influx of data.

To address these challenges, researchers and industry practitioners started exploring the concept of processing data closer to its source. Thus, giving rise to transformative area of edge computing. The idea is to distribute computing resources to the network edge. Processing data at the location where it has been generated and consumed enables faster data processing, reduced latency, and improved application performance.

Challenges and Opportunities

Edge computing distributes computing resources across multiple edge devices, allowing for local processing and decision-making at the network edge. It emphasizes performing computing tasks as close as possible to the data source. Thus, reducing latency (Cao et al., 2018). Its advantages are significant, but it also presents several challenges. It is crucial to address multiple challenges for the reliable deployment and adoption of edge computing solutions. Example issues are network connectivity, scalability, security, data management, standardization, edge intelligence etc. Overcoming these challenges will unlock the full potential of edge computing, enabling efficient and intelligent applications across various industries (Olaniyan et al., 2018).

Network Connectivity and Bandwidth

Ensuring robust and reliable network connectivity is one of the primary challenges in edge computing. Edge devices, edge servers, and the cloud infrastructure need to communicate seamlessly and efficiently. However, the performance and reliability of edge computing systems are impacted by network limitations such as low bandwidth, network congestion, and intermittent connectivity. Innovations in networking technologies such as 5G and Wi-Fi 6 are expected to address some of these challenges and provide higher bandwidth, lower latency, and improved network reliability for edge computing environments.

Scalability and Resource Constraints

Edge computing involves a distributed architecture with numerous edge devices and servers. Scaling these resources to handle varying workloads and accommodate increasing numbers of connected devices can be challenging (Shi et al., 2016). Resource constraints in terms of computational power, storage capacity, network connectivity, and energy efficiency need to be managed effectively. Techniques such as dynamic resource allocation, load balancing, and efficient utilization of resources can address scalability and resource constraints in edge computing.

Security and Privacy

The distributed nature of data processing and storage introduces novel security concerns in edge computing. This field involves distributed and heterogeneous devices. Thus, securing edge networks and mitigating potential vulnerabilities are paramount to building trustworthy and resilient edge computing systems (Mukherjee et al., 2020). Data traffic between edge devices, edge servers, and cloud infrastructure needs to be secure to protect sensitive information. Secured communication is crucial in mitigating security and privacy risks in edge computing. Researchers are exploring robust security mechanisms, privacy-preserving techniques, and trust management frameworks towards tackling this challenge.

Data Management and Analytics

Huge volumes of data are produced by edge devices, and this data needs to be efficiently managed and analysed. At the edge, there are ample challenges with data storage, data quality, data integration, and data analytics (Nayak et al., 2022). Traditional data management techniques may not be suitable for edge computing due to resource constraints and limited processing capabilities. Developing efficient data management and analytics frameworks tailored for edge computing environments is crucial for deriving meaningful insights and supporting real-time decision-making.

Standardization and Interoperability

As edge computing evolves, standardization and interoperability become essential for seamless integration of diverse edge devices, servers, and cloud infrastructure. Lack of standardized protocols, interfaces, and frameworks can hinder interoperability and hinder the development of a unified edge computing ecosystem (Douch et al., 2022). Common standards should be established. Compatibility and interoperability should be ensured across edge computing deployments.

Resource Management and Optimization

Edge resource management and optimization refer to the techniques and strategies employed to efficiently allocate, utilize, and optimize computing resources in edge computing environments. Developing efficient algorithms for resource management tasks such as task offloading, dynamic allocation, provisioning and adaptation, network-aware management etc is required to cope up with dynamic nature of edge.

Performance Evaluation and Metrics

With the increasing adoption of edge computing across various domains, it becomes essential to develop reliable metrics and evaluation methodologies to measure the performance of edge architectures, algorithms, and applications. This article provides an in-depth exploration of performance evaluation and metrics in edge computing, discussing the key aspects, challenges, and emerging trends in this field.

Performance Metrics for Edge Computing

A set of complex metrics are required to measure and evaluate different aspects of edge computing system behavior. Such metrics shall provide insights into the system's responsiveness, scalability, resource utilization, energy efficiency, and quality of service (Aslanpour et al., 2020). Some commonly used performance metrics in edge computing are discussed below.

- Latency: Latency is a critical metric that measures the delay between a request and the corresponding response in edge computing systems. Low latency is essential for time-sensitive applications such as remote surgery, telemedicine and remote healthcare, finance trading, smart grid and energy management, emergency response and public safety etc.
- Throughput: Throughput refers to the rate at which data can be processed or transmitted in edge computing systems. It quantifies the system's capacity to handle a large volume of data efficiently. Higher throughput ensures faster data processing and improved system performance.
- Reliability: Reliability assesses the system's ability to consistently deliver services without disruptions or failures. It takes into account factors such as fault tolerance, redundancy, and failover mechanisms (Jain and Smaranika, 2019). High reliability is crucial for mission-critical applications to ensure uninterrupted operation.
- Scalability: Scalability measures how well a system manages more devices, users, and data without slowing down. It evaluates how well the edge infrastructure can adapt to changing workloads and resource demands.
- Resource Utilization: Efficient and effective utilization of available resources is critical in an edge computing system as it supports time-sensitive applications. It involves maximizing the usage of computational resources, storage capacity, network bandwidth, and other system resources to achieve optimal performance, minimize wastage, and ensure cost-effectiveness. Optimal resource utilization ensures efficient use of available resources, minimizing wastage and maximizing system performance.

Benchmarking in Edge Computing

Benchmarking is an essential practice in performance evaluation, providing standardized procedures and datasets for comparing and evaluating the performance of edge computing systems. The distributed and heterogeneous nature of edge environment presents unique challenges to the design of benchmarks for edge computing. Researchers are developing benchmark suites that encompass various edge computing components, including edge devices, edge servers, and network connectivity, to capture the performance characteristics comprehensively (Hao et al., 2018).

Benchmarking also involves defining realistic workloads that simulate real-world scenarios and application requirements. These workloads help evaluate the system's performance under different conditions, such as varying data volumes, arrival rates, and processing demands. Realistic workload generation techniques, such as trace-based approaches or synthetic workload generators, are employed to ensure accurate performance evaluations.

Furthermore, benchmarking frameworks consider the diversity of edge computing applications and their specific requirements. For example, benchmarks may focus on latency-sensitive applications like video streaming, latency-insensitive applications like batch processing, or a combination of both. This approach enables targeted performance evaluation based on the application domain and its associated metrics.

Simulation and Modeling in Performance Evaluation

Simulation and modeling techniques are widely used in performance evaluation of edge computing systems. Simulations allow researchers to emulate complex edge architectures and analyze their performance under different conditions. They provide a cost-effective and controlled environment for testing various configurations, algorithms, and workload scenarios. Simulation frameworks like CloudSim, iFogSim, and EdgeCloudSim have been developed specifically for edge computing research (Sonmez et al., 2018; Gupta et al., 2017).

Modeling, on the other hand, involves creating mathematical or analytical models that capture the behavior and performance characteristics of edge computing systems. Models can be used to predict system performance, optimize resource allocation, and evaluate different design choices. Analytical models, queuing models, and stochastic models are commonly used to analyze and optimize various aspects of edge computing performance.

Challenges in Performance Evaluation

Edge environement is inherently distributed and dynamic in nature. It presents several challenges in terms of performance evaluation. Some key challenges are discussed below.

- Heterogeneity: Edge computing encompasses diverse devices, networks, and software platforms, leading to heterogeneity in performance characteristics. Developing evaluation methodologies that consider this heterogeneity and provide accurate performance insights is a challenge.
- Scalability: Evaluating scalability of edge computing systems is challenged by dynamic nature of edge networks. Scaling the evaluation methodologies to capture large-scale edge deployments is a significant challenge.
- Realistic Workload Generation: Generating realistic workloads that capture the diversity of edge computing applications, data volumes, and processing demands is a complex task. Workload generation techniques should accurately represent real-world scenarios to ensure meaningful performance evaluations.
- Dynamic Resource Allocation: Edge computing involves dynamic resource allocation to optimize performance and energy efficiency. Developing evaluation methodologies that capture dynamic resource allocation strategies and their impact on system performance is a research challenge.

Summary

Performance evaluation and metrics are essential components of edge computing research, enabling the assessment and optimization of system performance. This article discussed the key performance metrics, benchmarking approaches, simulation and modeling techniques, and the challenges associated with performance evaluation in edge computing (Aslanpour et al., 2020). By addressing these challenges and adopting comprehensive evaluation methodologies, researchers and practitioners can advance the field of edge computing, optimize system performance, and drive innovation in various application domains.

Research Trends in Edge Computing

Due to its ability to meet the growing demands of data-intensive and time-sensitive applications, edge computing has garnered significant attention. As a result, researchers worldwide are actively investigating various aspects of edge computing, including architectural design, resource management, security, data analytics, and application development. These research endeavors aim to push the boundaries of edge computing and capitalize on its promises for enhanced performance, scalability, and efficiency.

Convergence of Edge and Artificial Intelligence

One prominent research trend in edge computing is integration of AI at network edge. Researchers are exploring ways to enable intelligent decision-making, predictive analytics, and real-time analytics directly at the edge (Zhou et al., 2019; Harth et al., 2018). This can be achieved by deploying lightweight AI models and algorithms on edge devices.

Edge Computing for IoT

IoT is a key domain where edge computing plays a vital role. Many customized edge computing solutions have been developed using IoT, enabling local analytics, at the edge (Chakraborty et al., 2023). Edge-enabled IoT architectures, edge-based data management, and edge analytics techniques have emerged as key research areas to support the massive-scale deployment and efficient operation of IoT systems.

Edge computing brings computational capabilities nearer to IoT devices. In smart homes, it can enable intelligent automation, energy management, and enhanced security by processing sensor data locally (Kong et al., 2022). Edge computing also enables real-time data analysis in transportation systems, enabling intelligent traffic management and autonomous vehicles.

Edge-Cloud Collaboration and Integration

Cloud computing and edge computing are complementary paradigms in the world of computing. Each serves specific purposes and addresses distinct requirements. Edge-cloud collaboration allows for the efficient utilization of resources (Duan et al., 2020). This collaboration enables computationally intensive tasks to be relocated to cloud while maintaining real-time, low-latency processing at the edge. Developing effective frameworks and mechanisms for edge-cloud collaboration is vital for achieving optimal resource utilization and performance in edge computing deployments.

Energy Optimization in Edge Computing

Energy optimization has gained attention as a crucial aspect of edge computing research (Jiang et al., 2020). Researchers have explored energy-efficient strategies, including task scheduling, dynamic power management, and energy-aware resource allocation, to minimize energy consumption in edge devices. Such efforts are targeted to enhance edge computing systems sustainability and longevity; While addressing the resource constraints and limited power availability at the edge.

Federated Learning and Edge Intelligence

Federated learning empowers edge computing by enabling collaborative and privacy-preserving model training on distributed edge devices. It leverages the computational capabilities of edge devices and utilizes their local data while preserving data privacy (Nguyen et al., 2021). Investigating federated learning approaches that allow edge devices to collaboratively train and improve machine learning models while preserving data privacy is of utmost importance.

Edge Computing for 5G and Beyond

Another key research area focuses on the seamless integration and collaboration between edge computing and the telecommunication technologies 5G/6G networks, blockchain (Bhat et al., 2020; Aswathy et al., 2021). Researchers are investigating how edge computing can complement and synergize with these technologies to deliver novel capabilities and enable new use cases. In the 5G/6G telecommunications landscape, edge computing promises efficient network traffic control, distributed and collaborative intelligence, ultra-low latency, high-bandwidth connectivity, and network cost optimization (Alawadhi et al., 2023).

Summary

Research in edge computing is advancing rapidly, driven by the need for real-time, distributed computing capabilities at the network edge. This introduction has provided a glimpse into the current research trends in edge computing, highlighting the integration of AI/ML, synergy with other technologies, security and privacy concerns, resource management, and energy efficiency. By staying at the forefront of these research trends, researchers and practitioners can shape the future of edge computing, unlocking its full potential.

Applications of Edge Computing

This section explores various domains where edge computing finds practical applications and showcases its potential benefits.

Video Analytics and Surveillance

Edge computing offers significant advantages in video analytics and surveillance applications. Edge computing reduces latency and bandwidth requirements by processing video data near video sources (Chen et al., 2019). This enables real-time video analysis, object detection, facial recognition, and event detection. Edge computing in video surveillance allows for immediate response to security threats, proactive monitoring, and efficient utilization of network resources.

Smart Cities

Edge computing is a key enabler of smart city initiatives. Sensors, cameras and IoT devices may be installed at various corners of the city to collect real-time data. By deploying edge devices and servers throughout the city, edge computing facilitates real-time data analytics, and decision-making at the network edge. Edge computing supports various smart city applications such as quality lifestyle, sustainable energy generation, smart water management, environmental monitoring, public safety (Zhou et al., 2022). Localized edge computing resources reduce the reliance on centralized cloud infrastructure and enable efficient data processing and response in time-critical scenarios.

Augmented Reality (AR) and Virtual Reality (VR)

Edge computing has significant implications for AR and VR applications (Lehman et al., 2021; Mehrabi et al., 2021). By offloading computational tasks to edge servers, AR and VR experiences can benefit from reduced latency, improved responsiveness, and higher-quality graphics rendering. Edge computing enables real-time content delivery, object recognition, and spatial mapping, enhancing the overall user experience in AR and VR applications. This is particularly beneficial for gaming, training simulations, remote collaboration, and immersive experiences.

Healthcare

Edge computing has transformative potential in the healthcare domain. Edge computing enables real-time monitoring, personalized healthcare, and remote patient care by processing medical data at edge. Edge devices can collect and process data from wearable sensors, monitoring vital signs, and analyzing patient data locally (Abdellatif et al., 2019). This enables timely detection of health abnormalities, proactive healthcare interventions, and reduced dependency on centralized healthcare infrastructure.

Energy Management

Edge computing offers promising applications in energy management systems. Deploying edge devices and sensors in energy grids enables monitoring, control of energy generation, distribution, and consumption. Edge analytics can optimize energy usage, detect anomalies, and enable demand response mechanisms (Liu et al., 2019). Energy management systems can be enabled to respond quickly to changes in demand, incorporate renewable energy sources efficiently, and reduce energy wastage.

Edge Gaming

Edge computing provides exciting opportunities in the gaming industry. By leveraging edge servers, game developers can offload computational tasks, reduce latency, and enhance the multiplayer gaming experience (Spinelli et al., 2022). Edge computing enables real-time rendering, fast content delivery, and seamless gameplay across devices. Edge gaming also supports cloud gaming services, where games are streamed and processed at the edge, reducing the need for powerful gaming hardware on the user's end.

Autonomous Vehicles

Edge computing is instrumental in enabling autonomous vehicles to make real-time decisions. By processing sensor data locally, edge computing reduces response times and ensures the safety and efficiency of autonomous driving systems (McEnroe et al., 2022, Qiu et al., 2022).

Telecommunications

Edge computing is being adopted in the telecommunications industry to support low-latency applications such as online gaming, remote surgery, high-frequency trading, and video conferencing and telepresence (Song et al., 2022). Edge computing and 5G/6G are closely intertwined and complementary technologies that have the potential to revolutionize the way data is processed, transmitted, and utilized in the digital era.

Precision Agriculture

Edge devices can collect a wealth of agricultural data regarding soil conditions, weather patterns, crop growth, and livestock health. This data is processed locally at the edge, allowing for real-time analysis and actionable insights. By applying advanced analytics and machine learning algorithms, farmers can make informed decisions on irrigation, fertilization, pesticide application, and disease management, optimizing resource usage, reducing waste, and maximizing crop yields (O'Grady et al., 2019).

Edge computing also offers significant benefits in livestock management. By deploying edge devices equipped with sensors and wearables, farmers can continuously monitor the health, behavior, and location of individual animals. This enables early detection of diseases, identification of potential breeding issues, and timely intervention in case of emergencies. With edge computing, livestock farmers can improve animal welfare, optimize feeding regimes, and enhance overall productivity.

Summary

The challenges posed by data-intensive and time-sensitive applications are the reason for the evolution of edge computing. Its foundational concepts, including proximity, decentralization, heterogeneity, and edge analytics, enable low-latency processing, optimized bandwidth usage, and enhanced privacy and security. By adhering to key principles such as latency reduction, bandwidth optimization, resilience, and data privacy, edge computing offers a scalable and flexible computing model with diverse applications across various domains.

Implications of Edge Computing on Society

This section explores the various implications that edge computing has on society, encompassing areas such as connectivity, privacy, sustainability, healthcare, and smart cities. We may better prepare for the societal changes brought about by understanding the implications of the widespread adoption of edge computing.

One of the primary implications of edge computing on society is the provision of enhanced connectivity and ubiquitous services. This enhances user experiences, enables seamless interactions with digital services, and fosters the growth of emerging technologies. Improved connectivity empowers individuals, businesses, and communities to access and utilize advanced applications and services, bridging the digital divide and promoting digital inclusivity (Shanthakumar et al., 2023).

With the proliferation of edge devices and the collection of vast amounts of personal and sensitive data at the edge, privacy and data protection become critical concerns. Edge computing raises critical questions about data ownership, consent, and security as it moves computing capabilities closer to data sources. Safeguarding privacy in edge computing environments requires robust privacy-preserving mechanisms, secure data transmission protocols, and transparent data governance frameworks to protect individuals' rights and ensure compliance with privacy regulations (Mogilevskaia et al., 2022).

Edge computing has the potential to contribute to environmental sustainability (Arroba et al., 2023). Localized processing at the edge also enables energy-efficient operations, as edge devices can be optimized to operate at lower power levels, prolonging battery life and reducing overall energy consumption. These sustainable practices align with global efforts to reduce carbon footprints and promote eco-friendly technologies (Li et al., 2018).

The implications of edge computing on society are far-reaching, encompassing enhanced connectivity, privacy challenges, environmental sustainability, healthcare transformation, and the development of smart cities. These implications highlight the transformative power of edge computing in various domains, impacting individuals, businesses, and communities. Understanding and addressing these implications are crucial to harness the full potential of edge computing while ensuring privacy, security, sustainability, and societal well-being.

Conclusion and Future Directions

Edge computing has witnessed significant advancements in recent years, shaping the way data is processed, analyzed, and utilized at the edge of the network. Through a systematic exploration of the various topics related to edge computing, this article has provided a comprehensive overview of the field. We have discussed the evolution and concepts of edge computing, highlighted its key components and architecture, examined the challenges and opportunities it presents, explored the applications, identified emerging research trends, explored performance evaluation and metrics, and outlined future directions.

From the convergence of edge computing with artificial intelligence to the integration of edge and cloud resources, numerous exciting research avenues are on the horizon. Ensuring security and privacy, enhancing performance evaluation methodologies, and leveraging edge intelligence are crucial areas for further investigation. Additionally, federated learning at the edge and the collaboration between edge and cloud infrastructure offer promising opportunities for future exploration.

Edge computing finds diverse applications across various domains, revolutionizing the way data is processed, analyzed, and utilized. From IoT and video surveillance to smart cities, healthcare, and gaming, edge computing enables real-time, low-latency applications with improved efficiency and enhanced user experiences. Embracing edge computing technology opens up new avenues for innovation and transformative solutions in numerous industries.

By embracing these future directions, researchers and practitioners can contribute to the ongoing advancement of edge computing, overcome the existing challenges, and unlock its full potential. Edge computing holds tremendous promise in enabling real-time applications, improving efficiency, and facilitating intelligent decision-making at the edge. With continued research and innovation, edge computing will revolutionize industries and empower the development of transformative technologies for a connected and intelligent world.

Disclaimer

None.

References

Abdellatif, Alaa Awad, Amr Mohamed, Carla Fabiana Chiasserini, Mounira Tlili, and Aiman Erbad. "Edge computing for smart health: Context-aware approaches, opportunities, and challenges." *IEEE Network* 33, no. 3 (2019): 196-203.

Alawadhi, Abdulwadood, Abdullah Almogahed, and Etidal Azrag. "Towards Edge Computing for 6G Internet of Everything: Challenges and Opportunities." In *2023 1st International Conference on Advanced Innovations in Smart Cities* (ICAISC), pp. 1-6. IEEE, 2023.

Arroba, Patricia, Rajkumar Buyya, Román Cárdenas, José L. Risco-Martín, and José M. Moya. "*Sustainable Edge Computing: Challenges and Future Directions*." arXiv preprint arXiv:2304.04450 (2023).

Aslanpour, Mohammad S., Sukhpal Singh Gill, and Adel N. Toosi. "Performance evaluation metrics for cloud, fog and edge computing: A review, taxonomy, benchmarks and standards for future research." *Internet of Things* 12 (2020): 100273.

Aswathy, S. U., Amit Kumar Tyagi, and Shabnam Kumari. "The Future of Edge Computing with Blockchain Technology: Possibility of Threats, Opportunities, and Challenges."

Recent Trends in Blockchain for Information Systems Security and Privacy (2021): 261-292.

Bhat, Showkat Ahmad, Ishfaq Bashir Sofi, and Chong-Yung Chi. "Edge computing and its convergence with blockchain in 5G and beyond: Security, challenges, and opportunities." *IEEE Access* 8 (2020): 205340-205373.

Cao, Jie, Quan Zhang, Weisong Shi, Jie Cao, Quan Zhang, and Weisong Shi. "Challenges and opportunities in edge computing." *Edge Computing: A Primer* (2018): 59-70.

Chakraborty, Sanjay, and Lopamudra Dey. "Edge Computing with Internet of Things (IoT) and Data Analysis." In *Computing for Data Analysis: Theory and Practices*, pp. 51-73. Singapore: Springer Nature Singapore, 2023.

Chen, Jianguo, Kenli Li, Qingying Deng, Keqin Li, and S. Yu Philip. "Distributed deep learning model for intelligent video surveillance systems with edge computing." *IEEE Transactions on Industrial Informatics* (2019).

Douch, Salmane, Mohamed Riduan Abid, Khalid Zine-Dine, Driss Bouzidi, and Driss Benhaddou. "Edge computing technology enablers: A systematic lecture study." *IEEE Access* 10 (2022): 69264-69302.

Duan, Qiang, Shangguang Wang, and Nirwan Ansari. "Convergence of networking and cloud/edge computing: Status, challenges, and opportunities." *IEEE Network* 34, no. 6 (2020): 148-155.

Gupta, Harshit, Amir Vahid Dastjerdi, Soumya K. Ghosh, and Rajkumar Buyya. "iFogSim: A toolkit for modeling and simulation of resource management techniques in the Internet of Things, Edge and Fog computing environments." *Software: Practice and Experience* 47, no. 9 (2017): 1275-1296.

Hao, Tianshu, Yunyou Huang, Xu Wen, Wanling Gao, Fan Zhang, Chen Zheng, Lei Wang et al. "Edge AIBench: towards comprehensive end-to-end edge computing benchmarking." In *Benchmarking, Measuring, and Optimizing: First Bench Council International Symposium*, Bench 2018, Seattle, WA, USA, December 10-13, 2018, Revised Selected Papers 1, pp. 23-30. Springer International Publishing, 2019.

Harth, Natascha, Christos Anagnostopoulos, and Dimitrios Pezaros. "Predictive intelligence to the edge: impact on edge analytics." *Evolving Systems* 9 (2018): 95-118.

Jain, Kusumlata, and Smaranika Mohapatra. "Taxonomy of edge computing: Challenges, opportunities, and data reduction methods." *Edge Computing: From Hype to Reality* (2019): 51-69.

Jiang, Congfeng, Tiantian Fan, Honghao Gao, Weisong Shi, Liangkai Liu, Christophe Cérin, and Jian Wan. "Energy aware edge computing: A survey." *Computer Communications* 151 (2020): 556-580.

Kong, Linghe, Jinlin Tan, Junqin Huang, Guihai Chen, Shuaitian Wang, Xi Jin, Peng Zeng, Muhammad Khan, and Sajal K. Das. "Edge-computing-driven internet of things: A survey." *ACM Computing Surveys* 55, no. 8 (2022): 1-41.

Lehman, Sarah M., and Chiu C. Tan. "Leveraging Edge Computing for Mobile Augmented Reality." *Fog/Edge Computing for Security, Privacy, and Applications* (2021): 327-353.

Li, Wei, Ting Yang, Flavia C. Delicato, Paulo F. Pires, Zahir Tari, Samee U. Khan, and Albert Y. Zomaya. "On enabling sustainable edge computing with renewable energy resources." *IEEE communications magazine* 56, no. 5 (2018): 94-101.

Liu, Yi, Chao Yang, Li Jiang, Shengli Xie, and Yan Zhang. "Intelligent edge computing for IoT-based energy management in smart cities." *IEEE network* 33, no. 2 (2019): 111-117.

McEnroe, Patrick, Shen Wang, and Madhusanka Liyanage. "A survey on the convergence of edge computing and AI for UAVs: Opportunities and challenges." *IEEE Internet of Things Journal* 9, no. 17 (2022): 15435-15459.

Mehrabi, Abbas, Matti Siekkinen, Teemu Kämäräinen, and Antti yl̈-J̈ski. "Multi-tier cloudvr: Leveraging edge computing in remote rendered virtual reality." *ACM Transactions on Multimedia Computing, Communications, and Applications* (TOMM) 17, no. 2 (2021): 1-24.

Mogilevskaia, Iliana. "*Security and privacy challenges in Edge Computing*." Master's thesis, University of South-Eastern Norway, 2022.

Mukherjee, Mithun, Rakesh Matam, Constandinos X. Mavromoustakis, Hao Jiang, George Mastorakis, and Mian Guo. "Intelligent edge computing: Security and privacy challenges." *IEEE Communications Magazine* 58, no. 9 (2020): 26-31.

Nayak, Sabuzima, Ripon Patgiri, Lilapati Waikhom, and Arif Ahmed. "A review on edge analytics: Issues, challenges, opportunities, promises, future directions, and applications." *Digital Communications and Networks* (2022).

Nguyen, Dinh C., Ming Ding, Quoc-Viet Pham, Pubudu N. Pathirana, Long Bao Le, Aruna Seneviratne, Jun Li, Dusit Niyato, and H. Vincent Poor. "Federated learning meets blockchain in edge computing: Opportunities and challenges." *IEEE Internet of Things Journal* 8, no. 16 (2021): 12806-12825.

O'Grady, M. J., David Langton, and G. M. P. O'Hare. "Edge computing: A tractable model for smart agriculture?" *Artificial Intelligence in Agriculture* 3 (2019): 42-51.

Olaniyan, Richard, Olamilekan Fadahunsi, Muthucumaru Maheswaran, and Mohamed Faten Zhani. "Opportunistic edge computing: Concepts, opportunities and research challenges." *Future Generation Computer Systems* 89 (2018): 633-645.

Panetta, Kasey. "*Gartner Top 10 Strategic Predictions for 2021 and Beyond*." 2020 Oct.

Qiu, Tie, Jiancheng Chi, Xiaobo Zhou, Zhaolong Ning, Mohammed Atiquzzaman, and Dapeng Oliver Wu. "Edge computing in industrial internet of things: Architecture, advances and challenges." *IEEE Communications Surveys & Tutorials* 22, no. 4 (2020): 2462-2488.

Satyanarayanan, Mahadev. "The emergence of edge computing." *Computer 50*, no. 1 (2017): 30-39.

Shanthakumar, Chandana Sai Thondebhavi, Neha Harish, and Anandi Giridharan. "Internet of Things and Edge Computing for Real Time Applications." In *2023 International Conference on Intelligent and Innovative Technologies in Computing, Electrical and Electronics (IITCEE)*, pp. 1137-1141. IEEE, 2023.

Shi, Weisong, Dustdar, Schahram. "The Promise of Edge Computing." *Computer 49*, no. 13 (2016):78-81.

Shi, Weisong, Jie Cao, Quan Zhang, Youhuizi Li, and Lanyu Xu. "Edge computing: Vision and challenges." *IEEE internet of things journal* 3, no. 5 (2016): 637-646.

Song, Zhengyu, Xintong Qin, Yuanyuan Hao, Tianwei Hou, Jun Wang, and Xin Sun. "A comprehensive survey on aerial mobile edge computing: Challenges, state-of-the-art, and future directions." *Computer Communications* 191 (2022): 233-256.

Sonmez, Cagatay, Atay Ozgovde, and Cem Ersoy. "Edgecloudsim: An environment for performance evaluation of edge computing systems." *Transactions on Emerging Telecommunications Technologies* 29, no. 11 (2018): e3493.

Spinelli, Francesco, Antonio Bazco-Nogueras, and Vincenzo Mancuso. "Edge gaming: A greening perspective." *Computer Com*munications 192 (2022): 89-105.

Zhou, MengChu, Mohammad Mehedi Hassan, and Andrzej Goscinski. "Emerging edge-of-things computing for smart cities: Recent advances and future trends." *Information Sciences* 600 (2022): 442-445.

Zhou, Zhi, Xu Chen, En Li, Liekang Zeng, Ke Luo, and Junshan Zhang. "Edge intelligence: Paving the last mile of artificial intelligence with edge computing." *Proceedings of the IEEE* 107, no. 8 (2019): 1738-1762.

Chapter 2

A Taxonomy of Edge Computing

J. Avanija[1,*]
Sam Goundar[2]
Gurram Sunitha[1]
K. Reddy Madhavi[1]
Viswaksena Balaji[3]
and Palagiri Tharun Sai Reddy[4]
[1]Department of AI and ML, School of Computing, Mohan Babu University, Tirupati, A.P, India
[2]RMIT University, Hanoi, Vietnam
[3]University of Limerick, Limerick, Ireland
[4]Department of CSE, Sree Vidyanikethan Engineering College, Tirupati, A.P., India

Abstract

Edge Computing is termed as an important paradigm utilized to address the problems related to latency, bandwidth, and privacy. It is required to create a taxonomy that offers a thorough understanding of the various aspects and components of edge computing . This chapter focuses on the taxonomy of edge computing that captures its various aspects including deployment models, application domains, infrastructure, and services. The chapter also discusses the components such as edge servers, edge networks, edge analytics, and edge devices. The range of edge computing-enabled applications discussed in the chapter include as Internet of Things, autonomous driving, augmented reality, video surveillance, and more. By providing the systematic organization of edge

[*] Corresponding Author's Email: avans75@yahoo.co.in.

In: The Future of Mobile Computing
Editors: Sam Goundar, J. Avanija and K. Reddy Madhavi
ISBN: 979-8-89113-715-8

computing concepts, the taxonomy helps researchers, decision-makers to navigate the landscape of edge computing effectively (Varghese et al., 2016). It facilitates better understanding of different elements of edge computing and their relationship. It facilitates a better understanding of the relationships and interdependencies between different elements of edge computing, fostering knowledge sharing, collaboration, and innovation. This chapter provides an discussion on the taxonomy of edge computing, offering a structured framework for comprehending the various dimensions and elements of this evolving technique.

Keywords: Real-time data processing, low-latency communication, local data analytics, faster decision-making, reduced latency, IoT deployments, industrial automation, remote patient monitoring

Introduction

Edge computing represents a shift in the distributed computing, also strategically relocating the data storage and also computational will have the capabilities to closer of the sources where the data will be originates from the cloud. This innovation will redefine the conventional cloud model by the decentralizing of computing power, thar will be helps in bringing it nearer to the edge of the network, precisely where data will be generated (Vora et al., 2017).

This of the evolution a departure in the form that traditional centralized cloud architecture, aiming to the minimize of the data will be transit between the distances and enhance the

efficiency of data processing and storage at the data's point of creation. This will also improve the performance of the system and it will also reduce the usage of bandwidth (Cao et al., 2020).

Also, edge computing can be used as a method to optimize cloud computing systems. Edge can be the form of any device used for computing and can also be used as a network resource. Moreover, it is easy to expand the edge computing paradigm from individual to enterprise-wide applications. Edge computing can get around the limitations of conventional cloud computing models by processing data locally.

Applications that use real-time Applications such as internet connectivity, traffic monitoring, and surveillance that need prompt responses, which can be hindered by latency and mobile-related issues. Edge computing relocates processing to network's edge, and effectively addresses these application requirements. The issues due to cloud computing can be resolved using mobile-edge computing, fog computing, and edge-server model. A diverse range of technologies, components, and entities are included in edge computing. This chapter introduces the taxonomy of edge computing in terms of edge devices, infrastructure, edge services, and applications.

Background of Edge Computing

Being edge computing close to the source of the data can result in significant business benefits such as faster insights, faster response times, and better bandwidth availability (Jain et al., 2019). Gartner predicts that by 2025, 75% of data processing will occur outside of a traditional data center or the cloud. Massive amounts of data have been generated as a result of the rapid expansion and increasing computing power of IoT devices. Furthermore, as the number of mobile devices connected to 5G networks grows, there will be an increase in the volume of data.

Transmitting all the device-generated data to a centralised data center leads to issues related to latency and bandwidth. Edge computing, which processes and analyses data closer to the point of creation, is a more efficient substitute. In the past, automation and speeding up innovation through the creation of useful data insights was the potential of cloud computing and artificial intelligence (AI). However, network and infrastructure capabilities have not kept up with connected devices' ability to produce data at a scale and in a complexity never before seen. Edge computing makes it possible to analyse data more quickly and thoroughly, resulting in deeper insights, quicker responses, and improved customer experiences.

Characteristics and Paradigms of Edge Computing

Edge computing in its core, rechanges the traditional centralized computing paradigm by the changing of in computational resources be like the closer to the points of data in the generation of the edge. Its essence lies in the reducing of the distance that will be in data must also be in travel of minimizing latency, and also optimizing bandwidth usage. This proximity sensors enable the fundamental shifts in how the data will be processed, fostering a decentralized in the architecture distributed of the across various edge devices, servers, and network infrastructure. This distributed nature enhances scalability, fault tolerance, and resource utilization, by providing a robust foundation for a multitude of applications.

One of the main traits of edge computing is the ability to significantly less latency. By the processing of the data closer to its origin that will get out of the edge, it will also minimizes the time taken for the data to traverse from the edge devices to the centralized data centers and also back. This feature will help us for the instrumental in the applications of requiring in the real-time or the near-real-time responses, such as IoT devices and, autonomous vehicles, and in the industrial automation systems. This will enable the enable the delivery of timely responses in the critical of enhancing user for the experience of the edge and enabling swift decision-making in various domains. The tasks of the network administrators will be made easy without traversing the entire Wide Area Networks using the mobility services. Real-time analytics and big data analytics can be executed with enhanced accuracy and scalability. Monitoring of the IoT-based applications and Machine Learning pipeline becomes easier through this characteristic of edge computing Figure 1 represents the characteristics of edge computing.

The next important characteristic is provided through the support extended for mobility in edge computing. This characteristic is rendered through the LISP (Locator ID Separator) protocol which provides direct communication with mobile devices by implementing the distributed directory system. The mobility support is extended through the LISP by the process of decoupling the host and location identity. This characteristic is termed a key principle in edge computing. The property location-awareness is used to access the services from edge servers near the location of the users. The devices can be tracked by the users through technologies such as GPS or using wireless access points. This particular characteristic proves highly beneficial for applications like vehicular safety and disaster management that rely on edge-based solutions.

The proximity characteristic of edge computing improves the users experience by making the resources available for computation at their levels of proximity. Also, the users can make service decisions comfortably since the resources required for computation are available in the local vicinity. Moreover, this can help the service providers to analyze the behavior of mobile users by extracting their device information in order to improve the process of allocating resources and services to users. The most important property of edge computing is low latency achieved by bringing the services nearer to the user. Also, data-intensive tasks can be executed by the users easily on the edge devices like access point, router and server. Context-awareness enables edge to work with mobile traffic patterns at different levels of spatiotemporal scalability. The context-aware services can be rendered to edge users by providing network information such as location of the user and network load. Edge computing uses varied platforms such as architectures, networks, infrastructures, communication methods and computational resources. The heterogeneity in edge computing is achieved by dynamic API support, network, platform, and technologies. The major possible challenge is interoperability issues in edge computing due to heterogeneity.

Cloudlet computing and Edge AI are represented in Figure 2. Using a decentralized infrastructure called fog computing, data sources like application users and sensors are located at the cloud's edge, where storage and processing components are located (Pan et al., 2018). Fog computing is the process of storing data locally before sending it to the cloud. The load of the cloud is shared by fog computing through devices with minimal processing capabilities. Also, the goal is to use the cloud for data-intensive analytics. The system's overall efficiency is increased and the amount of data transported through it is reduced through the fog computing architecture. Fog computing acts as a layer of computing between cloud and edge (Vora et al., 2017).

Mobile Edge Computing (MEC) represents in the cutting-edge tech approach the focused in th immediate processing of the extensive volumes for data generated on edge devices and applications will be closed in proximity for their origin. This paradigm will help to prioritizes in the swift analysis and also handling of data at the edge of the network, precisely in where it's captured or created. By executing the computational tasks in closer in the for taking to the point for data generation, in MEC significantly uses in the process of reducing latency, enabling near-real-time responsiveness for a wide range in array of applications across various industries. Network operators now have a new option in mobile edge computing to help them economically meet the growing demand for better coverage and to give more bandwidth to consumers. The contextualized services of mobile edge computing are tailored based on individual needs and the utilization of network resources. Mobile edge computing possesses various characteristics such as proximity, location awareness, High throughput, low latency, high reliability, energy efficiency, and less backhaul network congestion.

A cloudlet is considered as an enhanced small scale data centre used to quickly deliver cloud computing services to nearby mobile devices, including smartphones, wearable devices and tablets. The main aim of cloudlet is to reduce the latency and provide high bandwidth by hosting the virtual machines closer to the devices accessing them. Traditional cloud computing model facing latency delays in wide area network can be avoided using cloudlet computing. The major difference between cloudlet and public cloud is that the cloudlet is self-managed by users employing it but the public cloud the data center is managed exclusively by cloud service provider. Moreover, cloudlet computing uses local area network for connectivity as specified in Figure 2. Augmented/virtual reality and high-quality service applications are supported by cloudlet computing.

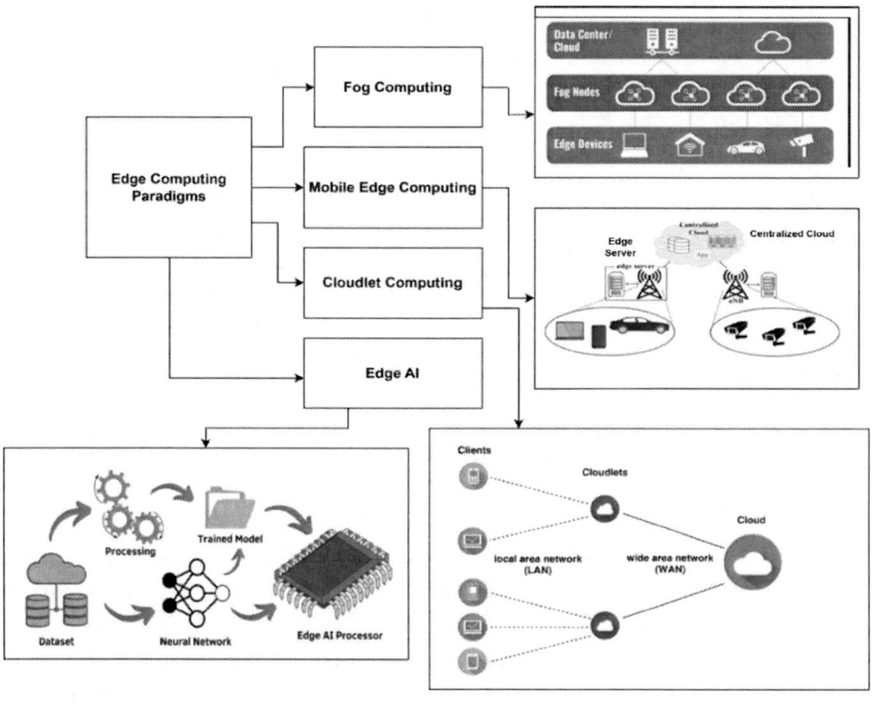

Figure 1. Edge Computing Characteristics.

The paradigm Edge AI can be used to deploy artificial intelligence applications in devices. The name Edge AI specifies that the AI-based computation is performed at the edge of the network nearer to the location of the data. The organizational requirement of improving the safety and efficiency of process automation can be achieved easily by Edge AI. Moreover, it is difficult to deploy real-time applications in a centralized cloud provider due to several issues such as privacy, bandwidth and latency. The deployment of edge ai based models is required due to raise in computing infrastructure, IoT devices and neural networks. The working of the Edge AI technique is depicted in Figure 2. The major advantages of using Edge AI are reduced cost, privacy, intelligence, high accuracy and availability.

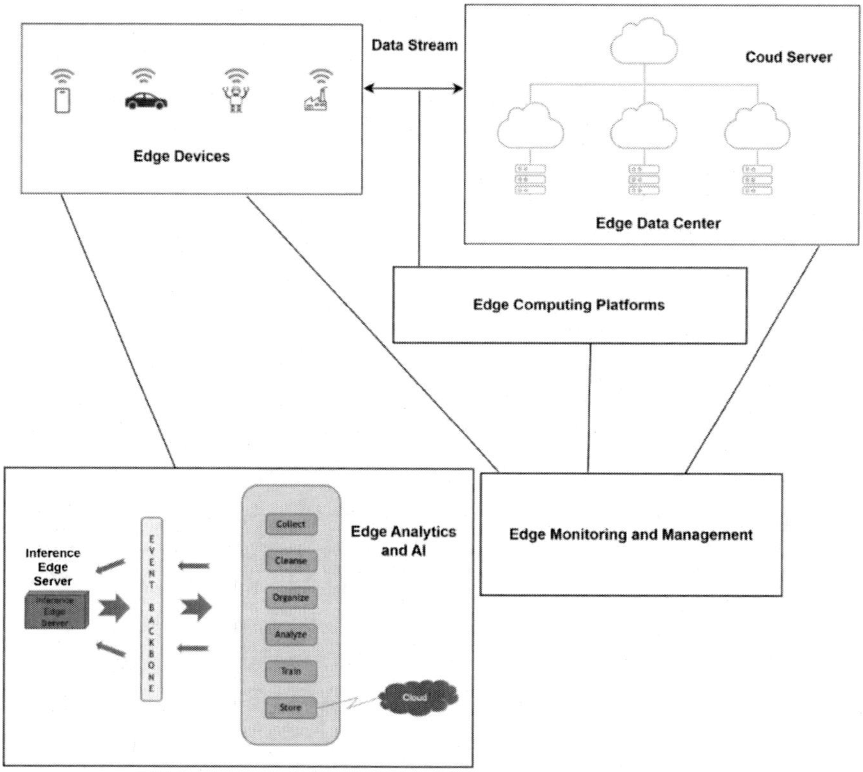

Figure 2. Edge Computing Paradigms.

Edge Devices

An edge device can be used as a networking device to control the flow of data efficiently at the boundary of two networks. They are frequently employed in situations requiring real-time or nearly real-time processing as well as those with bandwidth, latency, or connectivity limitations. The networks with different protocols become highly incompatible and can be managed with the help of edge device. Moreover, edge devices provide interconnectivity between two different networks to carry out operations such as data transmission, monitoring and filtering between networks. Also, edge devices act as an interface between data center and real-world. It can be used for simple to complex industrial applications. Some of the edge devices are Smartphones, the Internet of Things (IoT), Security cameras, Industrial control systems, Autonomous vehicles, Edge servers and gateways. Edge devices can act as the boundary between physical environment and digital processes. They take end-user instructions and return back the information. The machinery can be monitored and controlled using edge devices. As devices are becoming advanced, they are more capable of processing and using data at the edge, avoiding latency and bandwidth restrictions. For storage and analysis, the majority of edge devices must share data with an edge server (as a component of an edge cloud). IoT data must be protected and transmitted with the help of an efficient and secure connection. Wireless networks or 5G connectivity can be used across edge networks for faster data exchange.

The edge devices use industrial IoT for data transmission on the cloud or can be used to perform the functions directly at edge. Edge routers, switches, firewalls, and multiplexers are some of the traditional edge devices. An edge router is a common type of traditional edge device that can be used to connect the campus network to the internet and acts as a gateway between these networks. A routing switch is also an edge device that has minimal features than normal routers. A firewall can also be termed an edge device used to filter the movement of data between both external and internal networks. Also, multiplexers can be used to merge data from various sources into a single signal. These integrated access devices can improve the performance of advanced IoT networks and automated systems. Intelligent edge devices can be used to perform edge computing tasks in close proximity to data sources which helps in industrial automation. These devices facilitate advanced automation and analytics in IIOT platforms and smart factories. Intelligent devices include sensors, actuators, IoT gateways and M2M devices. Both traditional and intelligent edge devices can be used to connect machinery and asset.

The edge devices connected at different points in the network architecture are shown in Figure 3. The cloud server represents the centralized cloud infrastructure where data can be processed and stored. The gateway serves as an intermediary between the edge devices and the cloud, and aggregates and preprocesses the data before transmitting it to the cloud server. The edge devices present in the edge of the network consist of devices such as IoT devices, smartphones, IoT device controllers and sensors. There are three layers that can be used for an edge device setup. The edge layer includes the edge of the network representing the edge devices. This layer is responsible for data collection from various data sources, processing the data locally and sending data to the network layer making relevant decisions. The network layer connects the edge devices with the cloud and specifies the network infrastructure. Also, organizations can make decisions more quickly, reduce the cost of data transfers, and address privacy concerns by storing sensitive data locally by processing data locally. The rising demand for real-time analytics, low latency, enhanced security, and reduced use of network bandwidth leads to the rapid increase of edge devices.

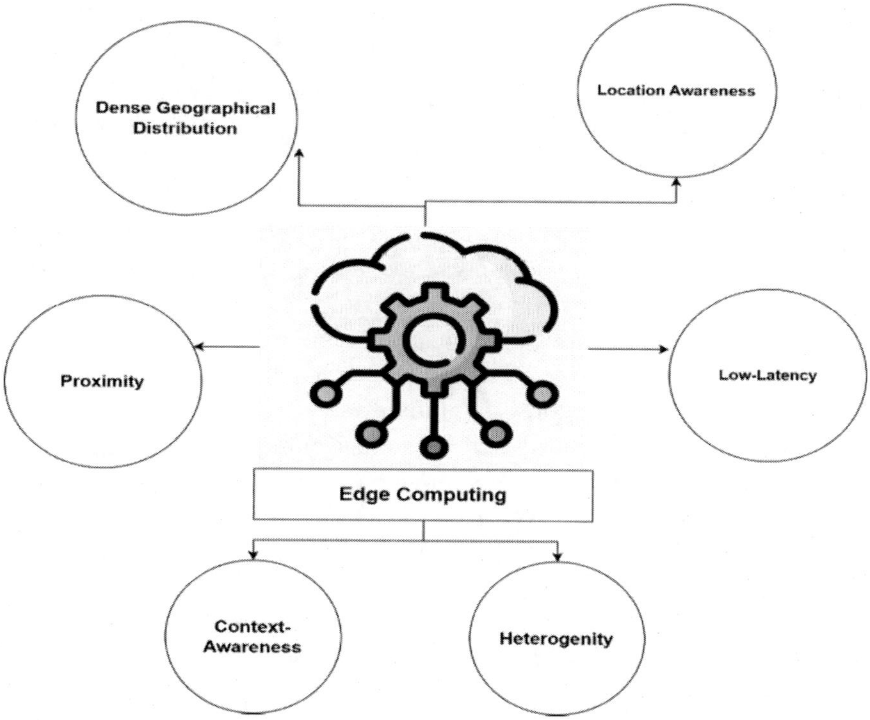

Figure 3. Connectivity of Edge Devices in Network Architecture.

Edge Infrastructure

In order to support edge computing and other edge-related technologies, edge infrastructure is used. It refers to the physical and virtual components that are deployed at networks edge. A distributed computing model known as edge infrastructure brings computing power and data storage closer to a location usually at the edge of a network. Data processing and also the storage are typically centralised in data centers that will have been situated in the specific and geographic locations in the traditional cloud computing. However, there are some growing demands for faster data processing and also real-time decision-making due to the emergence of Internet of Things (IoT) devices, autonomous vehicles, and other latency-sensitive applications. This is met most by edge infrastructure, which uses the decentralizes computing things and relocates them close to the data-generating and -consuming devices. The use of the edge servers, small data centres, or even specialised hardware like the routers or the gateways with computing the capabilities which can accomplish the edge devices. These edge nodes will also be carefully positioned at various locations, including cell towers, network hubs, or close to end users or Internet of Things devices. The benefits of edge infrastructure include reduced latency, bandwidth optimization, scalability, enhanced privacy and security and offline capabilities. Smart cities, autonomous vehicles, industrial automation, augmented reality/virtual reality (AR/VR), and healthcare are few applications for edge infrastructure. Edge computing creates new opportunities for real-time data processing, quicker decision-making, and enhanced user experience for enterprises (Stankovski et al., 2020).

Edge infrastructure consists of hardware, software, and networking elements that make data processing and storage closer to the source of the data and supports the process of edge computing (Liu et al., 2019). In order to reduce latency, increase responsiveness, and improve system performance, edge infrastructure aims to process and analyse data closer to its source. The important elements of edge infrastructure specified in figure 4 include Edge data centers, Edge devices, Edge networks, Edge computing platforms, Edge analytics and AI, Privacy and security, and Monitoring and management tools. Edge data centers are smaller-scale data centers deployed at the edge. To facilitate local data processing and storage, edge data centers host computing resources, storage, and networking hardware. The characteristics of edge data centers include, Compact, energy-efficient, and able to operate in complex environments. Edge devices are actual hardware components, such as edge servers, gateways, routers, or switches, that are situated at the network's edge. By handling data processing and management locally, these devices offload the workloads from the centralised data centers (Jain et al., 2019). They might be equipped with specialised hardware, like GPUs or FPGAs, to support particular computing needs.

Edge computing platforms include, operating systems, middleware, and software frameworks that support edge computing features. It enables the orchestration, management, and service deployment at the edge. Utilisation of resources is optimised, handling data distribution, effective processing and communication between edge devices are all made possible by edge computing software. To connect edge devices, edge data centres, and the centralised cloud or data centres, edge infrastructure depends on robust networking capabilities. This might include both wired and wireless technologies, including cellular networks, Ethernet, Wi-Fi, and specialised protocols like LoRaWAN or Zigbee. Security measures are incorporated into edge infrastructure to secure data and devices there. This includes intrusion detection systems, access controls, authentication methods, and encryption (Varghese, 2016). Moreover, management systems will be used to monitor and control edge devices, collects the telemetry data, perform the updates, and ensure the total health of the patients and will also performance of the edge in the infrastructure (Khan et al., 2017). Edge management is specified as the practices, technologies, tools used to manage edge computing infrastructure. At the network edge, edge devices and applications must be provisioned, monitored, configured and updated (Satyanarayanan, 2017). The performance, security, and efficiency of the distributed computing environment are all made possible by effective edge management. For edge infrastructure to remain such as reliable, secure, and performant, effective edge management will be essential for the edge. It enables the businesses to take over the advantage of the edge computing deployments, manage distributed computing environments effectively, and also it will also guarantee us the smooth operation. Thus, The Edge computing is built on the edge infrastructure, which enables us businesses to process us and analyse act on data in real-time, closer to the point of generation. It offers reduced latency, enhanced performance, and improved data privacy and security, supporting the development of edge-related technologies and applications. Edge analytics and AI (Artificial Intelligence) are complementary technologies that enable data analysis and smart decision-making at the network edge. In comparison the sending data to a centralised cloud or data centre for the processing of the edge analytics refers to the practise of analysing data or close to the source. When the data is processed through locally, either on edge devices or in edge data centres, edge analytics enables real-time insights, prompt action, and decreased latency. This strategy is especially helpful within applications like IoT deployments, autonomous vehicles, industrial automation, and smart cities where low latency, bandwidth optimisation, and real-time decision-making are essential.

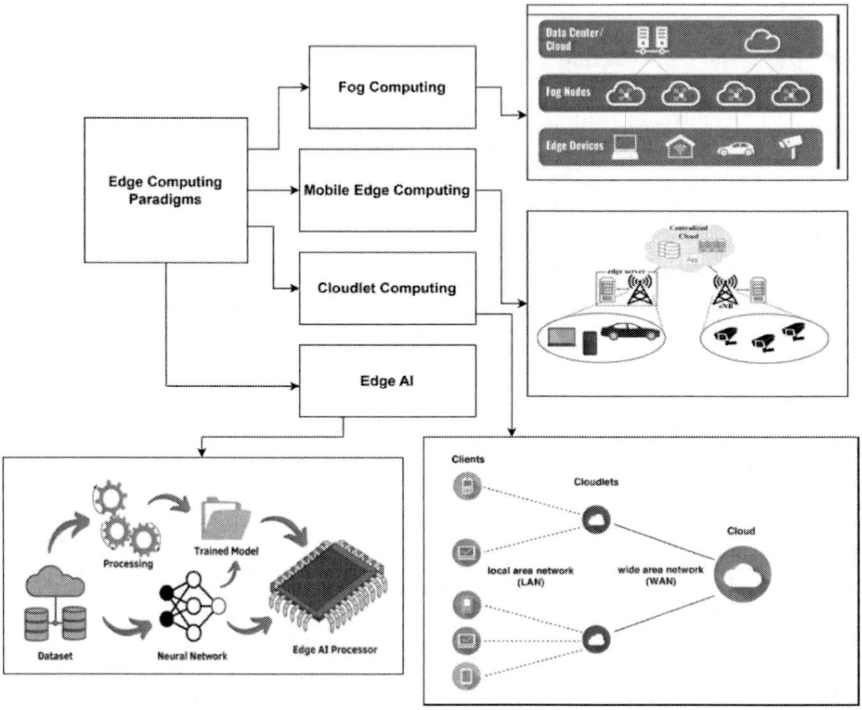

Figure 4. Edge Infrastructure.

Edge Services and Applications

Edge as a Service (EaaS) is the term used to describe the on-demand cloud-based delivery of edge computing resources, capabilities, and services to users. Without having to maintain the underlying hardware and software components, it enables companies and developers to take advantage of edge computing infrastructure. The users can access edge computing resources remotely like cloud services. To bring computation closer to the data source or end users, the edge infrastructure is typically deployed across a distributed network of edge locations or devices. The benefits of edge as a service include on-demand resource provisioning, reduced latency, simplified development and deployment, cost efficiency, scalability and agility, edge analytics and AI, and enhanced security and privacy. Edge service providers include Cloud service providers, telecommunications firms, or providers of specialised edge computing platforms.

Users can focus on creating and deploying their applications while these providers take care of managing the underlying infrastructure, which includes edge devices, networks, and software platforms. Also, the adoption of a new computing paradigm that produces better digital experiences and ultimately enhances the Internet as a whole is made simpler for modern engineering teams by the introduction of edge as a service. Overall, edge computing benefits are made available to developers and companies through edge as a service, giving them flexible, scalable, and cost-effective access to edge resources and capabilities. It enables enterprises to take advantage of edge computing's potential without having to make costly upfront investments and manage their own infrastructure.

Edge Computing has a multilayered architecture to distribute the workload among the edge devices, edge servers and enterprise servers which forms the components of edge as a service as specified in Figure 5. With the rapid development of edge computing, a single intelligent platform that offers full edge-as-a-service solution management capability is required. The tools support in rendering services such as operation management, data analytics, automation, orchestration, management and security. The popular tools used to provide edge-as-a-service include Kubernetes, Apache OpenWhisk, Tensor FlowLite, AWS Greengrass, Azure IOT Edge, Google Cloud IOT Edge, EdgeX Foundry, and Eclipse ioFog. The selection of tools depends on different factors, including the requirements for particular use cases, the infrastructure that supports them, programming languages, and the desired integration level with cloud services.

Edge applications are created specifically to run on edge servers or devices as part of an edge computing infrastructure. These applications make use of the computing resources and edge computing capabilities to process data, run analytics, and provide services closer to the source or consumer of the data. Edge application deployment at the edge has several advantages, including decreased latency, improved performance, and increased data privacy. Edge applications can span across many domains and industries. Few examples of edge applications include IoT applications, Autonomous vehicles, Augmented reality and Virtual reality, Video surveillance, Edge Analytics, Content delivery and Edge caching and Edge gaming. Edge computing is frequently used by IoT applications to process sensor data and carry out real-time analysis. Edge applications, for instance, can monitor traffic flow in smart cities, optimise energy use, and recognise environmental changes. Edge applications can improve production processes, monitor the health of the machines, and enable predictive maintenance in industrial settings. For autonomous vehicles, where timely decision-making is crucial, edge applications are essential. With the help of edge computing, sensor data can be processed onboard so that vehicles can make important decisions without relying on cloud connectivity. Algorithms for computer vision, AI-based object detection, and sensor fusion for enhanced perception are examples of edge applications for autonomous vehicles (Goundat et al., 2021).

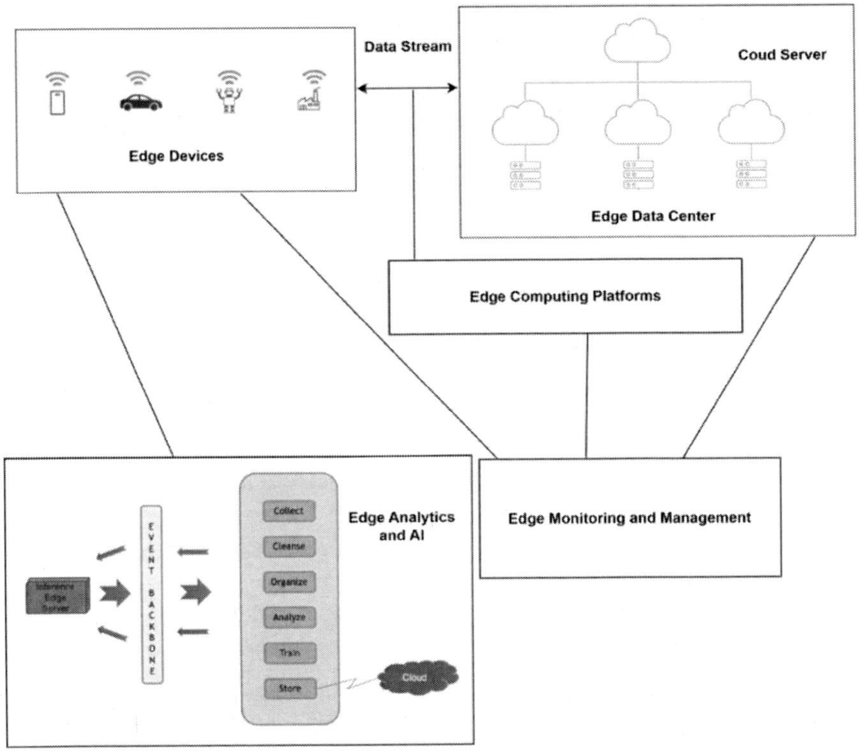

Figure 5. Edge-as-a-Service Architecture.

For an immersive experience, AR and VR applications frequently need low latency and high bandwidth. Rendering, object tracking, and gesture recognition are examples of computation-intensive tasks that edge applications can offload to edge servers, reducing latency and improving user experience. This enables responsiveness and real-time interaction in AR/VR applications. Video surveillance systems perform video processing and real-time analysis using edge applications. The need to send huge amounts of video data to a centralised server can be minimised by using edge servers to run algorithms for object detection, facial recognition, and anomaly detection. This makes it possible to use network bandwidth effectively, respond more quickly, and increase security. Edge applications can analyse data locally and produce insights (Mao et al., 2017). In situations where real-time analysis is necessary, like in industrial automation, healthcare monitoring, and retail analytics, this is especially helpful. In order to save bandwidth and facilitate quicker decision-making, edge analytics applications can process data locally and transmit only the pertinent information to the central/cloud infrastructure.

Edge applications are used by content delivery networks (CDNs) to cache and distribute content closer to end users. In order to reduce latency and enhance the performance of content delivery, edge caching applications can store popular web content, videos, and software updates at edge servers. This makes it possible for quicker load times, better streaming quality, and improved user experiences. In cloud gaming services, where game rendering and processing are delegated to edge servers, edge applications are being used. This reduces the processing load on client devices and makes it possible for devices with limited computing power to provide high-quality gaming experiences. Low-latency gameplay, multiplayer communication, and real-time streaming of game content are all possible with edge gaming applications. Applications that need real-time processing, low latency, and resource efficiency can be deployed using edge computing. As the edge computing ecosystem develops there is a possibility of more innovative and industry-specific applications emerging.

Conclusion

A taxonomy offers a structured framework for organising and understanding the complexities of edge computing systems through the analysis and classification of various edge computing-related elements, including edge devices, edge architectures and edge services. Also, a taxonomy improves understanding and management of the heterogeneous nature of devices present at the network edge by classifying edge devices based on their capabilities, characteristics, and functionalities. Making informed decisions about the choice of device, allocation of resources and distribution of tasks in edge computing environments is made easier though this categorization.

The architectural approaches used in edge computing, such as cloud-centric, fog computing, and mobile edge computing, can also be identified and distinguished using a taxonomy of edge architectures. In order to make the best architectural decisions and optimisations based on particular use cases and requirements, it is helpful to understand the trade-offs, benefits, and limitations associated with each architecture. Data analytics, real-time processing, AI inference, and IoT services are just a few of the numerous services and applications that can be deployed at the edge. The taxonomy of edge services also helps in categorising these services and applications. A taxonomy can effectively place and manage these services in edge computing systems by classifying them and providing information about their unique features, resource needs, and performance considerations.

Thus, a comprehensive taxonomy of edge computing offers a structured framework that improves our knowledge of the various elements and facets of this developing field. It supports better resource management, optimisation, and decision-making in edge computing environments, enhancing system responsiveness, scalability, and user experience. An up-to-date and flexible taxonomy will be necessary for successfully navigating the complex landscape of edge computing technologies and applications as edge computing continues to develop and become more pervasive.

References

Cao K, Liu Y, Meng G, Sun Q. "An overview on edge computing research." *IEEE Access*.(2020) May 1;8:85714-28.

Goundar, Sam, J. Avanija, Gurram Sunitha, K. Reddy Madhavi, and S. Bharath Bhushan, eds. *Innovations in the industrial Internet of Things (IIoT) and smart factory*. IGI Global, 2021.

Jain, Kusumlata, and Smaranika Mohapatra. "Taxonomy of edge computing: Challenges, opportunities, and data reduction methods." *Edge Computing: From Hype to Reality* (2019): 51-69.

Khan, Wazir Zada, Ejaz Ahmed, Saqib Hakak, Ibrar Yaqoob, and Arif Ahmed. "Edge computing: A survey." *Future Generation Computer Systems* 97 (2019): 219-235.

Liu, Fang, Guoming Tang, Youhuizi Li, Zhiping Cai, Xingzhou Zhang, and Tongqing Zhou. "A survey on edge computing systems and tools." *Proceedings of the IEEE* 107, no. 8 (2019): 1537-1562.

Mao, Yuyi, Changsheng You, Jun Zhang, Kaibin Huang, and Khaled B. Letaief. "A survey on mobile edge computing: The communication perspective." *IEEE communications surveys & tutorials* 19, no. 4 (2017): 2322-2358.

Pan, Yi, Parimala Thulasiraman, and Yingwei Wang. "Overview of cloudlet, fog computing, edge computing, and dew computing." In *Proceedings of The 3rd International Workshop on Dew Computing*, pp. 20-23. 2018.

Panchali, B. "Edge computing-background and overview." In *2018 International Conference on Smart Systems and Inventive Technology* (ICSSIT), pp. 580-582. IEEE, 2018.

Satyanarayanan M. The emergence of edge computing. *Computer*. 2017 Jan 5;50(1):30-9.

Singh, Raghubir. "Edge AI: a survey," *Internet of Things and Cyber-Phy*. (2023).

Stankovski, Stevan, Gordana Ostojić, Igor Baranovski, Mladen Babić, and Miloš Stanojević. "The impact of edge computing on industrial automation." In *2020 19th International Symposium Infoteh-Jahorina* (Infoteh), pp. 1-4. IEEE, 2020.

Varghese, Blesson, Nan Wang, Sakil Barbhuiya, Peter Kilpatrick, and Dimitrios S. Nikolopoulos. "Challenges and opportunities in edge computing." In *2016 IEEE international conference on smart cloud* (SmartCloud), pp. 20-26. IEEE, 2016.

Vora, Jayneel, Sudeep Tanwar, Sudhanshu Tyagi, Neeraj Kumar, and Joel JPC Rodrigues. "FAAL: Fog computing-based patient monitoring system for ambient assisted living." In *2017 IEEE 19th international conference on e-health networking, applications and services* (Healthcom), pp. 1-6. IEEE, 2017.

Wang, Tian, Yuzhu Liang, Xuewei Shen, Xi Zheng, Adnan Mahmood, and Quan Z. Sheng. "Edge Computing and Sensor-Cloud: Overview, Solutions, and Directions." *ACM Computing Surveys* (2023).

Chapter 3

Edge Computing: Transforming Enterprises and Personal Tech Applications

J. Avanija[1,*]
Sam Goundar[2]
Ch. Prathima[3]
Palagiri Tharun Sai Reddy[4]
Trinadh Mummareddy[4]
and Viswaksena Balaji[5]

[1]Department of AI and ML, School of Computing, Mohan Babu University, Tirupati, A.P, India
[2]RMIT University, Hanoi, Vietnam
[3]School of Computing, Mohan Babu University, Tirupati, A.P, India
[4]Department of CSE, Sree Vidyanikethan Engineering College, Tirupathi, A.P, India
[5]University of Limerick, Limerick, Ireland

Abstract

Edge computing is a concept that brings computer power and data processing closer to the source of the data, enabling rapid analysis, quicker decision-making, and lower latency. This abstract investigates how edge computing is used in numerous fields. Edge computing improves data analytics, promotes IOT installations, and facilitates industrial automation in enterprise-level applications. It enables telemedicine, real-time data processing, and remote patient monitoring in the healthcare industry for better healthcare delivery. Precision farming, resource management, and crop analysis are all supported by

---

* Corresponding Author's Email: avans75@yahoo.co.in.

In: The Future of Mobile Computing
Editors: Sam Goundar, J. Avanija and K. Reddy Madhavi
ISBN: 979-8-89113-715-8

edge computing in agriculture. In areas like real-time data processing, autonomous driving, and the automotive industry benefit from edge computing. In addition, edge computing is essential in a variety of industries, including smart cities, retail, logistics, and others. Overall, edge computing transforms industries by enabling localised data processing, lowering dependency on cloud connectivity, and enabling real-time decision-making for improved productivity, efficiency, and user experiences.

Keywords: real-time data processing, low-latency communication, local data analytics, faster decision-making, reduced latency, IoT deployments, industrial automation, remote patient monitoring

Introduction

Edge computing, a paradigm-shifting technology, has emerged in response to the issues caused by the increasing volume of data created by connected devices in the modern world. The internet of things (IoT) and the proliferation of smart devices have caused problems with real-time data processing, bandwidth, and latency for traditional cloud-based computing infrastructures. By moving computation and data processing closer to the source, at the network edge, edge computing seeks to get around these constraints.

In its most basic form, edge computing is a decentralised computing architecture that distributes computation and data storage among a network of edge devices, such as sensors, gateways, and routers, positioned close to the data source. These edge devices act as mini data centres that can analyse data in real time close to its source (Cao K et al., 2020). Edge computing does this by minimising the need for data to travel over vast distances to centralised cloud servers, which decreases latency, boosts reaction times, and improves system performance as a whole.

Pushing intelligence closer to the network's edge, where data is being created and consumed, is the underlying idea behind edge computing. A variety of applications and use cases that were previously not possible or realistic utilising conventional cloud computing technologies are now possible thanks to this paradigm shift in computing.

One of the key advantages of edge computing is its capacity to handle mission-critical and real-time applications. Edge computing offers quicker decision-making and prompt responses to events or anomalies by processing data locally at the edge. Real-time capabilities can help sectors like manufacturing, energy, healthcare, transportation, and smart cities by increasing efficiency, optimising operations, strengthening monitoring and analysis, and making choices quickly. Real-time monitoring, autonomous control systems, predictive maintenance, and intelligent resource allocation are all made possible by it.

The capacity of edge computing to solve the problems associated with network connectivity and bandwidth constraints is another important advantage of the technology (Varghese B et al., 2016). Only pertinent and useful data is delivered to the cloud or data centre by processing and analysing data at the edge, reducing the amount of data that must cross the network. Edge computing is excellent for situations with sporadic or weak network access since it not only optimises bandwidth utilisation but also lessens the dependence on continual high-speed connectivity.

Additionally, edge computing enables improved data protection and privacy. Businesses can have more control over their data and lower the danger of sensitive data being compromised or exposed during transmission by processing and storing it locally at the edge. In fields like healthcare and finance, where data privacy and regulatory compliance are crucial, this is especially significant.

Significance of Edge Computing

An important technical development with broad consequences in many fields is edge computing. Its significance comes from its ability to deal with important concerns including data processing, latency, bandwidth, privacy, and real-time decision-making (Khan WZ et al., 2019). The following salient features underline the importance of edge computing:

Reduced Latency

By bringing computation closer to the data source, edge computing cuts down on the amount of time data must travel to and from a central cloud server. This decreased latency makes it possible to evaluate data in real-time and make decisions more quickly, which is essential for applications like autonomous vehicles, industrial automation, and remote monitoring that call for quick responses (Stankovski S et al., 2020).

Real-Time Data Processing

Edge computing makes it possible to process and analyse data right at or close to the data source. Predictive maintenance, anomaly detection, and real-time analytics are applications that significantly benefit from this capacity. Organisations can increase overall efficiency, optimise processes, and make quicker choices by processing data at the edge.

Optimisation of Bandwidth

With the proliferation of connected devices and the exponential rise in data generation, sending all data to a single cloud server might put a pressure on network capacity. Edge computing resolves this issue by minimising the amount of data transmitted across the network by doing local data processing, filtering, and summarization at the edge. This optimisation results in significant cost savings and improved network performance, reducing reliance on high-bandwidth connections. These upgrades help create a network architecture that is efficient and affordable.

Enhanced Privacy and Security

Edge computing tackles privacy and security issues by keeping sensitive data localised and minimising data exposure during transmission. By processing data locally, businesses may keep control of their data and put security safeguards in place right at the edge devices. This regional strategy reduces the dangers of data breaches and assures adherence to data privacy laws.

Decentralised Architecture

Edge computing makes it possible for a decentralised design by dispersing processing power and brainpower across the network. By reducing reliance on a single, central cloud server, this architecture improves fault tolerance, scalability, and flexibility. In the event of network outages or problems with cloud access, edge devices' independence enables the creation of more durable and resilient systems.

Cost Savings

Edge computing can result in substantial cost savings by lowering the demand for high-bandwidth network infrastructure and lowering data storage and transmission expenses. The amount of data transferred to the cloud is reduced via localised data processing and analytics, which lowers the cost of cloud services. As an additional means of lowering operational expenses, edge computing also gives businesses the ability to allocate resources more efficiently and minimise downtime through preventative maintenance.

Offline Operation and Edge Intelligence

Applications can run offline or with sporadic connectivity thanks to edge computing, which also enables edge intelligence. Edge devices are able to continue operating even in the event of restricted or non-existent network connectivity by processing and storing data locally. Edge intelligence enables devices to make informed decisions locally, ensuring responsiveness and uninterrupted operation. It is powered by local processing capabilities.

Scalability and Flexibility

Edge computing delivers scalability and flexibility by enabling organisations to deploy edge devices and infrastructure as required. This makes it possible for edge networks to rapidly expand in order to handle the increasing number of IoT devices and data sources. Edge computing also offers dynamic resource allocation, enabling businesses to distribute computer resources in accordance with demand, optimising resource utilisation and adaptability.

In general, edge computing is significant because it can overcome the drawbacks of conventional, centralised cloud computing (Pan Y et al., 2018; Jain K and Mohapatra S, 2021). Organisations can achieve decreased latency, real-time decision-making, improved privacy and security, bandwidth optimisation, cost savings, and scalability by moving compute and data processing closer to the edge. Edge computing is a game-changing technology that opens up a wide range of applications and revolutionises numerous industries. It opens the door for creativity, increased effectiveness, and greater user experiences.

Industrial Automation

Industrial automation relies heavily on edge computing, which has transformed how factories and production lines run. Edge computing allows real-time analysis, quicker decision-making, lower latency, and increased operational efficiency by moving computation and data processing closer to the source as specified in Figure 1. Here is a thorough explanation of how edge computing is applied to industrial automation:

Massive volumes of data are produced by industrial automation systems from sensors, equipment, and manufacturing lines. PLCs or industrial gateways are examples of equipment that can process real-time data directly at the edge-thanks to-edge computing (Stankovski S et al., 2020). Edge devices can react to events, spot anomalies, and take rapid action by evaluating data locally. Low latency is necessary for real-time control and decision-making in industrial automation. Edge computing eliminates the need to send data to a distant cloud server for processing, thereby lowering the latency involved with delivering data over a network. This enables quicker response times, enabling quick actions to handle process variances or key events.

Figure 1. Industrial Automation.

In industrial automation, edge devices serve as localised control units that are capable of taking independent choices. Based on real-time sensor data, they can run control algorithms, put logic into place, and carry out directives. This localised control increases system responsiveness and robustness overall by reducing reliance on a centralised control system. In industrial automation, edge computing optimises the use of network bandwidth. Only pertinent data must be communicated to the central system or the cloud when data processing and analysis are done at the edge devices. Because less data needs to be delivered, network congestion is reduced, and communication expenses are decreased.

Machine learning algorithms can now be implemented at the edge devices in industrial automation thanks to edge computing. Real-time data can be evaluated and used to inform local decisions by putting machine learning models directly on the edge devices. Predictive maintenance, anomaly detection, and production process optimisation are made easier as a result, increasing productivity and lowering downtime (Shakarami A et al., 2020; Kozik R et al., 2021). Edge computing equips edge devices with the ability to perform advanced analytics. Data can be analysed in real-time to gain insightful knowledge, spot trends, anticipate equipment problems, and enhance production procedures by running analytics algorithms locally (Wang F et al., 2020). Industrial automation systems can make intelligent decisions at the edge thanks to edge analytics, which eliminates the need for constant data transfer to a distant server.

Robotics applications in industrial automation are improved by edge computing. Real-time data processing and decision-making can happen onboard by putting edge devices nearby or directly aboard robots. This reduces the need for constant communication with a central system, improves robot autonomy, and enables faster response times, enabling more sophisticated and efficient robotic automation. Not every piece of data produced by sensors and machines is crucial in industrial automation. Data prioritisation and filtering are made possible by edge computing at the edge devices. To the central system or cloud for additional analysis and storage, only pertinent and essential data is communicated. This lessens the need for bandwidth, improves data transfer, and makes sure that the most pertinent data is used to provide insightful conclusions.

The fault tolerance and dependability of industrial automation systems are improved via edge computing. The system is less prone to single points of failure by dispersing computational power among a number of edge devices. Edge devices have the ability to continue operating autonomously in the case of network or cloud connectivity problems, ensuring ongoing production and process control. Edge computing focuses on local data processing and control, but it can also interact with cloud-based systems for more comprehensive analytics, historical data storage, and centralised management. For long-term analysis, proactive maintenance, and performance improvement, compiled data from numerous edge devices can be sent to the cloud. A strong and complete ecosystem for industrial automation is produced by this integration of edge and cloud computing.

In industrial automation, edge computing enables scalable and adaptable implementation. To adapt to changes in production lines, machinery, or industrial layouts, edge devices can be quickly added or withdrawn. Without major disruptions or infrastructure changes, its scalability and flexibility allow for the seamless extension or reconfiguration of automation systems. Edge computing improves industrial automation system security by limiting the exposure of sensitive data to external networks. Sensitive data can stay within the factory network when edge devices process data locally, reducing the possibility of unauthorised access or data breaches. Edge computing also enables localised security mechanisms, such as firewalls, access controls, and encryption, that are specifically designed to safeguard the industrial environment and the relevant edge devices.

In industrial automation, edge computing aids cost optimisation. Edge computing lowers the cost of data transmission by lowering the requirement for constant high-bandwidth network connections and minimising data transfer to the cloud. Additionally, it lessens the need for cloud infrastructure, which may lead to possible savings on the price of cloud processing and storage.

Edge Cybersecurity

Edge cybersecurity refers to the security measures and strategies implemented at the edge of a network to protect edge devices, data, and applications from cyber threats. Edge computing creates new security concerns and needs by moving computation and data processing closer to the edge devices. The processing power, memory, and security capabilities of edge devices, such as sensors, actuators, gateways, and IoT devices, are frequently constrained by available resources. These devices are particularly susceptible to assaults because they may not have built-in security mechanisms and may not have the processing power to run complex security software (Cao K et al., 2020).

Therefore, protecting edge devices is essential to guaranteeing the overall security of the edge computing infrastructure.

There are several key aspects to consider in edge cybersecurity:

- Device Hardening: To reduce vulnerabilities, edge devices should be hardened. In order to avoid unauthorised access, this entails turning down unused services, installing security patches and updates, setting up strong passwords, and putting in place access controls.
- Secure Communication: To transport data and communicate with other devices or cloud services, edge devices must first create secure communication channels. Implementing encryption methods like Transport Layer Security (TLS) and using secure communication protocols with the proper authentication and authorisation processes, such as HTTPS or MQTT, are required for this.
- Access Control: Mechanisms for access control should be in place to guarantee that only authorised people and devices can access and communicate with edge devices. Access control lists, role-based access control (RBAC) policies, and authentication techniques like username and password, biometric authentication, and two-factor authentication are all included in this.
- Data encryption: To prevent unauthorised access to sensitive information, data should be encrypted both at rest and while in transit. Advanced Encryption Standard (AES) and other encryption methods can be used to protect data being held on edge devices or sent across a network.
- Intrusion Detection and Prevention: Intrusion detection and prevention systems (IDPS) can be placed at the edge to monitor and analyse network traffic, detect malicious activity, and block or mitigate possible threats in real-time.
- Edge Firewalls: Edge firewalls can be used to filter and manage network traffic between the edge devices and external networks. These firewalls support the enforcement of security policies, the blocking of harmful traffic, and the prevention of unauthorised access.
- Threat intelligence: Edge cybersecurity methods should keep track on and incorporate recent updates on new threats and vulnerabilities. Organisations may actively reduce potential risks and vulnerabilities by remaining educated on the most recent attack vectors and trends.

- Security analytics: Implementing security analytics tools and technologies at the edge can assist in spotting unusual behaviour, spotting security events, and giving out early warnings of possible cyber attacks. To evaluate data patterns and spot suspect activity, these analytics solutions employ machine learning and artificial intelligence algorithms.
- Enhanced efficiency: Edge computing enables real-time data analysis and decision-making at the edge devices, reducing the need for data to travel to a central server or cloud. This localized processing improves system response times and enables faster automation control, leading to enhanced operational efficiency and productivity.
- Predictive Maintenance: Industrial automation can employ predictive maintenance techniques thanks to edge computing. Machines and apparatus can be continuously checked for indications of probable faults or anomalies by doing local data analysis at the edge. This proactive strategy aids in avoiding unplanned downtime, streamlining maintenance plans, and lowering maintenance expenditures.
- Improved Quality Control: With edge computing, firms may put in place real-time quality control systems. Instantaneous analysis of data from edge sensors and devices enables the quick detection of errors or departures from desired parameters. This makes it possible to take rapid corrective action, reduce waste, and guarantee a constant level of product quality.
- Offline Operations: Edge computing enables offline operations in situations when dependable network connectivity is not guaranteed. Edge devices can store and analyse data locally, ensuring that automated processes continue even during brief network interruptions. The synchronised data can be sent to central systems for analysis and synchronisation after connectivity has been restored.
- Reduced Network Traffic: Edge computing reduces the amount of data transmitted over the network by filtering and processing data at the edge devices. Edge computing optimises network bandwidth utilisation, lowers latency, and lessens the stress on the network infrastructure by only transmitting information that is pertinent and useful to central servers or the cloud.
- Physical Security: To guard against physical tampering or unauthorised access, physical security measures should be in place. To prevent theft, damage, or unauthorised manipulation, this

comprises physical locks, access restrictions, video surveillance, and environmental controls.

Remote Patient Monitoring

A medical procedure known as remote patient monitoring (RPM) enables medical professionals to keep an eye on patients' health away from conventional healthcare facilities. In order to gather patient data and send it to healthcare professionals for analysis and decision-making, it entails the use of linked devices, sensors, and mobile applications. By putting computational power and data processing closer to the patient's location, edge computing is essential for improving the effectiveness and efficiency of remote patient monitoring (Vora J et al., 2017). Here is a detailed explanation of how edge computing is beneficial for remote patient monitoring.

Edge computing facilitates the processing and analysis of patient data at the edge devices, such as wearable technology or home monitoring systems. As a result, healthcare professionals can get quick insights into a patient's health status and use that information to spot possible problems, monitor trends, and take prompt action. Real-time data analysis is crucial in urgent circumstances, such as identifying irregularities in vital signs or responding to emergencies. With edge computing, patient data can be processed locally instead of being sent to a central cloud server. To cut down on latency and enable faster reaction times, it is instead handled locally at the edge devices (Goundar et al., 2021). As a result, healthcare providers can get timely notifications and take appropriate action in time-sensitive circumstances.

Edge computing makes it possible to continuously monitor the health status of patients. A complete picture of the patient's health status throughout time is provided by connected devices and sensors, which collect data in real-time. With the use of continuous monitoring, medical personnel can spot small changes in a patient's health and take early action to avoid complications or hospital stays. Even when network access is spotty, edge computing ensures that patient data is continuously analysed and examined. Edge computing handles privacy and security issues with remote patient monitoring. Sensitive data can be retained inside the boundaries of the edge devices and the patient's home network by processing patient data locally, lowering the risk of data breaches. By using this strategy, privacy laws are respected, and patient health information is protected. Additionally, edge computing lessens the need to send sensitive data over open networks, lowering the risk of intrusion.

Network bandwidth may be strained when sending a lot of patient data to a central cloud server for processing. Edge computing addresses this problem by processing data locally and sending only pertinent or summarised data to the cloud or healthcare providers. This data transmission optimisation increases system performance by reducing network congestion, cutting costs, and lowering costs. Edge computing enables offline capabilities for remote patient monitoring in circumstances where network connectivity is constrained or sporadic. Even when connectivity is briefly disrupted, edge devices may locally store and analyse data. The gathered data may be synchronised with the main system after the connection has been restored. With this offline capabilities, vital patient data is protected from loss and can be easily included into the whole monitoring process.

Scalable deployments are made possible by edge computing as more patients use remote patient monitoring. In order to ensure effective data processing and analysis without taxing centralised systems, edge devices can handle the increasing volume of data supplied by numerous patients. This scalability makes it possible to expand remote patient monitoring to a bigger population without sacrificing the standard of care or system performance. Patients can participate in remote patient monitoring and receive personalised care thanks to edge computing. Edge devices assess patient-specific data in real time and offer individualised insights and recommendations by processing data locally. Improved patient participation, proactive interventions, and treatment plans that are specific to each patient are made possible. Patients are able to actively manage their own treatment, receive rapid feedback, and monitor their progress.

Real-time anomaly or deviation identification in healthcare is made possible by edge computing. Healthcare professionals can quickly detect anomalies by examining patient data at edge devices and receiving alerts or messages when they do. This enables early action and prompt medical support. The development of illnesses or consequences might be stopped with this preventive approach. Edge computing gives patients the power to actively manage their own healthcare. Patients can track their progress, check their health problems, and make well-informed decisions if they have access to real-time health data via wearable technology or mobile applications. Better health outcomes and higher patient satisfaction may result from this elevated engagement and self-management.

Edge - Controlled Irrigation and Water Management

Edge-controlled irrigation and water management, which harnesses the power of edge computing technology, offers numerous benefits for optimizing water usage in agriculture as specified in Figure 2. Here are the key points that highlight the significance of edge-controlled irrigation.

Local data processing and analysis by edge devices allows for real-time decision-making based on recent sensor data. As a result, irrigation decisions are made quickly and correctly in response to shifting environmental factors and crop requirements. Edge-controlled systems give Edge computing allows for local irrigation decision-making at the edge devices, eliminating the need for constant connection with a central system or the cloud (Munir MS et al., 2021). This allows for quicker response times and guarantees that irrigation adjustments can be made in response to current environmental conditions or plant requirements. accurate insights into the need for irrigation by gathering data from soil moisture sensors and meteorological stations. Through tailored water distribution to particular fields, over-irrigation and water waste are prevented.

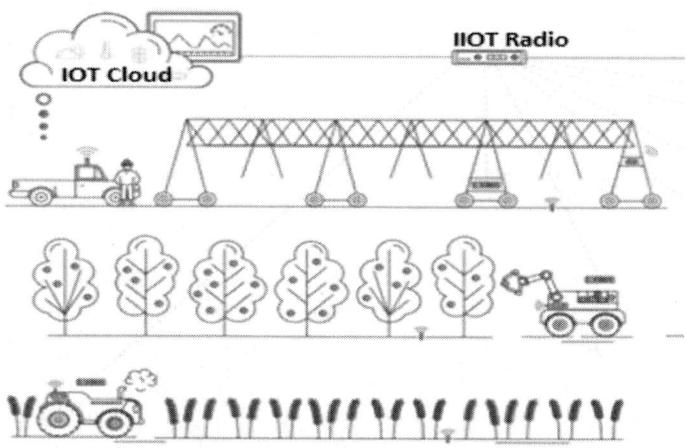

Figure 2. Irrigation and Water Management Architecture.

Crop health and productivity are enhanced by a water supply that is optimised based on real-time data. By ensuring that crops receive the proper amount of water at the appropriate time, edge-controlled irrigation helps to prevent water stress, encourages healthy growth, and, ultimately, increases yields. With edge computing, irrigation decisions may be performed locally at edge devices, eliminating the requirement for constant connection with a central system or the cloud. This offers quicker response times and guarantees that irrigation adjustments can be done in real-time based on current environmental conditions or plant needs.

Edge-controlled irrigation systems reduce water waste by carefully controlling irrigation, which aids in water conservation. Water scarcity is a problem that affects the entire world, and effective irrigation techniques help preserve this essential resource for sustainable agriculture. Energy Efficiency: Local data processing at the edge minimises the requirement for data transmission to the cloud, resulting in less energy use. The irrigation system's environmental impact is diminished thanks to its energy efficiency. Based on real-time sensor data, edge-controlled systems continuously monitor and modify irrigation parameters. This flexibility makes it possible to quickly alter irrigation decisions in response to shifting soil moisture levels, weather patterns, or crop circumstances. Integration with cloud-based platforms enables extra analysis, monitoring, and long-term data storage while data processing and decision-making are done at the edge. The creation of long-term water management strategies and complete data insights are made possible through cloud integration. To accommodate various field sizes, crop varieties, and farming techniques, edge-controlled irrigation systems are easily scaled and customized. The modular design of edge devices enables adaptable deployment to changing agricultural requirements.

Edge-controlled systems lower the amount of physical labour needed and operating costs related to water use by automating and improving irrigation procedures. Farmers gain from this cost-effectiveness, which also encourages wise resource use. Edge-controlled irrigation encourages effective water management strategies, which is in line with the objectives of sustainable agriculture. These technologies assist long-term agricultural profitability by maximising water use, reducing waste, and increasing crop output. To produce data-driven insights, edge computing enables edge-controlled irrigation systems. These systems can analyse data at the edge to find trends, patterns, and correlations that can help with irrigation strategy optimisation. Long-term planning, predictive analytics, and continual practice improvement of water management techniques can all benefit from these findings.

Even in scenarios where there is little network access, edge-controlled watering systems provide resilience and operational continuity. In the event of network outages or disturbances, these systems' local processing capabilities allow them to carry on and make irrigation decisions on their own.

Synchronised data can be sent to central systems for additional analysis or historical records after connectivity has been restored.

Conclusion

Edge computing is a game-changing technology that has enormous advantages in a number of industries, to sum up. It revolutionises industrial automation by allowing for real-time data processing, localised control, and increased operational effectiveness. With regard to cybersecurity, edge computing offers a distributed and pro-active strategy to protect critical data and reduce online threats. Real-time analysis and individualised care are made possible via remote patient monitoring, which improves patient outcomes and lowers costs. Edge computing also enhances irrigation water management, supporting resource conservation and sustainable practises. Overall, edge computing improves efficiency, security, and response times across a variety of industries, spurring innovation and meeting changing needs in our interconnected world. Edge computing also offers scalability and flexibility, allowing for seamless system expansion and reconfiguration. By reducing infrastructural and data transport dependencies, it also helps with cost optimization. Edge computing is paving the way for cutting-edge technology, wise decision-making, and a more connected and effective future as it is incorporated into a variety of industries.

References

Cao, Keyan, Yefan Liu, Gongjie Meng, and Qimeng Sun. "An overview on edge computing research." *IEEE Access* 8 (2020): 85714-85728.

Goundar, Sam, J. Avanija, Gurram Sunitha, K. Reddy Madhavi, and S. Bharath Bhushan, eds. *Innovations in the industrial Internet of Things (IIoT) and smart factory*. IGI Global, 2021.

Jain, Kusumlata, and Smaranika Mohapatra. "Taxonomy of edge computing: Challenges, opportunities, and data reduction methods." *Edge Computing: From Hype to Reality* (2019): 51-69.

Khan, Wazir Zada, Ejaz Ahmed, Saqib Hakak, Ibrar Yaqoob, and Arif Ahmed. "Edge computing: A survey." *Future Generation Computer Systems* 97 (2019): 219-235.

Kozik, Rafał, Michał Choraś, Massimo Ficco, and Francesco Palmieri. "A scalable distributed machine learning approach for attack detection in edge computing environments." *Journal of Parallel and Distributed Computing* 119 (2018): 18-26.

Munir, M. Safdar, Imran Sarwar Bajwa, Amna Ashraf, Waheed Anwar, and Rubina Rashid. "Intelligent and smart irrigation system using edge computing and IoT." *Complexity* 2021 (2021): 1-16.

Pan, Yi, Parimala Thulasiraman, and Yingwei Wang. "Overview of cloudlet, fog computing, edge computing, and dew computing." In Proceedings of *The 3rd International Workshop on Dew Computing*, pp. 20-23. 2018.

Satyanarayanan, Mahadev. "The emergence of edge computing." *Computer* 50, no. 1 (2017): 30-39.

Shakarami, Ali, Mostafa Ghobaei-Arani, and Ali Shahidinejad. "A survey on the computation offloading approaches in mobile edge computing: A machine learning-based perspective." *Computer Networks* 182 (2020): 107496.

Stankovski, Stevan, Gordana Ostojić, Igor Baranovski, Mladen Babić, and Miloš Stanojević. "The impact of edge computing on industrial automation." In *2020 19th International Symposium Infoteh-Jahorina (Infoteh)*, pp. 1-4. IEEE, 2020.

Varghese, Blesson, Nan Wang, Sakil Barbhuiya, Peter Kilpatrick, and Dimitrios S. Nikolopoulos. "Challenges and opportunities in edge computing." In 2016 *IEEE international conference on smart cloud (SmartCloud)*, pp. 20-26. IEEE, 2016.

Vora, Jayneel, Sudeep Tanwar, Sudhanshu Tyagi, Neeraj Kumar, and Joel JPC Rodrigues. "FAAL: Fog computing-based patient monitoring system for ambient assisted living." In *2017 IEEE 19th International conference on e-health networking, applications and services (Healthcom)*, pp. 1-6. IEEE, 2017.

Wang, Fangxin, Miao Zhang, Xiangxiang Wang, Xiaoqiang Ma, and Jiangchuan Liu. "Deep learning for edge computing applications: A state-of-the-art survey." *IEEE Access* 8 (2020): 58322-58336.

Chapter 4

Smart Agriculture: Mobile Solutions for Sustainable Farming

J. Avanija[1,*]
Sam Goundar[2]
Padaga Sri Sai Sankar[4]
Vakati Revanth Reddy[4]
D. Ganesh[3]
and Viswaksena Balaji[5]
[1]Department of AI and ML, School of Computing, Mohan Babu University, Tirupati, A.P, India
[2]RMIT University, Hanoi, Vietnam
[3]Department of CSE, School of Computing, Mohan Babu University, Tirupati, A.P, India
[4]Department of CSE, Sree Vidyanikethan Engineering College, Tirupati, A.P, India
[5]University of Limerick, Limerick, Ireland

Abstract

Smart farming is becoming more and more significant for the agricultural sector in India. It is a great deal more efficient than traditional farming methods. Smart farming involves the use of sensors and automatic watering procedures to monitor temperature, moisture content in the soil, and other aspects of agricultural land. At that point, farmers could monitor their crops from anywhere. The inability of India's small and marginal farmers to integrate digital and physical infrastructures prevents them from earning more money. This number has expanded significantly over the last two years due to an increase in financing and investments in

[*] Corresponding Author's Email: saicorporate26@gmail.com.

In: The Future of Mobile Computing
Editors: Sam Goundar, J. Avanija and K. Reddy Madhavi
ISBN: 979-8-89113-715-8

the business. Tech-driven agribusiness firms have transformed farming practices and provided farmers with innovative support. They have also used climate-smart farming to address one of the major challenges, which is climate change (Sharma et al., 2022, Rahman et al., 2022, Qazi et al., 2022).

Keywords: smart farming, mobile computing, IoT, mobile sensors, artificial neural networks

Introduction

In order to modernize and improve farming's efficiency, mobile solutions are essential. They also greatly increase agricultural output and sustainability. By giving farmers access to real-time data, tools for making decisions, and connection, these solutions take advantage of the growing popularity of mobile devices and transform conventional agricultural methods. Furthermore, mobile solutions that integrate technologies like GPS and sensors make precision agriculture easier. Farmers can ensure accurate fertilizer and pesticide application by using mobile devices to remotely monitor and manage equipment. On smartphones, a plethora of futuristic apps may be downloaded for free, such as Kisan Suvidha, Krishi Mitra, Aqua Mini, Krishi, Life Tools, Sanchar Shakti, Pusa Krishi, and Shetkari. Additionally, these apps encourage and enable farmers to use ICT to promote improved agriculture.

All a farmer needs to do to report crop interruptions or get farming-related information is to take a picture, upload it, or send a text message using the app. Mobile-focused Smart Agriculture is a game-changer in farming, utilizing the-strength of mobile tech to boost sustainability and e-ffectiveness. Mobile- apps for agriculture equip farmers with instant acce-ss to crucial data, letting them make real-time decisions driven by facts. These apps usually offer details on we-ather trends, soil wellbe-ing, and crop status, letting farmers adjust watering plans, ke-ep an eye on pe-st risks, and apply precise farming methods.

Mobile solutions in smart agriculture also contribute to sustainable agricultural practices. Through the integration of mobile apps, farmers can adopt more precise agricultural practices to reduce the impact of agricultural activities on the environment.

Current Challenges in Agriculture

Farmers need to adapt to the shifting demands of the environment as well as those of regulators, consumers, food processors, and retailers. The effects of soil erosion, biodiversity loss, and climate change are all becoming more and more of a burden, as are consumer preferences for food and worries about its production as specified in Figure 1. Furthermore, the natural world that farming interacts with—plants, pests, and diseases—continues to present difficulties. Farmers face a variety of challenges, such as addressing soil erosion, biodiversity loss, and climate change:

- Meet the evolving tastes and expectations of customers
- Satisfy the growing desire for more upscale food.
- Remain resilient in the face of external economic shocks.

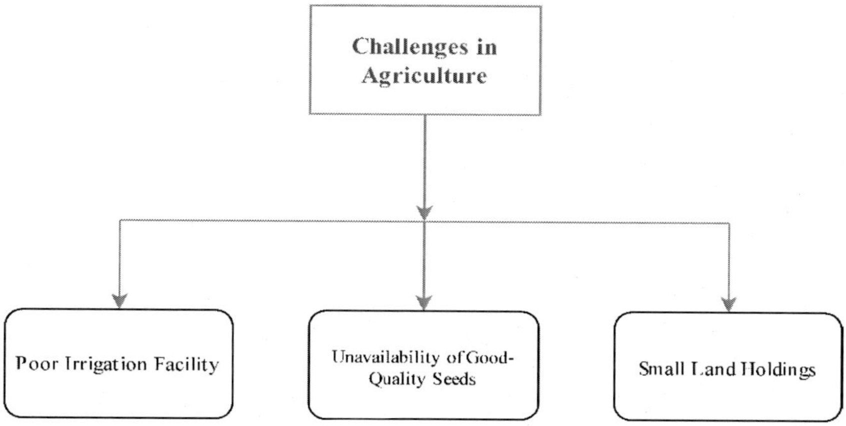

Figure 1. Current Challenges in Agriculture.

Resource Constraints

Benefits for farmers include guaranteed markets for their produce, reduced production risks, knowledge transfer about cutting edge farming technology, and access to essential agricultural inputs, frequently on credit. Additionally, they exert control over the production system to ensure that it complies with relevant standards for market access. Not withstanding the evident advantages, several limitations in the connections between farms and agribusinesses have been noted in the cases examined. There are two types of constraints: internal and external.

Internal Constraints

Lack of Business Management Skills

Inadequate production planning and marketing expertise, particularly among small-scale processors, leads to an inability to consider the inputs required for the scheduled processing of raw material quantities. During the harvest season, agribusiness entities need to be particularly adept at financial planning.

Raw Material Procurement

During harvest season, there are frequently surpluses of unprocessed farm produce, and setting up continuous processing activities is challenging due to a lack of pre-processing and storage facilities. Agribusiness and farmers have different socioeconomic backgrounds, which makes it challenging to build lasting business partnerships. For many processors, farmers are just a source of raw materials; they have no financial or other incentive to assist or develop them.

Quality Constraints

Farmers frequently don't know that processors have precise requirements when it comes to crop varieties, quality standards, production volumes, and delivery timeliness. Farmers who lack knowledge and expertise may also harvest crops too soon, handle them poorly after harvest, and fail to separate crops into different quality grades.

External Constraints

Adverse Macroeconomic Conditions

Business development is generally hampered by inconsistent and opaque business rules and regulations. Any economic development is stifled in nations with high tax rates, inefficient tax administration, and high levels of corruption. The depreciation raises the price of imported inputs. In the majority of agriculturally based nations, declining government spending on agriculture is more common than unusual.

Market Constraints

Low demand for processed goods is a result of consumers in developing nations having limited purchasing power. As a result, agribusiness's profitability is constrained. Agribusiness development is further hampered by the lack of large enough processing companies to sustain local producers or suppliers of ingredients, packaging, and processing equipment.

Limited Availability of Inputs

The agricultural and business sectors are not very profitable due to high raw material costs in both farming and processing. Since local intermediary goods suppliers cannot compete with imports in terms of both price and quality, imports are frequently the source of inputs needed to add value to primary products.

Environmental Impact

Agriculture has had a huge environmental impact, which is why we need to evaluate it and work to make it as sustainable as we can for future generations. Agriculture encompasses the raising of animals, the cultivation of plants, and any afferent activity. Since humans have lived there for centuries, many animals have evolved to live on farms as a natural consequence. Across the world, agricultural practices vary according to the species that are available and the environmental conditions.

Depending on the environment we have positive impact and negative impact on agriculture.

Positive Effects:

- Reduce carbon dioxide (CO2) levels in the atmosphere by storing carbon (C) in soils.
- Improve air quality

Negative Effects:

Negative effects of agriculture include water pollution and soil erosion. Through the atmospheric release of greenhouse gases, it can also exacerbate climate change.

- Changes to the hydrological cycle.
- Soil quality loss

Around the world, war, environmental "fickleness," and other natural or man-made factors all interfere with agriculture. Air pollution, deforestation, and the use of fertilizers and pesticides are just a few ways that agriculture affects the environment. Additionally, agriculture can benefit the environment by lowering air pollution and giving some wild species a habitat rich in resources. An extreme illustration of the consequences of unsustainable agriculture is the Aral Sea. They caused a whole landlocked sea to evaporate.

Technological Gaps in Traditional Farming

Significant technological gaps frequently exist in traditional farming methods, impeding their productivity, sustainability, and efficiency. The limited application of sophisticated machinery and smart agriculture (Abbasi et al., 2022) technologies is one obvious gap. This results in inefficient resource utilization in addition to adding to the workload. Another technological shortcoming in traditional farming is the lack of access to real-time data and information. Using sensors, satellite imagery, and weather forecasts, data-driven decision-making is essential to modern agriculture.

Role of Mobile Computing in Agriculture

The Use of Mobile Computing in Agriculture

94% of farmers currently own a smartphone or other mobile device, according to a USA Today article. This high percentage demonstrates the growing use of mobile computing in the agricultural industry. It has expanded so quickly. Farmers are now aware of the specialized impact mobile computing can have on both their personal and farm productivity. Farmers must be able to download the included tracking apps in order to be able to track these particular items on their farms. The more than a million apps in the agriculture category on Google Play and the Apple App Store can be categorized to explain their purpose and benefits.

Mobile Sensors and IoT in farming

A sensor is an apparatus that detects a physical quantity and converts it into a signal that can be read and used by other apparatuses. These days, a huge range of sensors are accessible, and many well-known smartphones already have a number of sensors installed, including gyroscopes, barometers, accelerometers, light sensors, temperature sensors, and GPS.

Smart phones are equipped with three different types of sensors: environmental, motion, and location sensors. Motion sensors, which make up the first category are monitor rotational and acceleration forces. This includes the ambient air temperature measured by a thermometer, the pressure measured by a barometer, and the light level measured by a photometer. The third type of sensors, known as position sensors, measures the actual position of the gadget. These sensors include orientation sensors, GPS, and magnetometers.

IoT in Farming

Smart Agriculture is the common term used to denote the application of IoT solutions in agriculture. Farmers may collect machine and environmental measurements using Internet of Things (IoT) sensors, as specified in Figure 2 will enable them to improve nearly every aspect of their operations, from livestock to crops, and make more informed decisions. Numerous parts of agriculture could be transformed by technologies (Padhy et al., 2022) and the Internet of Things. Specifically, there are four ways that IoT (Farooq et al., 2022) might enhance agriculture:

- Many data points gathered by intelligent agricultural sensors.
- Reduced manufacturing hazards and improved internal process control.
- Increased quantity and quality of the products.
- Smaller environmental impact.

Some of the use cases in agriculture under IoT are shown in the below diagram.

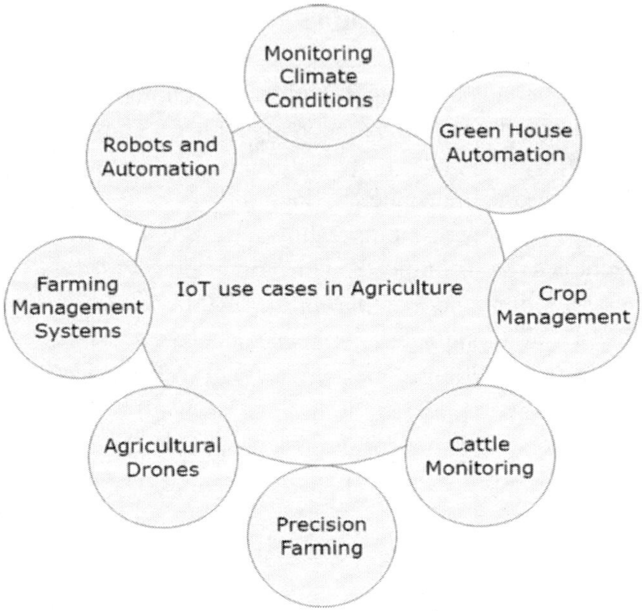

Figure 2. IoT use cases in Agriculture.

Data Analytics for Precision Farming

The process of gathering, transforming, cleaning, and modelling data with the aim of obtaining the necessary knowledge is known as data analysis. Data analytics is the process of examining huge data sets using a variety of data kinds to uncover hidden correlations, market trends, consumer preferences, and other important business information. Figure 3 specifies the most widely used and closely related machine learning methods for forecasting agricultural illnesses and pests that utilize weather data analysis are logistic regression, artificial neural networks (ANN), fuzzy technology for recognition, and support vector machines (SVM).

Precision agriculture involves the precise application of agricultural inputs to yield higher average yields than traditional cultivation methods. Regression-based analyses are used in machine learning to precisely control agricultural output by elucidating how the value of the dependent variable varies in response to an independent variable when other independent variables are held constant.

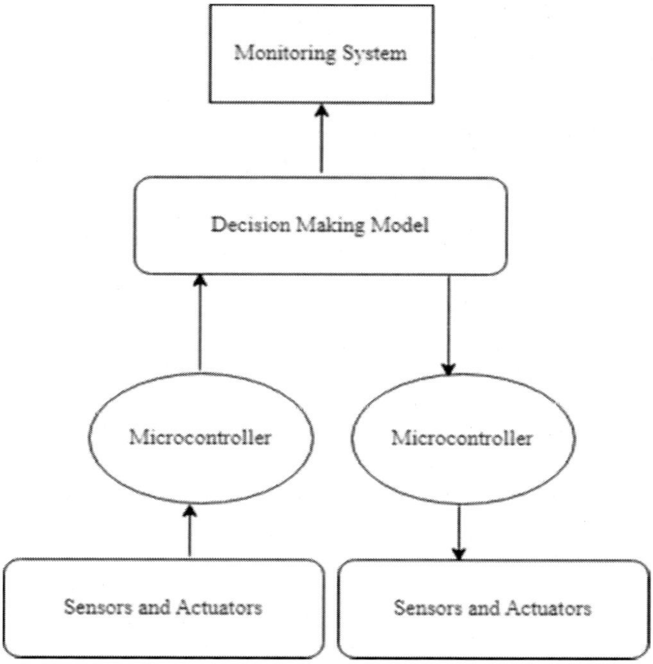

Figure 3. A Representation for Precision Farming using Data Analytics.

Remote Monitoring and Control Systems

By using remote monitoring, users can cut labour costs, boost productivity, improve operational efficiency, and spend more time where it matters most. Although each day is a little different and calls for different schedules and approaches to ensure ideal crop health, seasoned farmers have learned how to best utilise the relationship between these variables to yield an optimal crop yield.

Control Systems in Agriculture

The development of agricultural technology will lessen risks in the agricultural sector while also enhancing the farming system. Production will become sustainable and be able to meet population demands with the help of an effective system specified in Figure 4 explains that can give farmers security in their output and monitoring sensors that will help minimise the hazards in their working environment (Goundar et al., 2021). For forecasting crop production and analysing crop growth, a feedback crop simulation system is useful. Because of the real-time monitoring feature, this system's monitoring feature enhances data collection and allows for accurate crop growth stage display.

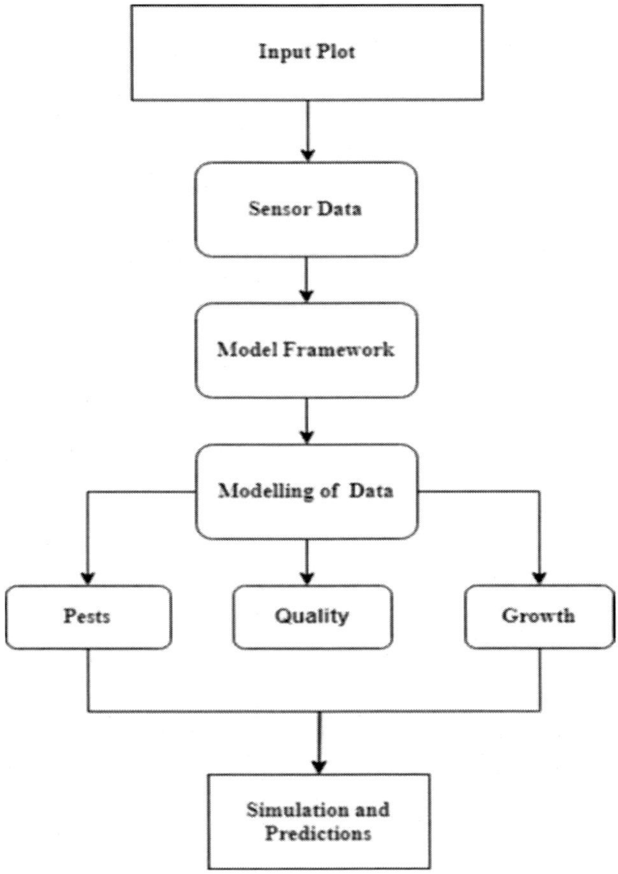

Figure 4. Sample Representation of Crop Simulation System.

Mobile Apps for Farmers

With the global availability of 3G and 4G mobile networks, farmers have been reached, informed, and empowered by mobile and cloud-based applications.

In addition to addressing current sustainability issues, the use of smartphone apps in agriculture generates revenue for small farmers as well as large agriculture-based businesses. A farming software might prove to be a farmer's best ally in the field, boosting productivity without requiring any financial outlay. You can easily download it for free from the Google Play Store.

Some of the best agriculture mobile application for Farmersare specified in Table 1.

Table 1. Agriculture Based Mobile Applications

Name of the Application	Features
IFFCO KISAN	The user can access variety of modules including weather, market prices. User can access audio and video in the selected language.
KRISHI JAGRAN	It offers comprehensive details on agricultural mechanization, crop subsidies, pest and disease control, and crop protection. For tractor enthusiasts, the Krishi Jagran app's model information area is the ideal place to browse. It has details about every model currently on the market.
CROP INSURANCE	It can be used to determine all available cover information as well as, in the event that a farmer is a loanee, to compute the insurance premium for notified crops based on area, coverage amount, and loan amount.

Crop Monitoring and Management Apps

Apps (Michels et al., 2020) for crop management and monitoring are essential to contemporary agriculture because they use technology to improve farming practices' sustainability, efficiency, and productivity. These applications are made to help farmers monitor different parts of their crops, make data-driven decisions, and maximize the use of their resources. Some of the Crop Monitoring and Management Apps are:

- EOSDA CROP MONITORING
- CROP IN
- MAP MY CROP.

EOSDA Crop Monitoring

A cutting-edge precision farming platform for food producers, insurance providers, input suppliers, and other agricultural stakeholders is called EOSDA Crop Monitoring. It is driven by satellite technology. Get data on crop health, weather, crop rotation, field operations, elevation, soil moisture, and more with ease. All of this data is smoothly integrated into an intuitive interface.

CROPIN

Pioneers in the worldwide Ag Tech space, CROPIN created CROPIN. Cloud, the first industry cloud specifically designed for agriculture in history. With the help of CROPIN Cloud, different agri-ecosystem stakeholders may effectively use digitization and predictive intelligence to make decisions that improve sustainability, manage risk and environmental changes, raise farming efficiency, and scale productivity.

Map My Crop

Map My Crop is a cutting-edge Ag Tech startup that provides farmers with advanced crop monitoring solutions through the use of satellite images, artificial intelligence, and machine learning. Farmers will be able to better understand their crops and make more educated decisions about their operations with the software's help.

Weather Forecasting and Advisory Apps

Weather forecasting and advisory apps play a crucial role in providing users with real-time and future weather information, helping them plan and prepare for various atmospheric conditions. These apps (Singh et al., 2023) leverage advanced meteorological technologies, satellite data, and computational models to analyse and predict weather patterns. Some of the Weather forecasting Apps are:

- Megh Doot
- Weather Bug

Megh Doot

Megh Doot is a straightforward and user-friendly smartphone software that gives farmers crop advisories based on meteorological data. In addition to the crop advisory, the app offers current meteorological data, wind direction, and speed—all of which are vital for agricultural operations.

Weather Bug

Offering weather warnings for lightning, wind chill, local temperature, pollen count, UV index, precipitation, and much more, WeatherBug positions itself as a comprehensive app. The weather can also be seen on a user's home screen by using the weather widgets. The software is free however it contains advertisements. Some of the Advisory Apps are:

- Strawberry Advisory System
- Custom Weather Alerts.

Strawberry Advisory System

Producers of strawberries can protect their crops from damaging fruit roots like botrytis and anthracnose with the help of this incredibly helpful free software. The software keeps track of the weather, so it can recommend fungicides based on the climate in the area and alert users when their crops are most vulnerable. The business provides a limited-edition, free pro version that is limited to the state of Florida.

Custom Weather Alerts

Custom Weather Alerts is fantastic software that examines the weather at a specific time of day and alerts users if the temperature is too low. It is especially helpful for people who have to keep a close eye on their fields and soil for fear of sudden cold weather. Since the app may report on high temperatures or any temperature outside of a user-defined custom range, it can also be utilized during droughts.

Market Information and Price Tracking Apps

Market information and price tracking apps play a crucial role in the agriculture sector by providing farmers, traders, and other stakeholders with real-time data on market trends, commodity prices, weather conditions, and relevant news. These apps empower users to make informed decisions, optimize their crop management strategies, and enhance overall productivity. Some of the Mobile Applications used are:

- Kisan Suvidha
- Agri Market
- The Farms.com

Kisan Suvidha

An omnibus smartphone app called Kisan Suvidha was created to assist farmers by giving them access to pertinent information rapidly. They can obtain the current day's and the next five days' weather information by just clicking a button. To best enable farmers, special features have been incorporated, such as alerts for extreme weather, commodities market prices in the closest area, and the maximum price in both the state and India.

Agri Market

The market price of crops in markets within 50 kilometers of the device's location can be found using the Agri Market mobile app. Using a mobile GPS, this software automatically determines the user's location and retrieves the market price of crops in any markets that are within a 50-kilometer radius. If someone prefers not to use a GPS location, there is another way to find the price of any market or crop.

The Farms.com

Get the most recent pricing for agricultural commodities with the Farms.com Markets app. Commodity level data, such as pricing for corn, wheat, soybeans, canola, live cattle, lean hogs, and more, are available on the app. To see the most recent stories and news about agriculture, download the app (Misaki et al., 2021). Additionally, add commodity prices to your watch list to personalize your home screen.

Precision Farming Technologies

Precision farming makes use of a wide range of cutting-edge instruments and technologies to track many factors and gather data about crop development (such as pH, soil moisture, etc.). It is called "precision" because its main goal is to provide the appropriate intervention (such as watering crops) at the appropriate time and location while addressing the unique needs of each crop and each piece of land with the highest degree of precision (Blasch et al., 2021) possible.

GPS Technology in Agriculture

GPS technology has completely transformed the agricultural landscape, revolutionizing traditional farming practices. One of its key applications empowers farmers with accurate positioning information for their tractors, planters, and other machinery. This allows for optimal allocation of resources, such as water, fertilizers, and pesticides, by targeting specific areas in need. Moreover, the integration of GPS technology in Variable Rate Technology (VRT) has further enhanced efficiency in farming.

- Auto-Steer Systems: Tractors and other farm equipment can precisely follow predefined routes thanks to Auto-Steer Systems, which use GPS technology.
- Soil Head Management: GPS devices reduce crop damage and soil erosion by better monitoring variations in soil head and revolving machinery at the proper angles and locations.
- Yield monitoring: During harvest, crop rotation in the field is tracked and observed using GPS. In the future, these data will be useful for making well-informed decisions and assessing the effectiveness of implementation activities.
- Tracking equipment: GPS enhances fleet management by assisting farmers in tracking the location and movement of farm equipment.

Planning for maintenance, logistics, and preventing theft all depend on this.

- Data Processing: Transparency in the supply chain is achieved by tracking the origin of agricultural products using GPS technology. All things considered, GPS technology has significantly improved the productivity, sustainability, and efficiency of agricultural practices and helped modernize the agricultural sector.

Drones and Aerial Imaging for Crop Analysis

Aerial photography and drones have developed effective agricultural equipment that provides farmers with important information about crop health and field conditions. Drones are mobile aerial units similar to flying cameras. Farmers can obtain a comprehensive view of their fields with the aid of aerial photos (Kirkaya et al., 2020, Maloku et al., 2020). Drone images reveal whether crops are doing well or if there is an issue. This brief examination is similar to seeing the doctor for plants. A drone helps farmers decide where to use more or less water and fertilizer based on what they see in the images. This is so that each plant gets exactly what it needs, no more, no less. Drones give farmers a quick way to monitor their crops. If there is a problem, they can respond quickly, like a superhero to the field. Data from drones can be viewed on mobile devices. Farmers can analyse their fields and make decisions wherever they are, as if they had an agricultural dashboard in their pocket.

Smart Irrigation Systems

Intelligent irrigation systems are like intelligent irrigation assistants. They know exactly when each plant needs it and how much water it needs. Farmers can control these systems using their mobile devices. They seem to have the remote control of the farm's water supply in the palm of their hands. Smart irrigation systems target delivery of water where plants are thirsty. It's just like giving drinks to plants in areas where they really need it. By being prudent about water usage, these schemes help farmers conserve water. The faucet appears to be turned off when not in use at home.

Smart irrigation enables farmers to use water wisely. It's like leaving a room and turning off the lights to make sure you don't waste electricity. By managing water efficiently, farmers contribute to a sustainable future. Today is like planting seeds for a healthy field tomorrow. Smart irrigation systems can help farmers save money by using water more efficiently. It's like looking for ways to reduce monthly expenses. Specifically, smart irrigation brings a future and an efficient approach to agriculture by putting power in the hands of farmers through mobile solutions. It's about wise use of water, conservation, and a sustainable and productive future for agriculture.

Challenges and Future Prospects

- Limited network usage: Many rural areas lack robust mobile networks, making it difficult for farmers to access smart agricultural solutions (Yigezu Wendimu et al., 2021, Kheya et al., 2023) Limited connectivity prevents the real-time use of crops, weather and smart technologies.
- Low bandwidth: Even with coverage, rural areas can suffer from low bandwidth, affecting data speeds and reliability. Slow data transfer can hinder smart agricultural systems, delaying decision-making and response times.
- Material differences: Rural areas often lack the necessary infrastructure for robust and stable connectivity, including 4G/5G towers and reliable internet service. Inadequate infrastructure may limit the use of advanced mobile solutions for precision agriculture and data-driven decision making. Government and telecommunication companies can invest in network expansion to reach remote rural areas. The improved network and reliability can provide easy connectivity and data transfer for smart agricultural applications.

Data Security and Privacy Concerns

Risk associated with smart agriculture systems' access or data breaches (Yadav et al., 2020, Chakraborty et al., 2021). There is a compromise of sensitive farm data, which could result in financial loss and privacy concerns. Concerns concerning the way farmers use information are raised by ambiguities in as repsented in Figure 5 explains data ownership and management (Han et al., 2021). Farmers do not have sufficient control over their data, they can be hesitant to implement smart agricultural technologies. Integrating blockchain to offer transparency and data security. Blockchain can solve worries about data integrity by offering a decentralized, tamper-resistant ledger.

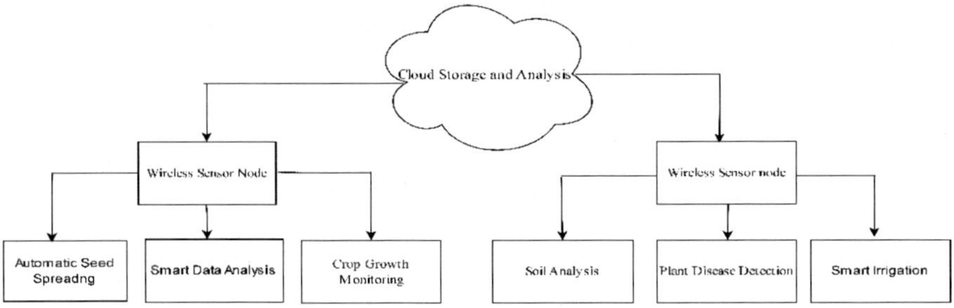

Figure 5. Cloud Storage and Analysis.

Future Innovations and Trends in Smart Agriculture

Integration of AI and ML has increased for advanced data analysis and decision making in agriculture (Han et al., 2021). AI-powered solutions help maximize resource allocation and offer insights into crop health. In summary, as technology advances for agriculture to optimize these data-driven, sustainable solutions, it will be critical to address connectivity issues, ensure data security and privacy, and adopt new technologies focused on mobile solutions for sustainable agriculture. Furthermore, it appears more and more likely that changing careers will be successful (Sott et al., 2020).

Policy Implications and Regulatory Framework

Governments can encourage farmers to use smart agricultural technologies by offering financial incentives and subsidies. Impact: Financial incentives facilitate farmers' investments in mobile solutions and promote more productive and sustainable farming methods. Governments can spend money on mobile network use and better communications in rural areas. Improved infrastructure makes it easier to use mobile solutions in isolated locations, which supports intelligent farming techniques. Financing research and development initiatives focused on mobile applications and environmentally friendly farming methods. It promotes creativity, which results in the creation of practical and reasonably priced mobile solutions for farmers.

Establish stringent guidelines and regulations for smart agriculture's data security and privacy. Having clear policies in place guarantees that farm data is secure, that issues are resolved, and that the use of mobile solutions is trusted. Provide farmers with incentives to use mobile-enabled sustainable farming techniques. Justification: Encourages the use of technology to lessen the impact on the environment and to support agriculture's long-term viability. Make plans of action to improve farmers' digital literacy. It facilitates farmers' adoption and effective use of smart agriculture technologies by providing them with the tools they need to deploy mobile solutions.

To provide a mechanism for tracking and assessing the effects of intelligent farming technologies. Ongoing assessment guarantees that the system will continue to operate as intended and can be modified to accommodate new requirements and technological advancements. To effectively integrate mobile solutions for smart agriculture, governments must play a major role in fostering an enabling environment. The aforementioned policy recommendations seek to bolster sustainable farming methods, augment technological utilization, and guarantee that the advantages of intelligent agriculture are realized by farmers throughout diverse settings.

Conclusion

In the field of smart agriculture, the integration of mobile solutions has revolutionized the field by resolving enduring problems in traditional farming. Mobile computing's importance in the agricultural sector is highlighted by its potential to eliminate technological gaps in farming processes, lower environmental impact, and alleviate resource limits. Given the current challenges of limited resources, environmental degradation, and technological shortcomings, farming must adopt innovative approaches in order to remain sustainable and productive. As we look ahead to new trends and advancements in this field, the continuous advancement of technology foreshadows further discoveries that will transform the agricultural environment into one that is more connected, sustainable, and productive. In conclusion, mobile solutions and precision farming technology are advancing agriculture toward a more resilient and productive future.

References

Abbasi, Rabiya, Pablo Martinez, and Rafiq Ahmad. "The digitization of agricultural industry–a systematic literature review on agriculture 4.0." *Smart Agricultural Technology* 2 (2022): 100042.

Blasch, Julia, Bianca van der Kroon, Pieter van Beukering, Rens Munster, Sergio Fabiani, Pasquale Nino, and Silvia Vanino. "Farmer preferences for adopting precision farming technologies: a case study from Italy." *European Review of Agricultural Economics* 49, no. 1 (2022): 33-81.

Farooq, Muhammad Shoaib, Shamyla Riaz, Adnan Abid, Tariq Umer, and Yousaf Bin Zikria. "Role of IoT technology in agriculture: A systematic literature review." *Electronics* 9, no. 2 (2020): 319.

Goundar, Sam, J. Avanija, Gurram Sunitha, K. Reddy Madhavi, and S. Bharath Bhushan, eds. Innovations in the industrial Internet of Things (IIoT) and smart factory. *IGI Global*, 2021.

Kalyani, Yogeswaranathan, and Rem Collier. "A systematic survey on the role of cloud, fog, and edge computing combination in smart agriculture." *Sensors* 21, no. 17 (2021): 5922.

Kirkaya, Aylin. "Smart farming-precision agriculture technologies and practices." *Journal of Scientific Perspectives* 4, no. 2 (2020): 123-136.

Michels, Marius, Vanessa Bonke, and Oliver Musshoff. "Understanding the adoption of smartphone apps in crop protection." *Precision Agriculture* 21 (2020): 1209-1226.

Misaki, Ezra. "Assessment of the Used Mobile Applications by Small-Scale Farmers at Miono and User Requirements in the Present and Future Mobile Apps." In 2021 *IEEE AFRICON*, pp. 1-6. IEEE, 2021.

Oteyo, Isaac Nyabisa, Matteo Marra, Stephen Kimani, Wolfgang De Meuter, and Elisa Gonzalez Boix. "A Survey on Mobile Applications for Smart Agriculture: Making Use of Mobile Software in Modern Farming." *SN Computer Science* 2, no. 4 (2021): 293.

Padhy, Chitrasena, M. D. Reddy, R. K. Raj, and K. P. Pattanayak. "Role of Digital Technology in Agriculture." *Indian Journal of Natural Sciences* 13, no. 71 (2022): 40287-40290.

Qazi, Sameer, Bilal A. Khawaja, and Qazi Umar Farooq. "IoT-equipped and AI-enabled next generation smart agriculture: A critical review, current challenges and future trends." *IEEE Access* 10 (2022): 21219-21235.

Rahman, Md Momtazur, Imran Khan, David Luke Field, Kuaanan Techato, and Kamal Alameh. "Powering agriculture: Present status, future potential, and challenges of renewable energy applications." *Renewable Energy* 188 (2022): 731-749.

Singh, Dharmender, P. S. Shehrawat, Joginder Singh Malik, Dangi Pooja Arun, and Dinesh Kumar. "Utilization Pattern of Mobile Apps Among Farmers for Agricultural Production." *Indian Journal of Extension Education* 59, no. 1 (2023): 150-153.

Sharma, Vivek, Ashish Kumar Tripathi, and Himanshu Mittal. "Technological revolutions in smart farming: Current trends, challenges & future directions." *Computers and Electronics in Agriculture* (2022): 107217.

Thar, So Pyay, Thiagarajah Ramilan, Robert J. Farquharson, Alexis Pang, and Deli Chen. "An empirical analysis of the use of agricultural mobile applications among smallholder farmers in Myanmar." *The Electronic Journal of Information Systems in Developing Countries* 87, no. 2 (2021): e12159.

Chapter 5

Emerging Trends in Mobile Hardware and Design

P. Dhanalakshmi[1,*]
U. Janardhan Reddy[2]
G. Ravikanth[3]
Chevuru Nandini[4]
Gurram Sunitha[1]
and J. Avanija[1]
[1]Department of AI and ML, School of Computing, Mohan Babu University, Tirupati, A. P, India
[2]Gitam University, Bengaluru, India
[3]BVC College of Engineering, Tirupati, Andhra Pradesh, India
[4]Department of CSE, Sree Vidyanikethan Engineering College, Tirupati, A. P, India

Abstract

This book chapter offers an in-depth investigation of the most recent patterns forming the scene of versatile equipment and plan. Centered on current and future improvements, the chapter examines the effect of cutting-edge advances like 5G and progressed processors on versatile equipment components, upgrading gadget execution and capabilities. At the same time, it digs into the advancing standards of portable plans, emphasizing user-centric approaches and the integration of expanded reality (AR), virtual reality (VR), and blended reality (MR) for immersive client encounters. The chapter too addresses the expanding accentuation on maintainability inside portable equipment, talking about

* Corresponding Author's Email: mallidhana5@gmail.com.

In: The Future of Mobile Computing
Editors: Sam Goundar, J. Avanija and K. Reddy Madhavi
ISBN: 979-8-89113-715-8

eco-friendly materials and hones. By giving a comprehensive diagram of these rising patterns, the chapter points to cater to a different gathering of people, counting analysts, industry experts, and innovation devotees, cultivating a more profound understanding of the energetic advancement of portable equipment and plan.

Keywords: mobile hardware, augmented reality, design trends, user-centric design, sustainable practices

Introduction

The most recent and anticipated developments, discoveries, and paths in the field of mobile device technology and design are referred to as "emerging trends" in mobile hardware and design. These developments could include hardware advancements like faster processors, better displays, longer battery lives, and networking capabilities, as well as design concepts and techniques that increase the usability and appeal of mobile devices. It is possible that mobile hardware and design may see some new developments, such 5G technology, biometric authentication, foldable smartphones, and environmentally friendly design.

The advent of foldable tablets and smartphones allows for larger screen sizes without sacrificing portability. The screens of these devices may fold or unfurl because of their inventive hinge mechanics and flexible display technologies (El Khaddar et al., 2012). Mobile devices will have more potential with 5G networks in place because of their higher data capacity and lower latency. This trend may lead to the development of devices that can handle an increasing number of data-intensive applications, such as augmented reality (AR) and virtual reality (VR) experiences.

Biometric features, including fingerprint sensors integrated into displays and facial recognition, are found in an increasing number of mobile devices. These features make device unlocking and transaction approval easier and safer. Ecologically responsible and sustainable design approaches are becoming more popular in the mobile industry. Using recyclable materials, energy-efficient components, and modular designs that enable simple component replacements and repairs are a few ways to reduce electronic waste.

Foldable Displays

A type of display technology called "foldable displays" can be bent or folded without damaging the display or negatively impacting its performance. Typically, these screens are employed in electronic devices like laptops, tablets, and smartphones to give users a more adaptable and varied experience (Kingslin et al., 2023). OLED (Organic Light Emitting Diode) technology, which is flexible and does not require a backlight like LCD (Liquid Crystal Display) screens do, is the key technology that makes foldable displays possible. OLEDs are composed of organic compounds that emit light when an electric current is applied (Back et al., 2023).

The following are a few products related to foldable displays:

- Samsung Galaxy Fold and Z Fold Series
- Huawei Mate X
- Motorola Razr
- Microsoft Surface Duo
- Developments in Foldable Technology

The advantage of foldable displays is that their unfolded screen area is larger than their folded profile (Huang et al., 2021). There are still problems to be fixed, like ensuring the foldable components are sturdy and long-lasting. In the future, foldable display technology might develop and expand much further.

5G Connectivity and the Future of Mobile Networking

In compared to its predecessors, 5G (fifth generation) connection offers faster speeds, lower latency, and larger capacity. This is a big advance in mobile networking technology. The future implications of 5G's primary features for mobile networking are as follows:

Speed and Throughput:

- Improved Data Rates
- Low Latency

Density of connections and capacity:

- Greater Capacity
- Connection Density

Network Slicing:

- Customized Networks

Edge Computing:

- Distributed Processing

Enhanced Mobile Broadband (eMBB):

- Improved Coverage

Industry 4.0 and IoT:

- Industrial Applications
- Massive IoT Deployment

Challenges and Considerations:

- Infrastructure Deployment
- Spectrum Availability

Finally, 5G is poised to revolutionize mobile networking by offering faster speeds, lower latency, and increased capacity. Its impact goes beyond consumer smartphones, extending to diverse industries and applications that rely on advanced connectivity. As 5G infrastructure continues to be deployed globally, we can expect a transformative shift in how we connect, communicate, and leverage digital technologies (Wiencek et al., 2023).

Multiple Camera Systems and the Evolution of Mobile Photography

The integration of numerous camera systems in smartphones is a fundamental component of the evolution of mobile photography, which has been greatly influenced by advancements in camera technology (Parulski et al., 2000). Some important information about multiple camera systems and how they impact mobile photography is as follows in Figure 1.

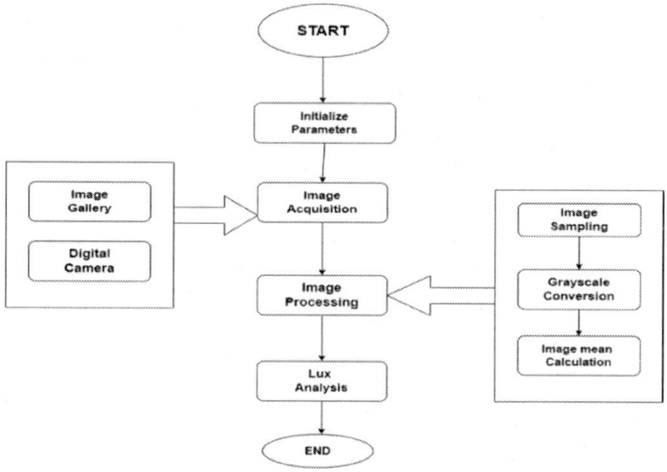

Figure 1. Mobile-application-to-obtain-luminance-through-the-digital-camera.

- Dual, Triple, and Quad Camera Setups: The majority of early cellphones had a single rear camera. But the fashion moved toward two-camera, then three-, and ultimately four-camera arrangements. Diverse lenses have diverse functions; examples include telephoto, depth-sensing, wide-angle, and ultra-wide-angle lenses.
- Enhanced Photography Capabilities: Because wide-angle lenses catch more in a single frame, they are ideal for group shots and landscape photography. These lenses allow users to get up close and personal with distant subjects without sacrificing the quality of their photos by enabling optical zoom (Delbracio et al., 2021).
- Depth Sensing and Portrait Mode: When in portrait mode, the blend of multiple cameras and depth-sensing technology creates a bokeh effect that looks realistic.

- Low-Light Performance: Smartphone cameras with multiple lenses sometimes come with advanced low-light shooting options such as Night Mode. Using computational photography techniques, these settings capture and enhance features in low light.
- Computational Photography: Multiple camera systems are combined with advanced image processing techniques and AI.
- Pro and Manual Modes: Owners of multiple camera smartphones can choose the pro or manual modes, which give them more control over settings like ISO, shutter speed, and white balance. This is especially advantageous for people who are more passionate about photography.
- Video Features: It's not only about still photos when using multiple cameras. By offering features like improved stabilization, smooth lens transitions, and simultaneous recording from many lenses, it further enhances video capabilities.

Future Innovations:

- Foldable Devices
- Advanced Sensors.

In-Display Fingerprint Scanners and Improved Device Security

Under-display or in-screen fingerprint scanners, sometimes referred to as in-display fingerprint scanners, are a type of biometric authentication technology that is built into the display of a device, like laptops or smartphones (Yeh et al., 2023). The introduction of this technology aims to improve device security in a more seamless and practical manner in Figure 2.

- Biometric Authentication: Fingerprint Recognition, In-display fingerprint scanners use each user's unique fingerprint patterns to authenticate and unlock a device. This biometric authentication solution is more convenient and often faster than typing in a password or PIN (Ni et al., 2023). Seamless Integration: Integration into the Display, unlike traditional fingerprint scanners, which are often located on a device's front or back, in-display fingerprint scanners are embedded beneath the screen of a smartphone. This link enables more efficient and aesthetically pleasing design.

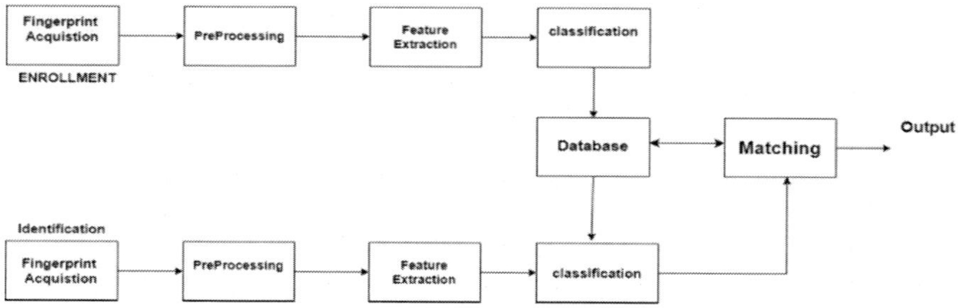

Figure 2. Basic components of the A-flowchart fingerprint identification system.

- User Convenience: Quick and Simple Unlocking, to unlock a smartphone, users simply need to touch the designated area of the screen with their registered finger. This method is often faster and more convenient than entering a passcode while the device is in use.
- Enhanced Security Protocols: Cutting-Edge Sensor Technology, In-display fingerprint scanners use sophisticated sensor technology, such as optical or ultrasonic sensors, to capture a detailed image of the user's fingerprint. This enhances the accuracy and security of the authentication process.
- Counteracting Spoofing: Distinguishing Properties, Anti-spoofing measures are implemented by manufacturers to prevent unauthorized access through the use of fake fingerprints or other biometric spoofing methods. One of these safety measures is the use of advanced algorithms to distinguish between authentic and fraudulent fingerprints.
- Biometric Data Protection: Secure Enclave, Fingerprint data is typically kept in a secure enclave within the device to add an extra layer of protection. This ensures that the biometric data cannot be easily obtained by malicious actors.
- Dual Authentication Techniques: Together with Other Security Features: In-display fingerprint scanners are often used in conjunction with other security features like as facial recognition or traditional PIN/password verification, to allow users to choose the most convenient method.
- Integration with Different Devices: Going Beyond Smartphones: In-display fingerprint scanners are becoming more common in goods other than smartphones, like laptops and tablets. On a variety of

devices, this technology contributes to a dependable and safe user experience.

Upcoming Developments:

- Constant Improvement The speed
- Precision
- dependability of in-display fingerprint scanners

Even though in-display fingerprint scanners provide a practical and safe biometric authentication mechanism, users should understand how important it is to keep their devices updated and maintain good security hygiene in order to ward against potential security vulnerabilities. Biometric authentication techniques ought to become increasingly important in guaranteeing the security of personal devices and data as technology advances.

Augmented Reality: Advancements and Potential Uses

"Augmented reality" (AR) refers to a technology that overlays digital or virtual information on the physical world. This is viewed on a tablet, smartphone, or AR headset. AR has advanced significantly over time, and a wide range of sectors may benefit from its application in Figure 3.

Advancements in Augmented Reality

- Hardware Upgrades: AR Goggles and Headsets using the development of AR technology, users may now enjoy AR in a more immersive and hands-free way using devices like smart glasses and headsets. Companies like Microsoft (HoloLens) and Magic Leap have developed augmented reality glasses for usage in both consumer and professional contexts (Crofton et al., 2019).
- Better Sensing and Tracking: Improved tracking and sensing technologies have made it possible for augmented reality (AR) systems to have a better understanding of and interaction with the real world. Augmented reality applications can now recognize and track real-world objects, resulting in a more smooth and natural experience.

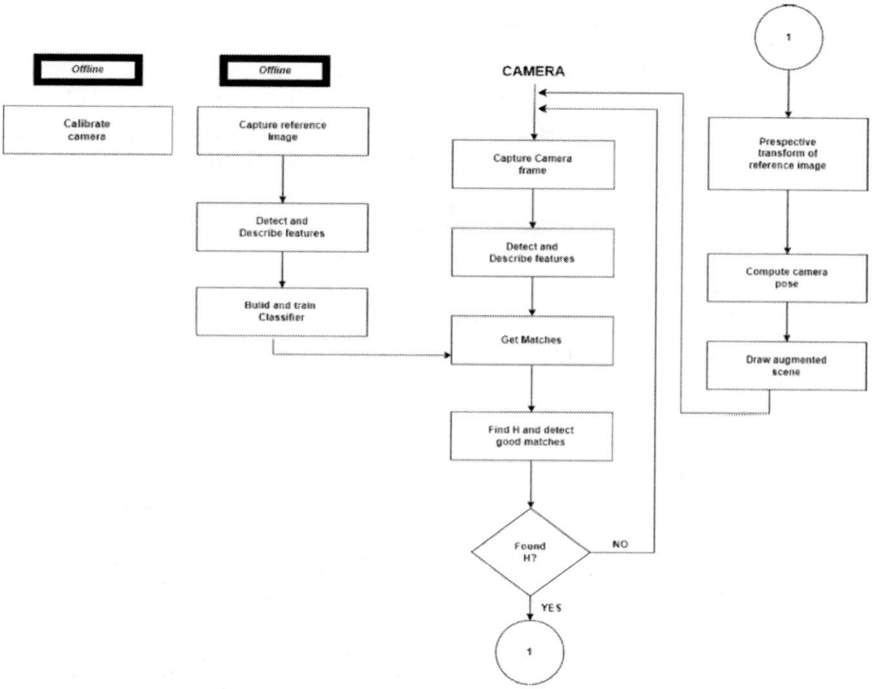

Figure 3. Augmented Reality.

- AI and Machine Learning Integration: Object Recognition, Augmented reality (AR) systems combine machine learning (ML) and artificial intelligence (AI) approaches to enhance object detection and enable more complicated interactions with the physical environment. Artificial intelligence (AI) helps digest real-time data so that augmented reality apps can respond fast to changes in their surroundings.
- Cloud-Based AR: Processing Offloading, Cloud-based augmented reality reduces reliance on device capabilities by offloading laborious processing tasks to the cloud. This opens up the possibility of using augmented reality (AR) on additional devices, including smartphones and lightweight glasses.
- AR Software Development Kits (SDKs): Accessible Development Tools, Developers may now create AR applications more easily because of the availability of AR SDKs from major tech companies like Google's ARCore and Apple's ARKit. As a result, there is now a growing ecosystem of AR content and creativity is encouraged.

Potential Uses of Augmented Reality

- Gaming and Entertainment: Immersive Gaming, Augmented reality (AR) enhances game experiences by superimposing virtual elements on the real world. Pokémon GO and other games have demonstrated the augmented reality's broad appeal and potential in the gaming industry.
- Education and Training: Students can interact with three-dimensional (3D) models, explore historical sites, and see complex concepts through Augmented Reality (AR), which literally brings the classroom to life. Training Simulations, Companies use augmented reality (AR) to give consumers the opportunity to practice in a realistic but virtual environment.
- Retail and E-Commerce: By allowing users to digitally try items on before making a purchase, augmented reality-enabled virtual try-ons enhance online shopping. In-Store Navigation, Customers can utilize augmented reality (AR) to traverse store spaces in order to locate products and get relevant information.
- Healthcare: Surgical Planning, Surgeons can use augmented reality (AR) to visualize and plan surgeries by superimposing medical pictures onto a patient's body. Medical Education, Procedure guidance, anatomical visualization, and simulations are all supported by AR in medical education.
- Manufacturing and Maintenance: Assembly Assistance, by providing real-time guidance for maintenance and assembly tasks, AR lowers errors and increases productivity. Remote Assistance, Technicians can receive professional guidance in real-time through the use of augmented reality, which facilitates remote troubleshooting and repairs.
- Architecture and Design: Visualization, by employing augmented reality (AR), designers and architects may view and present their creations in a physical space. Interactive Design Assessments, Augmented reality (AR) allows collaboration design assessments by superimposing digital models on real-world locales.
- Social media and Communication: Augmented reality (AR) filters and effects are incorporated into social media networks to promote creativity and engagement. Virtual Meetings, by overlaying

information, pictures, or avatars on participants' real environments, augmented reality (AR) can enhance virtual meetings.

- Tourism and Navigation: Users of AR navigation apps can get up-to-date directions and details about neighboring points of interest. Historical Augmentation, Augmented reality (AR) enhances tourist experiences by superimposing historical or cultural material on locations.
- Marketing and Advertising: Interactive Ads, Augmented reality (AR) opens up new methods for consumers to connect with products by enabling immersive and interactive advertising. Virtual Try-Before-You-Buy, Businesses use augmented reality (AR) to allow clients to view products in their workspaces or homes prior to making a purchase.
- Remote Collaboration: Virtual Collaboration environments: By utilizing augmented reality, users may hold virtual meetings and engage with three-dimensional items in shared virtual environments. Users are able to collaborate remotely more easily as a result.

As augmented reality (AR) technology advances, its potential applications should increase, altering how people interact with both the digital and physical worlds.

Biometric Authentication for Enhanced User Privacy and Security

The method of confirming a person's identity using their distinct bodily traits or behavioral patterns is known as biometric authentication. Although there are many security and privacy benefits to biometric authentication, it is important to take into account any possible hazards, such as biometric spoofing or false positives. Strong security protocols, ongoing biometric technology development, and adherence to industry standards may all work together to reduce these dangers and provide an environment that is safe and respectful of users' privacy when it comes to authentication in Figure 4 (Rui et al., 2018).

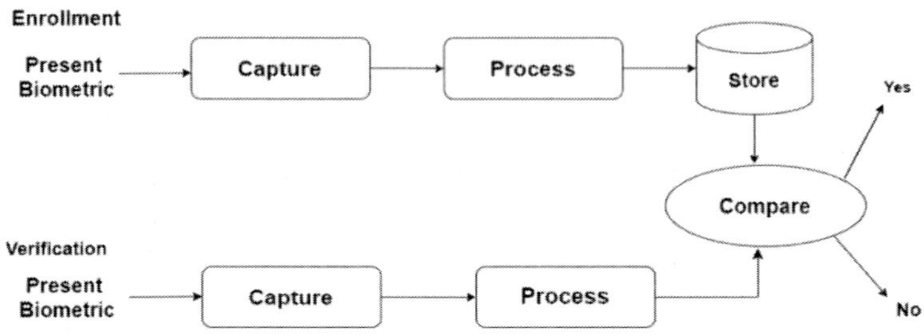

Figure 4. Biometric Authentication System Architecture.

Distinctive and innate qualities Face, Iris, Fingerprints, etc., The Biometric identifiers are unique to each individual and difficult to forge. They include fingerprints, iris patterns, and facial features. This uniqueness adds an additional layer of security to authentication processes. Less Dependency on Passwords: Login without the Need for Passwords By using biometric authentication, ordinary passwords which are prone to loss or unauthorized access—become less necessary (Ratha et al., 2001). Because they are no longer necessary to memorize complex passwords, users may now authenticate more quickly and securely. In the Improved User Experience, Speed and Convenience can Use biometric authentication methods like fingerprint or face recognition, users can access their devices or accounts with ease and speed. This enhances the entire user experience without compromising security. Two-Factor Authentication (2FA) in the Several Security Layers, several authentication factors, including passwords or PINs, can be linked with biometrics to give a multi-layered security strategy. An additional layer of protection is added with this two-factor authentication (2FA). Biometric Data Protection Can Secure Storage, Biometric data is typically stored on devices in secure enclaves, making it challenging for hackers to access or replicate. To further protect the data they store, some biometric systems additionally encrypt it. Dynamic Authentication, to enable ongoing authentication, some biometric systems continuously verify the user's biometric characteristics during a session in Figure 5. If a significant divergence causes the system to request re-authentication, this can offer an extra layer of protection.

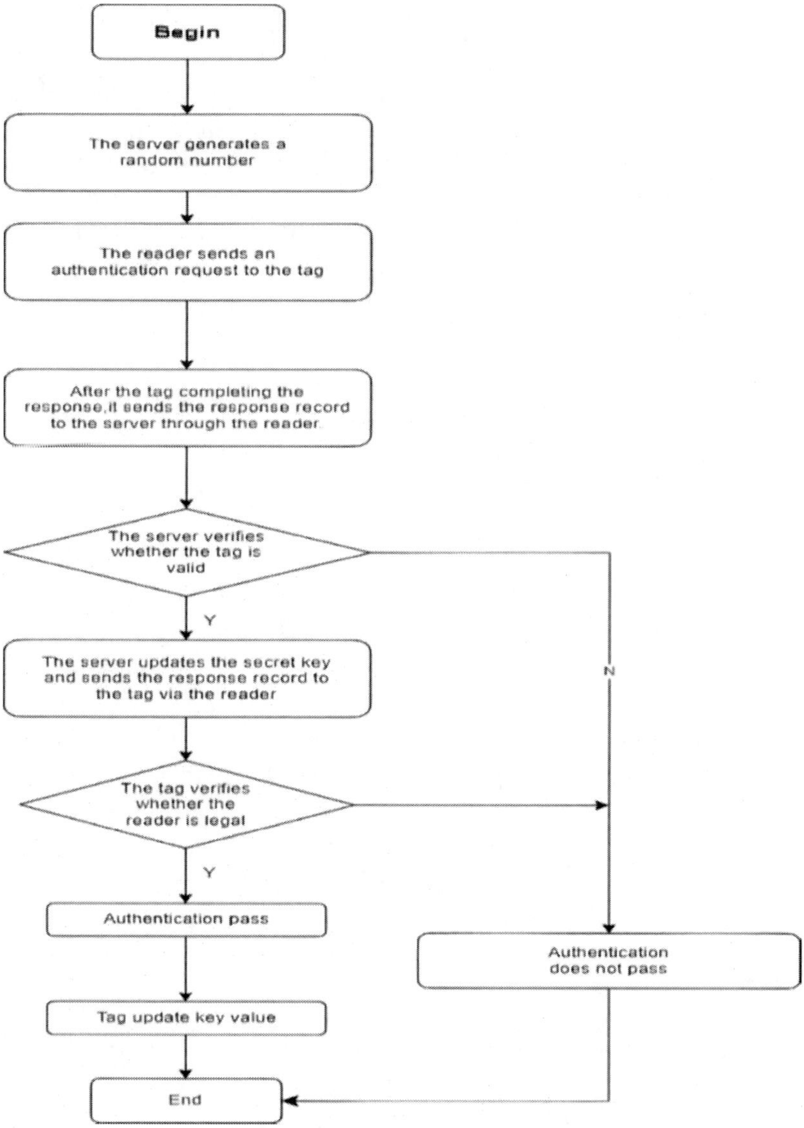

Figure 5. Security Authentication Protocol.

Behavioral Biometrics in Distinctive Behavior Patterns, for continuous identification, behavioral biometrics such as mouse clicks or typing patterns might be used. Every individual possesses a unique collection of patterns that allow them to recognize unwanted access by looking for deviations from the norm. Biometric Templates, Raw biometric data is not saved by biometric systems. Instead, templates are preserved. Instead, they use stored templates or mathematical representations of the biometric features. This adds an additional degree of anonymity because the preserved templates cannot be used to rebuild the original biometric data. By Remoting Authentication: Safe Access from Anywhere, Biometric authentication enables secure remote access to devices or systems. In today's mobile and remote work situations, this is extremely important. Biometric Encryption Biometric Cryptography, Biometric authentication can be combined with cryptographic techniques to further secure data transport and communication. This ensures that, in the absence of proper verification, intercepted data remains incoherent. Observance of Privacy Rules like GDPR and Additional Rules, Biometric systems that adhere to privacy rules, including the General Data Protection Regulation (GDPR), prioritize user privacy by ensuring that biometric data is collected and processed in a way that is both lawful and transparent.

Sustainable Design: Ethical and Environmental Considerations in Mobile Hardware

Sustainable design in the context of mobile hardware refers to considering ethics and the environment throughout the whole life cycle of a gadget, from manufacture to eventual disposal. As technology develops, the electronics industry is beginning to understand how critical it is to reduce its environmental impact and encourage moral behavior. By taking these aspects into account during the design and production phases, manufacturers can contribute to the development of a more moral and environmentally friendly mobile hardware market (Bask et al., 2013).

- Materials Selection: Materials with Renewable and Recyclable Properties Mobile device design can lessen its impact on the environment by utilizing recyclable materials and renewable resources. This involves utilizing resources like bioplastics and repurposed metal.
- Repairability and Modularity: Simple-to-Repair Parts, because modular component designs facilitate upgrades and repairs, devices using them have longer lifespans. Repairability reduces technological waste by enabling consumers to replace damaged pieces with new ones rather than discarding the entire thing.

- Energy Efficiency: Examples of energy-efficient hardware that ought to be incorporated into mobile device designs are low-power processors and displays. By doing this, the device uses less energy overall and the battery lasts longer.
- Durability and Adaptability: Extended Device Lifespan, by reducing the frequency of replacements, taking longevity into account during device design helps to minimize technological waste. By providing software updates and ensuring long-term hardware compatibility, manufacturers may aid with this.
- Conscientious Manufacturing Methods: Ethical procurement, producing more socially conscious goods are facilitated by the use of fair labor practices during the manufacturing process and ethical raw material procurement. Reduced Environmental Impact: Manufacturers should employ environmentally friendly production methods that reduce emissions, water and energy consumption, and emissions.
- End-of-Life Matters to Consider: Recycling and Getting Rid of, when devices are made with simple recyclability in mind, it is simpler to disassemble and reuse their materials at the end of their useful lives. Additionally, manufacturers can implement take-back programs for recycling and proper disposal.
- Sustainability in Packaging: Eco-Friendly and Minimalist Packaging, reducing unnecessary packing and utilizing eco-friendly packaging materials can help minimize waste. Manufacturers can employ recyclable or recycled packaging materials.
- Principles of the Circular Economy: Programs for Recycling and Reuse, putting circular economy principles into effect includes designing policies that promote electronic equipment recycling, refurbishing, and reuse. Manufacturers can set up projects to gather outdated gadgets, refurbish them, or recycle their components.
- Reducing Carbon Footprint: Carbon-Neutral Operations, Manufacturers might attempt to lessen their carbon footprint by investing in renewable energy sources or enrolling in carbon offset programs. This reduces the energy consumption of the production process and its detrimental impact on the environment.
- Transparency and Certification: Environmental Attestations, Customers can feel more at rest knowing that a product complies with environmental standards when it has environmental performance

certifications like ENERGY STAR or EPEAT (Electronic Product Environmental Assessment Tool).

- Technological Innovation in Sustainable Areas: Certifications in environmental and green technologies: When a device gets environmental performance certifications such as ENERGY STAR or EPEAT (Electronic Product Environmental Assessment Tool), customers may rest easier knowing that it conforms with environmental regulations.

Faster Processors and Increased RAM in Enhancing Mobile Performance and Multitasking

RAM (Random Access Memory) and processor speed increases are two important components that intensify mobile performance and facilitate multitasking on smartphones and other devices.

Faster Processors

Increased Speed and Responsiveness in Faster processors, measured in gigahertz (GHz) or other relevant metrics, enable faster program launches, UI navigation, and task execution. It also Enhanced computing Power in Faster CPU devices are more capable of handling increasingly complex computer tasks. This is particularly important for resource-intensive apps, like gaming, video editing, and augmented reality. The Smooth Multimedia Experience: Faster CPUs facilitate the playback of high-definition videos, graphic rendering, and other multimedia content, hence enhancing the multimedia experience on mobile devices. Optimized App Performance can have more computing power at their disposal, app developers are able to create more responsive and feature-rich applications. The user's ability to use various apps on the device is enhanced as a result. The Efficient Multitasking in Users can multitask more smoothly since speedier CPUs allow them to switch between apps without any lag or delays. This is quite beneficial in scenarios when productivity and multitasking are required. The Advanced Machine Learning and Artificial Intelligence in Modern CPUs sometimes have dedicated components for machine learning and artificial intelligence (ML) functions. This enables on-device processing of AI-driven features like speech recognition, predictive text input, and camera enhancements. So, the Energy Efficiency in Processing technology advances are often linked to increases in energy efficiency. Enabling devices to run at higher levels without significantly reducing battery life helps to improve the balance between power and efficiency (Asif et al., 2015).

Increased RAM

Multitasking Capacity in RAM serves as a short-term data and program storage medium. Because more RAM allows devices to manage more open applications at once, multitasking is improved. It has Less frequent App Reloading in More RAM-capable apps can operate in the background without always needing to be stopped and reloaded. Then more seamless user experience and faster app switching. Better App Performance in Apps can load and function faster when they have more RAM available to store important data. This is particularly noticeable in applications that utilize large databases or a lot of RAM. Better Experience with Games has More RAM and allows gaming apps—especially those with demanding graphics requirements—to store more models, textures, and other game elements. As a result, playing the game is more enjoyable and fluid. The Effective Management of Large files is better handled by devices with lots of RAM. This includes tasks like editing high-resolution photos or videos, where having enough RAM is essential for smooth performance. In Optimized Web Browsing: Web browsers that have more RAM are able to hold more tabs and content, which in faster page loading and more seamless navigation. Future-Proofing of More RAM ensures that a device can handle the growing complexity and resource demands of programs, making it more ready for new apps and software updates. A harmonious blend of faster processors and more RAM is needed to achieve a high-performance and responsive user experience on mobile devices. As technology advances, manufacturers strive to incorporate more RAM and powerful processors into their devices to meet the growing demands of users and applications.

Conclusion

New advancements in mobile design and hardware demonstrate a dramatic shift in the direction of smartphone and other portable electronics development. These trends demonstrate how the industry has adjusted to shifting consumer needs, technological advancements, and a growing emphasis on sustainability. As we look to the future, some key conclusions that can be made from these emerging trends include the convergence of innovation, the user-centric approach, and connectivity as a pillar, environmental consciousness, enhanced performance and multitasking, diverse form factors, biometrics as standard security measures, and holistic ecosystems. Because of the ongoing advancements in technology and the changing demands of consumers, these new trends are likely to continue changing in the years to come. Mobile devices will be helpful not only for communication but also as flexible hubs for various daily tasks that promote sustainability, creativity, and community. Manufacturers, developers, and other stakeholders in the mobile sector will play a critical role in shaping this exciting and dynamic future/

References

Asif, Muhammad, Imtiaz A. Taj, S. M. Ziauddin, Maaz Bin Ahmad, and M. Tahir. "A hybrid scheme based on pipelining and multitasking in mobile application processors for advanced video coding." *Scientific Programming* 2015 (2016): 22-22.

Bask, Anu, Merja Halme, Markku Kallio, and Markku Kuula. "Consumer preferences for sustainability and their impact on supply chain management: The case of mobile phones." *International Journal of Physical Distribution & Logistics Management* 43, no. 5/6 (2013): 380-406.

Back, Jong-Ho, Yonghwan Kwon, Hyeju Cho, Huesoo Lee, Dowon Ahn, Hyun-Joong Kim, Youngchang Yu, Youngdo Kim, Wonjoo Lee, and Min Sang Kwon. "Visible-Light-Curable Acrylic Resins toward UV-Light-Blocking Adhesives for Foldable Displays." *Advanced Materials* 35, no. 43 (2023): 2204776.

Crofton, Emily C., Cristina Botinestean, Mark Fenelon, and Eimear Gallagher. "Potential applications for virtual and augmented reality technologies in sensory science." *Innovative Food Science & Emerging Technologies* 56 (2019): 102178.

Delbracio, Mauricio, Damien Kelly, Michael S. Brown, and Peyman Milanfar. "Mobile computational photography: A tour." *Annual Review of Vision Science* 7 (2021): 571-604.

El Khaddar, Mehdia Ajana, Hamid Harroud, Mohammed Boulmalf, Mohammed Elkoutbi, and Ahmed Habbani. "Emerging wireless technologies in e-health trends, challenges, and framework design issues." In *2012 International Conference on Multimedia Computing and Systems*, pp. 440-445. IEEE, 2012.

Huang, Danny Ziyang. "Analysis of the Impact of Foldable Mobile Phones Design on People's Lives." In *2021 International Conference on Public Relations and Social Sciences (ICPRSS 2021)*, pp. 1155-1160. Atlantis Press, 2021.

Kim-Lee, Hyun-Joon, Seog Woo Hong, Dong Kyun Kim, Jinmyoung Kim, Hong Suk Kim, Seok-Whan Chung, Eun-Hyoung Cho, Hae-Sung Kim, and Byung-Kyu Lee. "On-screen fingerprint sensor with optically and electrically tailored transparent electrode patterns for use on high-resolution mobile displays." *Microsystems & Nanoengineering* 6, no. 1 (2020): 98.

Kingslin, M. Theodore. "A Review on Flexible and Foldable Displays." *Journal on Electronics Engineering* 13, no. 3 (2023).

Ni, Tao, Xiaokuan Zhang, and Qingchuan Zhao. "Recovering Fingerprints from In-Display Fingerprint Sensors via Electromagnetic Side Channel." In *Proceedings of the 2023 ACM SIGSAC Conference on Computer and Communications Security*, pp. 253-267. 2023.

Parulski, K., and Majid Rabbani. "The continuing evolution of digital cameras and digital photography systems." In *2000 IEEE International Symposium on Circuits and Systems (ISCAS)*, vol. 5, pp. 101-104. IEEE, 2000.

Ratha, Nalini K., Jonathan H. Connell, and Ruud M. Bolle. "Enhancing security and privacy in biometrics-based authentication systems." *IBM systems Journal* 40, no. 3 (2001): 614-634.

Rui, Zhang, and Zheng Yan. "A survey on biometric authentication: Toward secure and privacy-preserving identification." *IEEE access* 7 (2018): 5994-6009.

Wiencek, Richard, Sagnika Ghosh, Maria C. Laurent-Rice, Eden Black, Taheerah Mujahid, Sameer Kalyan, Monika Priya, Ayush Goyal, Cesar Luna, and Kanwalinderjit Kaur. "Simulation of the 5G Communication Link Between Solar Micro-Inverters and SCADA System." In *2023 5th Global Power, Energy and Communication Conference (GPECOM)*, pp. 311-316. IEEE, 2023.

Yeh, Chih-Chieh, Teng-Wei Huang, You-Ren Lin, and Guo-Dung Su. "The Design and Fabrication of Large-Area Under-Screen Fingerprint Sensors with Optimized Aperture and Microlens Structures." *Sensors* 23, no. 21 (2023): 8731.

Chapter 6

The Role of AI In Mobile Computing

P. Dhanalakshmi[1,*]
Chevuru Nandini[2]
U. Janardhan Reddy[3]
K. Reddy Madhavi[1]
Viswaksena Balaji[4]
and J. Avanija[1]

[1]Department of AI and ML, School of Computing, Mohan Babu University, Tirupati, A.P, India
[2]Department of CSE, Sree Vidyanikethan Engineering College, Tirupati, A.P, India
[3]Gitam University, Bengaluru, India
[4]University of Limerick, Limerick, Ireland

Abstract

The integration of Artificial Intelligence (AI) in mobile computing has revolutionized the way we interact with our devices and access information. This abstract explores the pivotal role of AI in enhancing mobile computing, focusing on its impact on user experience, efficiency, and functionality. Mobile computing's AI-driven features have completely rethought customization by enabling gadgets to recognize user preferences and modify features accordingly. Artificial Intelligence (AI) enables mobile devices to anticipate user demands, provide personalized suggestions, and automate repetitive operations using machine learning algorithms, therefore greatly improving user comfort. on order to maximize resource use on mobile devices, artificial

[*] Corresponding Author's Email: mallidhana5@gmail.com.

In: The Future of Mobile Computing
Editors: Sam Goundar, J. Avanija and K. Reddy Madhavi
ISBN: 979-8-89113-715-8

intelligence is essential. Artificial intelligence (AI) algorithms effectively manage device resources, from processor power to power management, providing peak performance while consuming the least amount of energy possible to extend battery life. Artificial Intelligence (AI) enables sophisticated features in mobile apps, like picture recognition, predictive analysis, and natural language processing. This allows cutting-edge apps that change how people engage with mobile technology in a variety of industries, including healthcare, banking, and entertainment. Security solutions powered by AI are becoming more and more important for protecting sensitive data on mobile devices. By seeing irregularities, spotting possible threats, and putting strong authentication mechanisms in place, AI algorithms support security procedures and make mobile computing environments more secure. Future developments have a plethora of prospects thanks to the combination of AI and mobile computing. The convergence of AI technologies with mobile devices is expected to have significant effects on the mobile computing environment by enabling increasingly more advanced apps, smoother user experiences, and better device capabilities as these technologies advance.

Keywords: AI, mobile computing, user experience, personalization, automation, security, privacy, augmented reality, edge computing, IoT

Introduction

Mobile computing refers to the use of computing devices, such as smartphones, tablets, and wearable devices, that are designed to be easily transported and used while on the move. It involves the creation, transmission, and access of information using a variety of wireless technologies and networks. Mobile computing has become increasingly prevalent in modern society, enabling users to access data and applications from almost anywhere. Portability, Wireless Connectivity, Location Awareness, Limited Resource Constraints, Touch Interfaces, Diverse Applications, Multitasking are some of the mobile computing. Mobile computing is changing the way people work, communicate and access information. It also facilitates the development of a broad mobile application ecosystem for a variety of needs and interests. Businesses continue to evolve with advances in hardware, software and network technology, making mobile devices an integral part of the daily lives of many people and businesses (Singh et al., 2022).

Evolution of Mobile Computing

The evolution of mobile computing has been a dynamic and rapid process, that was marked by significant advancements in hardware, software, and communication technologies. Mobile computing continues to evolve as artificial intelligence is integrated, security features improve, and new trends and technologies are discovered. The future will likely be integrated with new technologies such as artificial intelligence, the Internet of Things (IoT) and advances in data science, providing increasingly useful information and good uses.

- First Generation (1970s-1980s)
- Laptops and Notebooks (1980s-1990s)
- PDAs (Personal Digital Assistants) and Palmtops (1990s-early 2000s)
- Smartphones (2000s-2010s)
- Tablets (2010s)
- Wearable Devices (2010s-present)
- 5G and Enhanced Connectivity (2010s-present)
- Foldable Phones and Flexible Displays (2019-present)
- Edge Computing (2020s)
- Augmented Reality (AR) and Virtual Reality (VR) Integration (2020s).

Significance of AI in Mobile Computing

Artificial Intelligence (AI) is playing an important role in mobile computing by changing the way we interact with and use our mobile devices. The impact of artificial intelligence on mobile phone use; These include personalization, voice assistant, text prediction and self-correction, image and facial recognition, advanced stability security, mobile app development, chatbots and virtual assistants, health and wellness, cognitive computing, visualization., resource management, augmented reality (AR) and virtual reality (VR). The integration of artificial intelligence and mobile computing continues to evolve, providing users with smart, personalized and interactive technology. Artificial intelligence as a technology can play an important role in developing the future of mobile computing.

Fundamentals of Artificial Intelligence

Basics of AI and Machine Learning

Computer science research on artificial intelligence (AI) is essentially concerned with building machines that are capable of tasks that frequently call for human intelligence. Naturally, machine learning (Bhargava et al., 2021) is a subfield of artificial intelligence that develops statistical models and algorithms that allow computers to see patterns in data, learn from it, and make judgments. By training on datasets, a learning machine can gain knowledge over time while improving its performance. The three main methods of machine learning are reinforcement learning (teaching algorithms through trial and error based on environmental input), supervised learning (training models of recorded data), and unsupervised learning (finding patterns in unrecorded data). The combination of artificial intelligence (AI) and machine learning results in AI that can perform tasks such as natural language processing, image recognition, and predictive analytics as specified in Figure 1. These systems have revolutionized many industries and driven technology.

Types of AI: Narrow AI vs. General AI

The two main categories of artificial intelligence (AI) are general intelligence (strong intelligence) and narrow intelligence (weak intelligence). Systems that express intelligence in a strictly defined way and are specifically taught and adapted to one or more tasks are called narrow artificial intelligence (AI) systems. Image recognition, virtual assistants, and translation software are some examples. Although narrow AI is good at good tasks, its cognitive complexity is not as broad as human intelligence. General intelligence, on the other hand, seeks to apply human-like intelligence across a variety of tasks and the ability to understand, retrieve, and use information in a variety of ways. Any intellectual task that humans can do will be done through general intelligence. Although there are now numerous narrow-scope AI applications, general AI remains a challenging and evolving field. Scientists and engineers are working to create flexible and adaptable artificial intelligence (AI) that can demonstrate a wide range of knowledge (Kuusi et al., 2022).

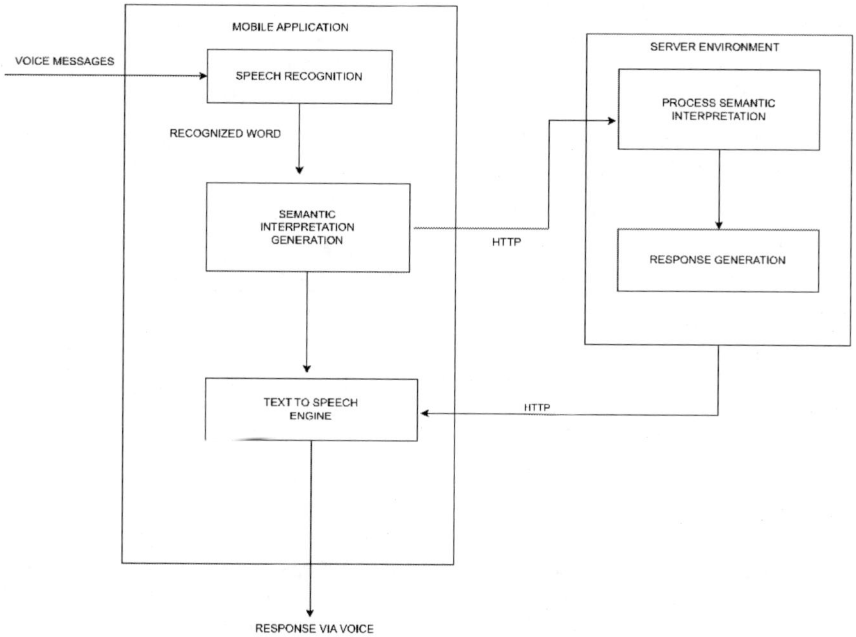

Figure 1. Basic Algorithm of AI.

Machine Learning Algorithms in Mobile Computing

Machine learning (ML) technology has greatly impacted mobile phone usage, allowing devices to learn from data and adapt to the user's behavior. Use different types of machine learning to improve mobile services and applications. For example, recommendation algorithms use user data to provide appropriate content or services in the context of personalized mobile applications, thus making the user experience more efficient. Users now have the ability to engage with their devices in a novel way, all thanks to the development of an intuitive interface made possible by picture and speech recognition algorithms. Because predictive algorithms anticipate user behavior and modify the device accordingly, they also contribute to increased battery life and resource allocation. Numerous machine learning algorithms have been used in mobile devices to improve their intelligence, efficiency, and usability as a result of advancements in mobile technology.

Support Vector Machines (SVM) and Relational Neural Networks (RNN) are popular methods of machine learning, they are important for mobile computing. Support vector technology is used to input text and images in other types of visualizations in mobile applications. SVM helps identify vulnerabilities in mobile security by identifying risks or patterns that indicate compromise. Recurrent neural networks are essential for language processing and speech recognition on mobile devices. Because RNNs are so good at understanding connections, they are useful for applications such as text prediction and command understanding. These algorithms improve user experience, increase the efficiency of mobile applications, and make mobile devices smarter.

Integration of AI in Mobile Devices

AI-Enabled Hardware Components

AI-capable hardware is essential for the success of AI applications in the future. AI efforts can be deployed more rapidly and effectively with systems that include powerful AI accelerators like GPUs and TPUs. Complex mathematical algorithms must be managed by highly qualified experts when using machine learning techniques. AI workloads employ memory designs like high bandwidth memory (HBM) and heterogeneous system architecture (HSA) that intensify data access and transfer. With capabilities like edge photography and speech recognition, AI-enabled sensors streamline device operations and lessen the need for cloud-based AI services. These hardware elements constitute a framework that facilitates the integration and optimization of AI algorithms on a range of platforms.

Embedded AI in Mobile Processors

The process of integrating specialist artificial intelligence technology straight into a mobile device's chipset is known as embedded artificial intelligence in mobile processors. These embedded AI components improve the on-device processing capabilities for machine learning applications. They frequently include specialized neural processing units (NPUs) or AI accelerators. Embedded AI on mobile processors allows AI-driven applications, like image recognition and natural language processing, to be handled more quickly and effectively without depending on cloud computing by execute AI algorithms locally (Chen et al., 2020).

Sensors and AI Integration

To intensify data processing and interpretation, mobile devices are being outfitted with hardware sensors and artificial intelligence algorithms. A clear picture can be obtained from sensor data from the integration of intelligence. Sensors such as accelerometers, gyroscopes, and cameras generate large amounts of data. More intelligent and sensitive mobile devices, this can allow for features like sensor-based interactions, gesture recognition, and context-aware applications.

Role of AI in Power Management:

Artificial intelligence aids in mobile power management, increasing device energy efficiency and battery life. Artificial intelligence systems adjust power settings and resource allocation based on analysis of user behavior, application usage, and device performance. AI improves the overall performance and usability of portable devices by intelligently managing power consumption and assisting in the increasingly continuous optimization of mobile power consumption (Elahi et al., 2021).

AI-Powered Mobile Applications

Overview of AI Applications in Mobile

The way we interact with our devices and the services they provide has been significantly altered by artificial intelligence (AI). These days, mobile applications incorporate AI. Mobile apps can now be more complex, user-friendly, and able to deliver personalized experiences because of AI technologies. As technology advances, it is anticipated that the use of AI in mobile applications will increase, offering users greater insight and personalization. In order to create mobile devices that are multi-user, effective, and efficient in a variety of settings, developers are looking for creative ways to credits AI's capabilities (Zhang et al., 2019).

- Voice Assistants
- Image and Facial Recognition
- Personalized Recommendations
- Chatbots and Virtual Assistants
- Predictive Text and Autocorrect
- Health and Fitness Tracking
- Augmented Reality (AR)
- Language Translation
- Mobile Gaming
- Security and Fraud Prevention
- Predictive Maintenance
- Emotion Recognition.

Personal Assistants and Virtual Agents

Personal Assistants

Software that helps with task management, information exchange, and natural language conversation is called a personal assistant. Artificial intelligence (AI) and natural language processing (NLP) are used by personal assistants to comprehend and react to human requests and queries. These applications make users' life easier by streamlining procedures and offering useful information. Mobile phones and smart speakers are two examples of platforms where personal assistants are often used. Some of the personal assistants are

- Siri (Apple)
- Google Assistant (Google)
- Alexa (Amazon)
- Cortana (Microsoft).

Virtual Agents

A virtual agent is an artificial intelligence program designed to interact with users and assist them in completing specific tasks or providing information for customers (Alsanousi et al., 2023). Digital technology is used by virtual agents and personal assistants to understand user input, deliver pertinent answers, and take action. Personal assistants are linked to the general operation of the device, whereas virtual workers are more specialized and can be integrated into different applications and workspaces to deliver specific services (Erol-kantarci et al., 2018).

- Chatbots
- Automated Customer Service Representatives
- Interactive Voice Response (IVR) Systems
- Virtual Sales Assistants
- Healthcare Virtual Assistants.

AI-Driven Health and Fitness Apps

Artificial intelligence (AI) technology is used by health and fitness apps to enhance the well-being of a number of users. These apps go beyond the rating system and utilizing machine learning algorithms, data analysis, and personalized suggestions to give users a better, more tailored experience. These are some of applications for fitness and health that are supported by artificial intelligence (Baldauf et al., 2020).

- Personalized Workout Plans
- Smart Coaching and Guidance
- Health Monitoring and Insights
- Nutritional Guidance
- Predictive Analytics
- Adaptive Workouts
- Behavioral Analysis and Habit Formation
- Emotional Well-being Support
- Integration with Wearable Devices
- Social and Community Features
- Remote Health Monitoring

- Continuous Learning and Improvement

AI-powered health and fitness apps include Nike Training Club, MyFitnessPal, and Fitbit. These apps might credit more artificial intelligence as technology develops to give users more helpful and individualized health and fitness experiences.

Mobile Security and AI

AI in Mobile Security Threat Detection

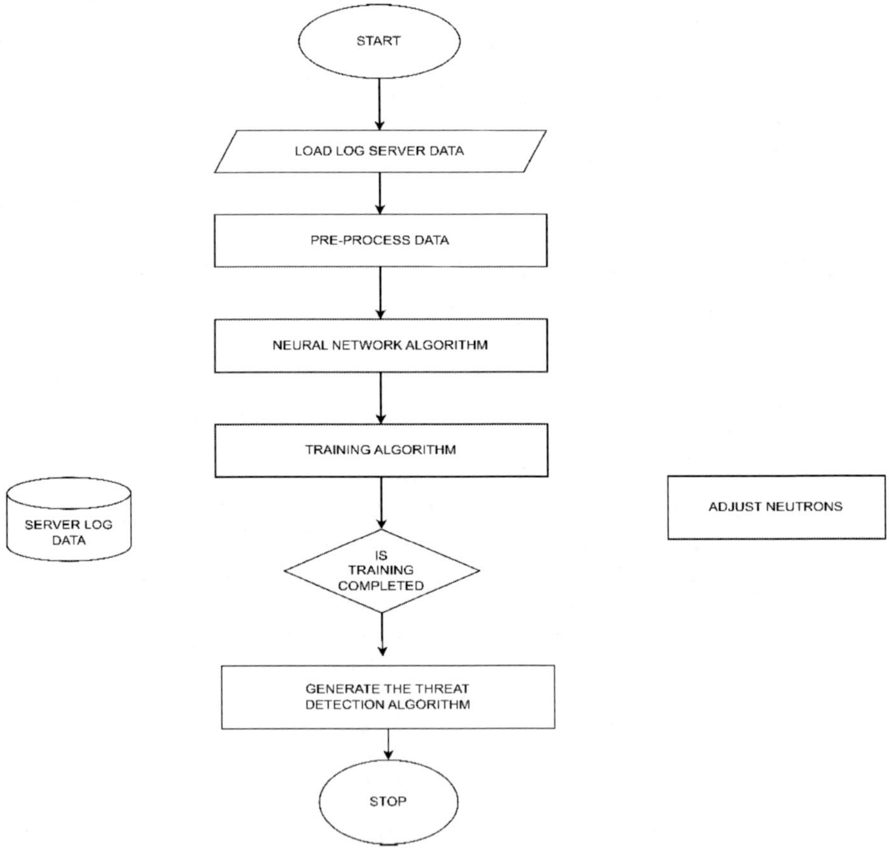

Figure 2. Threat Detection Algorithm.

The process of detecting, evaluating, and reacting to security threats in mobile devices by utilizing the hardware output of cutting-edge technologies, machine learning algorithms, and intelligent machines is known as artificial intelligence (AI) in mobile security research. The aim of mobile security threat is to shield smartphones, tablets, and other mobile devices from malware, scams such as phishing, hacking attempts, and other cybersecurity risks. In order to address the dynamic and ever-evolving nature of cybersecurity threats to mobile devices, artificial intelligence (AI) is crucial in mobile security research as specified in Figure 2. With the use of intelligent algorithms and real-time analysis, this technology fortifies the mobile platform's overall security and shields users from a range of dangers (Hu et al., 2021).

Biometric Authentication and AI

Biometric authentication and artificial intelligence (AI) are linked; AI intensifies the precision, safety, and usefulness of biometric systems. Biometric authentication is the process of confirming an individual's identity through their body or behavior. How artificial intelligence is applied to biometric technology specified in Figure 3:

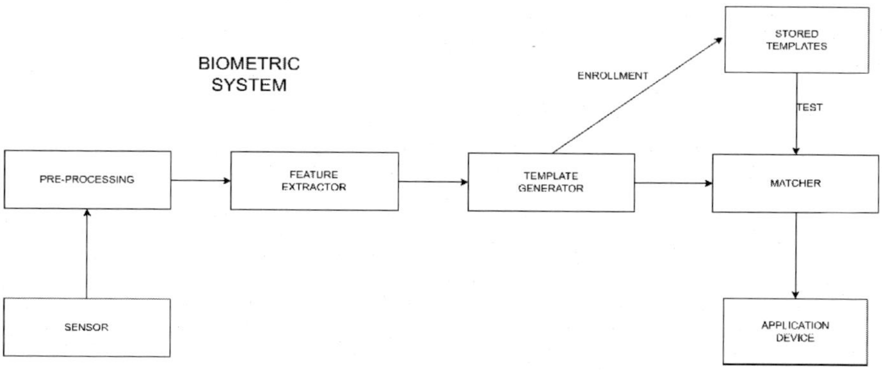

Figure 3. Biometric Technology and Authentication Process.

- Facial Recognition
- Fingerprint Recognition
- Voice Recognition
- Iris Recognition
- Behavioral Biometrics

- Continuous Authentication
- Security and Anti-Spoofing
- User Experience and Adaptability

Artificial intelligence (AI) can improve security and precision in biometric systems and moreover economical and effective applications of technology, such as financial transactions, administrative control, and mobile phones.

Privacy Concerns and AI in Mobile Computing

The primary areas of privacy concern in the fields of mobile computing and artificial intelligence (AI) are the risks and issues that may arise from the collection, processing, and storing of personal data on mobile devices and applications that enable AI capabilities. Using mobile phones and intelligence raises privacy concerns about data collection, processing, and analysis; understanding security issues; giving clear and informed consent; in Figure 4. following legal requirements; and monitoring different products. As mobile computing and artificial intelligence become more integrated, privacy concerns will necessitate the consideration of several technological, legal, and ethical issues. Security precautions must be taken, user privacy must be prioritized, and developers must be transparent about how they handle user data in order to win over customers' trust. Putting the finest privacy and compliance standards to use is necessary for preventing privacy issues in mobile applications driven by AI.

AI for Mobile Device Management

Utilize artificial intelligence (AI) in the mobile device management (MDM) industry to efficiently manage and safeguard mobile devices. Mobile device management is a crucial component of IT administration, particularly in settings where staff members utilize smartphones, tablets, and other mobile devices. A theoretical application of artificial intelligence (AI) in mobile device management includes statistical analysis, anomaly detection, dynamic policy enforcement, context-aware management, behavioral biometrics for authentication, automated threat response, user behavior analytics, and energy and resource optimization are the issues of the mobile device management. These applications use machine learning and analytics to boost productivity, enhance security, and offer an easier-to-use, context-aware method of managing mobile devices within the company.

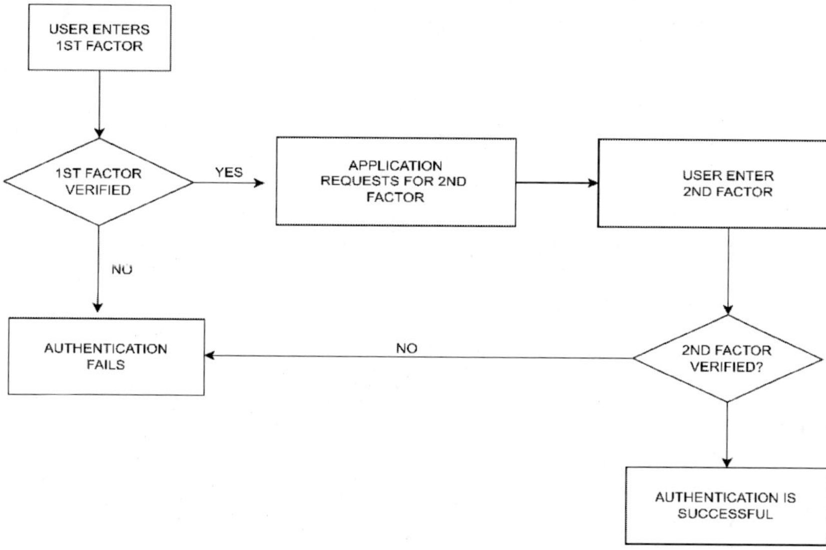

Figure 4. Two-Factor Authentication (2FA).

AI in Mobile User Experience

Personalization and AI

Personalization is the process of adjusting goods, services, or experiences to each user's or customer's unique requirements, preferences, and capabilities. The goal of personalization is to boost user satisfaction and engagement by offering advice or data that is relevant and helpful to each unique user. It can be applied to a wide range of responsibilities, including distribution of material, marketing, e-commerce, personalization, and user interface. Because artificial intelligence (AI) algorithms and computational models enable the analysis of vast volumes of data and the prediction or decision-making of the unique characteristics of users, their application is crucial for adaptability. AI may learn from user interaction and get better over time to offer more precise services or recommendations. Personal systems frequently employ machine learning, a subfield of artificial intelligence, to recognize trends and anticipate user preferences. When analyzing and interpreting user data, artificial intelligence (AI), and machine learning in particular, are strong tools for efficiency and personalization.

AI-Driven Content Recommendations

In order to offer or recommend tailored content, artificial intelligence (AI) algorithms and technology assess user behavior, preferences, and other pertinent data. Artificial intelligence-driven content suggestion is the term for this procedure. Content incorporates anything that viewers might find relevant or interesting, such as clothing, music, films, products, and other information. A number of online platforms, including news portals, forums, e-commerce sites, and streaming media services, frequently offer suggestions for content that is informed by intelligence. Intensify customer satisfaction, engagement, and overall experience through tailored information is intended to keep people interested and engaged.

Natural Language Processing for Mobile Interfaces

Natural Language Processing (NLP) is an application of technology that enables mobile devices to understand, interpret, and respond to human speech within and within the context of the mobile device. Natural Language Processing (NLP) allows users to be more interactive and interactive with computers and mobile devices. It targets the following NLP mobile interfaces:

- Text Understanding
- Speech Recognition
- Intent Recognition
- Conversational Interfaces
- Context Awareness
- Text Generation

Applications such as messaging apps, virtual assistants (like Siri and Google Assistant), translation services, and mobile interfaces make greater use of natural language processing (NLP). The intention is to make technology more approachable and receptive to human language by fostering a more natural and user-friendly relationship between people and their mobile devices.

Augmented Reality (AR) and Virtual Reality (VR) in Mobile

Virtual reality (VR) and augmented reality (AR) are immersive technologies that can generate whole new digital worlds or change how the user perceives the real world. They provide consumers with distinctive and engaging experiences when used with mobile devices.

Augmented Reality (AR) for Mobile

By fusing virtual and real-world elements together, augmented reality superimposes digital content on the outside world to improve the user's view. Mobile Applications for Augmented reality (AR) is frequently employed in mobile applications to give consumers access to contextually relevant information in real time. AR apps, for instance, have the ability to identify things using the camera on the device and present extra data or interactive features on the screen.

Virtual Reality (VR) for Mobile

Virtual reality isolates people from the real world and creates a wholly digital experience by submerging them in a computer-generated, simulated environment. Applications for Mobile VR on mobile devices usually require the use of a headset or a customized case that encloses the smartphone. Applications for mobile virtual reality (VR) can include educational materials, virtual tours, simulations, and immersive gaming.

AR and VR (Ardiny et al., 2018) technologies leverage mobile devices cameras, sensors, and computational power to create captivating and interactive experiences. The integration of AR and VR into mobile applications is evolving along with technology, offering users new and inventive ways to engage with digital content.

Edge Computing and AI in Mobile

Edge Computing Basics

Edge computing is a distributed computing paradigm that eliminates the need for a centralized data-processing warehouse by bringing computation and data storage closer to the point of demand. Edge computing adopts a distinct strategy by carrying out these operations on or close to the source of data generation, as opposed to typical cloud computing, which sends data to a distant server or data center for processing and analysis (Goundar et al., 2021). Edge computing is an example of cloud computing that enables greater distribution and efficiency when it comes to data processing across multiple applications and businesses as specified in Figure 5.

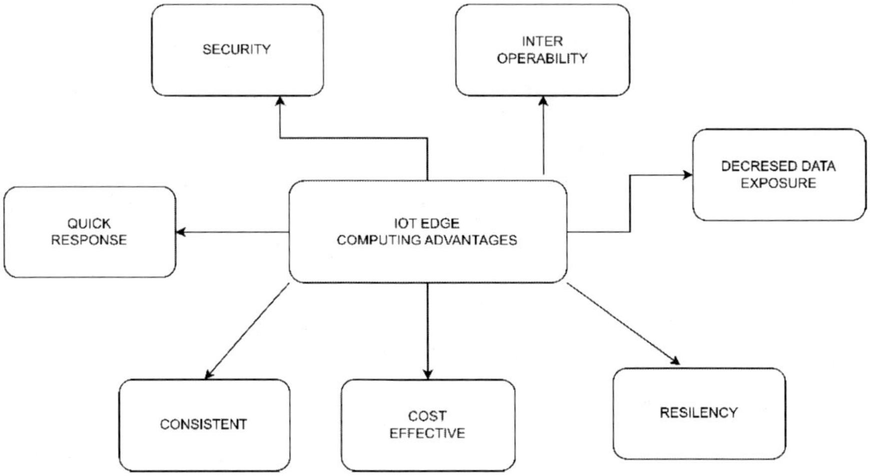

Figure 5. IoT Edge Computing Advatanges.

AI at the Edge: Benefits and Challenges

Rather than simply processing data on cloud servers in the middle, Edge AI uses AI capabilities directly at the edge of the device where data is created. This strategy has advantages and disadvantages of its own.

Benefits of AI at the Edge:

- Low Latency
- Bandwidth Efficiency
- Privacy and Security:
- Offline Operation
- Real-time Decision Making
- Scalability.

Challenges of AI at the Edge

Constrained Resources in Computing resources, such as memory, storage, and processor power, are frequently limited to edge devices. This can restrict the intricacy of AI models that are able to be used with these gadgets. Deploying AI models with substantial volumes and intricate structures on edge devices with restricted compute and storage capabilities may prove to be difficult. Optimization methods are frequently needed. The amount of power consumed is limited. The amount of power that certain edge devices can use is limited, particularly those run-on batteries. The device's usability may be impacted by resource-intensive AI algorithms that rapidly deplete the battery. Control and Upkeep, on a large number of dispersed edge devices, managing and upgrading AI models can be difficult. Careful maintenance of the edge infrastructure is necessary to ensure updates, security, and consistency. Cloud integration. Although edge computing moves processing closer to the data source, it is frequently necessary to integrate with cloud services for tasks like long-term storage, centralized analytics, or model training. Data Privacy Issues, Data security on the edge devices is an issue even when processing data at the edge improves privacy. Locally storing sensitive data is essential. The ecosystem of edge computing encompasses a range of platforms and devices and requires standardization and interoperability. It could be difficult to create universal solutions due to standardization and compatibility issues. Finally, edge AI has many advantages in terms of improved privacy, bandwidth efficiency, and reduced latency. However, it presents some challenges, such as energy consumption, model complexity, usage limitations, and requirements for good management and air integration. AI to reach at the cutting edge of numerous sectors and applications, these issues must be resolved.

Edge AI in Mobile Applications

Edge artificial intelligence (AI) refers to the use of artificial intelligence (AI) capabilities directly into mobile apps. As a result, mobile devices may function locally instead of relying on cloud computing. This idea offers a lot of benefits and opens up new possibilities for developing the most efficient and practical mobile applications (Avanija et al., 2022). These are some of edge AI in mobile applications

- Image and Video Processing
- Speech and Natural Language Processing
- Recommendation Systems
- Health and Fitness Tracking
- Offline Navigation
- Security and Authentication
- Gaming and Augmented Reality

While there are numerous advantages to employing Edge AI in mobile apps, while developing and implementing AI models for on-device use, developers must consider the constraints of mobile devices, such as memory and processing power restrictions. a combination between cloud-based services and on-device processing may be needed for certain functionality and scalability.

Edge-Based Machine Learning Models

Edge models are machine learning models loaded and executed directly on edge devices, which include sensors, cameras, smartphones, and other Internet of Things (IoT) devices. It will lessen the necessity for centralized processing on cloud servers by moving machine learning's processing capacity closer to the data center. Several edge-based machine learning models are as follows (Wang et al., 2019).

- Edge-based machine learning models that carry out on-device inference, or the act of generating predictions or judgments, do so directly on the device from which the data is obtained.
- By using model compression approaches, machine learning models can be deployed on edge devices with limited resources because of their smaller size.
- Reducing a model's numerical values' precision, usually from 32-bit floating-point integers to lower-bit representations, is known as quantization.
- Utilizing prior information from pre-trained models on one job to enhance performance on a related task is known as transfer learning.

- Without exchanging raw data, federated learning allows model training across dispersed edge devices. All that is transmitted are model updates.
- Collaboration from Edge to in some cases, cloud and edge-based machine learning models work with cloud servers. While inference is managed at the edge, model updates or training can be performed in the cloud.
- Energy Efficiency, the aim of creating learning models in edge-based systems is to reduce energy consumption in computing.
- Instant decisions, Edge-based models enable rapid decisions without the need for central servers or constant Internet connections.
- Adaptive Learning, it Adapting to Changing Environment or User Activity The edge-based machine learning model will include adaptive learning strategies.

The need for minimum latency, privacy protection, and resource efficiency is the driving force behind deploying machine learning models at the edge. As technology evolves, machine learning remains critical for intelligent use across multiple disciplines.

Challenges and Future Trends

Current Challenges in AI-Powered Mobile Computing

Today, mobile computing driven by artificial intelligence faces many challenges. Due to its reliance on the constrained resources of mobile devices, artificial intelligence algorithms provide a significant issue in light of the growing need for computational power and energy usage. Large-scale user data collection and processing by AI apps raises privacy and security concerns around data leaks and unauthorized access. Insufficient integration and compatibility will make it more difficult for AI solutions to be effectively integrated across various mobile devices. It is challenging to guarantee justice and accountability in AI-powered mobile applications due to ethical concerns about impartial algorithms and transparent decision-making procedures. To optimize the advantages of mobile intelligence while safeguarding user security, privacy, and ethical norms, these problems must be resolved (Elahi et al., 2021).

Ethical Considerations and AI

The ethical concerns surrounding artificial intelligence are growing in significance as technology advances and is integrated into more facets of society. Concerning factors include possible misuses of intelligence in areas like social media management and monitoring, as well as biases in algorithms and decision-making processes. A significant ethical challenge is ensuring artificial intelligence systems are unbiased and responsible, as prejudiced data might be utilized to create discriminating judgments. Large volumes of personal data are frequently collected and managed by AI programs, raising privacy concerns as well. The moral application of AI in society, it is essential to find a balance between the benefits of AI innovation and the protection of human rights and clean prosperity.

Future Trends and Innovations in AI for Mobile

The field of AI is rapidly evolving, and there are new developments. These some future trends and innovations in AI for mobile

- Edge AI
- AI-powered Personalization
- Natural Language Processing (NLP)
- AI-driven Camera Features
- AI in Mobile Gaming
- Healthcare Applications
- 5G Integration
- Security and Privacy
- AI-enhanced User Interfaces (UI)
- Collaboration with Other Technologies

The widespread adoption and practical application of these trends are contingent upon a number of factors, such as user acceptance, regulatory considerations, and technological advancements. Future developments in mobile AI should prioritize edge AI, greater personalization, and enhanced user experience. Personal assistants and services driven by artificial intelligence will be able to better understand their clients' needs, make recommendations, and work with them into their daily schedules. By reducing reliance on cloud services and enabling faster and more efficient AI applications, edge AI can help with privacy concerns. Edge artificial intelligence will also become more important in terms of device performance. Additionally, improving our knowledge of computer science, computer vision, and natural language processing will help to create mobile and interactive knowledge that will influence smart mobile innovation in the future (Gill et al., 2022).

Case Studies and Success Stories

Real-World Examples of AI Implementation in Mobile

The application of artificial intelligence on mobile devices is becoming more and more popular. Virtual assistants, like Google Assistant, Apple's Siri, and Amazon's Alexa, allow users to be productive and hands-free by understanding and responding to user requests through sophisticated machine learning and language processing algorithms. Google Photos is another noteworthy example of AI image recognition. It makes managing images easier for users by using sophisticated techniques to search and classify images based on content. Mobile keyboards (such as those found on smartphones) that use artificial intelligence (AI) for text prediction and autocorrection continuously learn from the way users type in order to provide messages that are more precise and clearer while also enabling faster and more accurate typing. In the healthcare industry, AI is employed for tasks including remote patient monitoring through mobile applications and early illness diagnosis. Smart algorithms in healthcare apps, for instance, may evaluate sensor data and wearable devices to deliver individualized health information and encourage preventative steps. These examples demonstrate how artificial intelligence (AI) (Marr et al., 2019), which boosts productivity, customization, and efficiency in enterprises, is now a crucial component of the mobile experience.

Impact of AI on Mobile Industries

Artificial Intelligence (AI) has had a significant impact on the mobile industry, transforming various aspects of the sector. In AI algorithms analyze user behavior and preferences to provide personalized content recommendations. In the mobile industry, this is evident in personalized app suggestions, content recommendations, and targeted advertisements. User Interface Enhancement, AI is used to optimize user interfaces by adapting to individual usage patterns. This leads to more intuitive and user-friendly mobile experiences. Voice Assistants, it is AI-powered voice assistants, such as Siri, Google Assistant, and Alexa, have become integral to mobile devices. They enable users to perform tasks, get information, and control their devices through NL interactions. Predictive Analytics, it helps mobile companies anticipate user needs and behavior. Chatbots, it provides instant customer support, answer queries, and assists users in various tasks. Intensify Security, it is also used to improve mobile security through features like facial recognition, fingerprint scanning, and behavioral biometrics. AI algorithms can detect unusual patterns of behavior, helping to identify and prevent security threats. Mobile App Development, Automated testing, code generation, and bug detection are some areas where AI can enhance efficiency and speed up development cycles. So finally, AI has brought about transformative changes in the mobile industry, impacting everything from user experience to security, development processes, and business strategies. The integration of AI technologies continues to shape the future of mobile technologies, offering new possibilities and opportunities for innovation.

Conclusion

The future of mobile technology is greatly influenced by artificial intelligence (Roy et al., 2020) which has the capacity to alter the device's functionality, user experience, and overall technological condition. Mobile devices with AI built in will be able to instantaneously adjust to the user's behavior, preferences, and surroundings, leading to previously unheard-of improvements. People's mobile device usage will be altered by augmented reality and better speech quality, which will facilitate conversation and make information retrieval more convenient. Furthermore, by enhancing energy management, security, and device performance, artificial intelligence will increase mobile phone performance and security. It's anticipated that mobile technology and artificial intelligence (AI) will work together to facilitate social engagement and make mobile devices more intimate and linked.

References

Alsanousi, Bassam, Abdulmohsen S. Albesher, Hyunsook Do, and Stephanie Ludi. "Investigating the user experience and evaluating usability issues in ai-enabled learning mobile apps: An analysis of user reviews." *International Journal of Advanced Computer Science and Applications* 14, no. 6 (2023).

Ardiny, Hadi, and Esmaeel Khanmirza. "The role of AR and VR technologies in education developments: opportunities and challenges." In *2018 6th RSI international conference on robotics and mechatronics* (ICROM), pp. 482-487. IEEE, 2018.

Avanija, J., Gurram Sunitha, K. Reddy Madhavi, S. Sreenivasa Chakravarthi, and R. Hitesh Sai Vittal. "Prediction and Analysis of Cervical Cancer: An Ensemble Approach." In *2022 4th International Conference on Inventive Research in Computing Applications* (ICIRCA), pp. 1734-1739. IEEE, 2022.

Avanija, J., Suneetha Konduru, Vijetha Kura, Grande NagaJyothi, and Bhanu Prakash Dudi. "Designing a Fuzzy Q-Learning Power Energy System Using Reinforcement Learning." *International Journal of Fuzzy System Applications* (IJFSA) 11, no. 3 (2022): 1-12.

Baldauf, Matthias, Peter Fröehlich, and Rainer Endl. "Trust me, I'ma doctor–user perceptions of AI-driven apps for mobile health diagnosis." In *Proceedings of the 19th International Conference on Mobile and Ubiquitous Multimedia*, pp. 167-178. 2020.

Bhargava, Cherry, and Pradeep Kumar Sharma, eds. *Artificial intelligence: fundamentals and applications.* CRC Press, 2021.

Chen, Yanjiao, Baolin Zheng, Zihan Zhang, Qian Wang, Chao Shen, and Qian Zhang. "Deep learning on mobile and embedded devices: State-of-the-art, challenges, and future directions." *ACM Computing Surveys* (CSUR) 53, no. 4 (2020): 1-37 (Chen et al., 2020).

Elahi, Haroon, Guojun Wang, Yang Xu, Aniello Castiglione, Qiben Yan, and Muhammad Naeem Shehzad. "On the Characterization and Risk Assessment of AI-Powered Mobile Cloud Applications." *Computer Standards & Interfaces* 78 (2021): 103538.

Erol-Kantarci, Melike, and Sukhmani Sukhmani. "Caching and computing at the edge for mobile augmented reality and virtual reality (AR/VR) in 5G." In *Ad Hoc Networks: 9th International Conference, AdHocNets 2017*, Niagara Falls, ON, Canada, September 28–29, 2017, Proceedings, pp. 169-177. Springer International Publishing, 2018.

Fasanella, Marco. "Dimensions of AI-enabled mobile and embedded devices: an integration design guide." (2022) (Fasanella and Marco, 2022).

Gill, Sukhpal Singh, Minxian Xu, Carlo Ottaviani, Panos Patros, Rami Bahsoon, Arash Shaghaghi, Muhammed Golec et al. "AI for next generation computing: Emerging trends and future directions." *Internet of Things* 19 (2022): 100514 .

Goundar, Sam, J. Avanija, Gurram Sunitha, K. Reddy Madhavi, and S. Bharath Bhushan, eds. Innovations in the industrial Internet of Things (IIoT) and smart factory. *IGI Global*, 2021.

Hu, Yupeng, Wenxin Kuang, Zheng Qin, Kenli Li, Jiliang Zhang, Yansong Gao, Wenjia Li, and Keqin Li. "Artificial intelligence security: Threats and countermeasures." *ACM Computing Surveys* (CSUR) 55, no. 1 (2021): 1-36.

Kuusi, Osmo, and Sirkka Heinonen. "Scenarios from artificial narrow intelligence to artificial general intelligence—reviewing the results of the international work/technology 2050 study." *World Futures Review* 14, no. 1 (2022): 65-79.

Roy, Palash, Sujan Sarker, Md Abdur Razzaque, Mohammad Mehedi Hassan, Salman A. AlQahtani, Gianluca Aloi, and Giancarlo Fortino. "AI-enabled mobile multimedia service instance placement scheme in mobile edge computing." *Computer Networks* 182 (2020): 107573.

Singh, Ashish, Suresh Chandra Satapathy, Arnab Roy, and Adnan Gutub. "Ai-based mobile edge computing for IoT: Applications, challenges, and future scope." *Arabian Journal for Science and Engineering* (2022): 1-31.

Wang, Xiaofei, Yiwen Han, Chenyang Wang, Qiyang Zhao, Xu Chen, and Min Chen. "In-edge AI: Intelligentizing mobile edge computing, caching and communication by federated learning." *Ieee Network* 33, no. 5 (2019): 156-165.

Chapter 7

Intelligent Mobile Assistants: The Power of Machine Learning

J. Avanija[1]
Kakarla Kavitha[2,*]
Katika Manasa[2]
Mogipalli Madhumitha[2]
Vanam Padma Teja[2]
and Viswaksena Balaji[3]
[1]Department of AI and ML, School of Computing, Mohan Babu University, Tirupati, A.P., India
[2]Department of CSE, Sree Vidyanikethan Engineering College, Tirupati, A.P., India
[3]University of Limerick, Limerick, Ireland

Abstract

"To reinvent mobile computing, intelligent mobile assistants are using machine learning to create a new form of communication." The synergy of the two is explored in this chapter, emphasising the crucial role played by machine learning (ML). The study examines the foundations of machine learning in mobile systems, including algorithm integration and intelligent mobile assistants (IMAs') evolutionary path. It highlights the essential components of natural language processing, speech recognition and computerised vision in order to demonstrate their importance. The multifaceted use of IMAs is shown by mobile ML applications such as personalised recommendations, adaptive interfaces. In addition, the growing domain of IMAs is further underlined by integration into the

* Corresponding Author's Email: kkavithakakarla477@gmail.com.

In: The Future of Mobile Computing
Editors: Sam Goundar, J. Avanija and K. Reddy Madhavi
ISBN: 979-8-89113-715-8

Internet of Things that includes household appliances and wearable devices. We address ethical considerations, security implications, challenges and future prospects leading to enhanced IMAs that will foresee a dynamic future shaped by the evolution of machine learning in mobile environments.

Keywords: natural language processing (NLP), speech recognition, mobile machine learning, personalization algorithms, IoT integration, adaptive user interfaces, data privacy in mobile computing, ethical AI in mobile environments, computer vision in mobile devices

Introduction

Intelligent mobile assistants (IMAs) are software applications that could apprehend and reply to consumer queries and commands in an herbal language. They are normally powered via a mixture of artificial intelligence (AI) technologies, including system gaining knowledge of (ML), herbal language processing (NLP), and speech recognition. IMAs have been around for many years, however they have got grow to be increasingly more popular in current years with the rise of smartphones and different cellular gadgets. Today, there are a number of distinctive IMAs available, such as Siri, Google Assistant, and Alexa.

IMAs can perform an extensive range of obligations, along with:

- Answering questions
- Setting reminders
- Playing song
- Making calls
- Sending text messages
- Navigating to locations
- Controlling clever home devices

Significance of Machine Learning in Mobile Assistance

Machine mastering plays a critical position in intelligent cell assistants. ML algorithms are used to train IMAs to understand and reply to user queries and instructions in an herbal manner. For example, ML algorithms are used to teach IMAs to understand special forms of speech, even in noisy environments. ML algorithms are also used to educate IMAs to recognize the means of consumer queries, even if they're ambiguous or incomplete. ML algorithms are also used to enhance the overall performance of IMAs over the years. For example, ML algorithms may be used to become aware of not unusual mistakes that IMAs make after which train the IMAs to keep away from those mistakes in the destiny.

Benefits of Intelligent Mobile Assistants

IMAs offer some of blessings, along with:

- Convenience: IMAs could make it simpler and faster for customers to finish responsibilities. For example, customers can use an IMA to set a reminder or play a music while not having to type or tap on their tool.
- Productivity: IMAs can assist users to be extra effective with the aid of automating repetitive responsibilities and imparting data on call for. For instance, users can use an IMA to test their calendar or get directions to a assembly while not having to stop what they're doing.
- Accessibility: IMAs can make mobile devices extra available to human beings with disabilities. For instance, human beings with visual impairments can use an IMA to govern their tool and get entry to information.

Future of Intelligent Mobile Assistants

IMAs are still under development, however they're rapidly becoming greater sophisticated and capable. In the destiny, IMAs are expected to turn out to be even more personalised and proactive. For instance, IMAs can be capable of anticipating person wishes and provide help before the user even asks for it. IMAs are also anticipated to become extra integrated with different devices and services. For example, IMAs can be able to manipulate smart domestic gadgets, control personal finances, and even offer clinical assistance. Overall, IMAs have the ability to revolutionize the manner we have interaction with our cell gadgets. As IMAs end up extra state-of-the-art and successful, they may possibly become an essential part of our lives (Sarker et al., 2021).

Foundations of Machine Learning in Mobile Computing

Overview of Machine Learning Algorithms

Machine learning algorithms can be categorized into three types: supervised learning, unsupervised learning, and reinforcement learning (Carbonell et al., 1983). Supervised learning algorithms are trained using labeled data and can predict outcomes based on input-output mappings. Examples include linear regression, logistic regression, decision trees, and support vector machines. On the other hand, unsupervised learning algorithms are trained on raw data without labeled outputs as specified in Figure 1. They discover patterns in the data without prior knowledge of those patterns. Examples include clustering, dimensionality reduction, and association rule learning specified in Table 1. Reinforcement learning algorithms learn through interaction with an environment. They take actions to maximize rewards and minimize punishments. Examples include Q-learning and policy gradient. Chooosing the most suitable algorithm for a specific problem depends on the data and desired outcomes, this is just a glimpse of the many machine learning algorithms available.

Table 1. Types of learning and machine learning algorithm

Type	Description	Example
Supervised learning	Algorithms are trained on a set of labelled data, where each data point has both an input and an output.	Linear regression, logistic regression, decision trees, support vector machines
Unsupervised learning	Algorithms are trained on a set of unlabeled data, where each data point only has an input.	Clustering, dimensionality reduction, association rule learning
Reinforcement learning	Algorithms are trained by interacting with an environment and learning to take actions that maximize reward and minimize punishment.	Q-learning, policy gradients

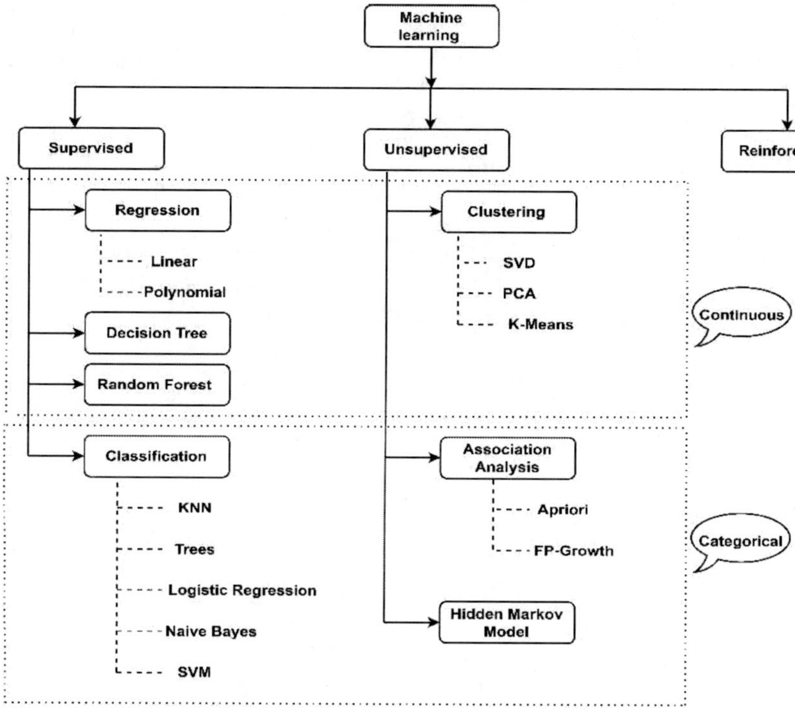

Figure 1. Overview of Machine Learning Algorithm.

Integration of Machine Learning in Mobile Systems

Mobile systems are integrating machine learning (ML), which offers a number of benefits. By decreasing latency and resource efficiency, automating activities, and enhancing user experience, machine learning algorithms can boost performance. Wearable technology that tracks fitness data and monitors health, cellphones that employ ML to optimize battery life and camera quality, and smart home gadgets that learn user preferences and control equipment are a few examples of ML integration. Machine learning (ML) models can be used to enhance functionality, personalize the user experience, or offer contextual support as specified in Figure 2. They're training to use data from a variety of sources (Będkowski, 2013). The processes of the integration of ML in mobile systems is problem selection, data collection and maintenance, ML algorithm selection, cloud Service based training, and mobile implementation of the model (Avanija et al.2022). Nevertheless, there are drawbacks such as a limited ability to use mobile devices, privacy issues, as well as security risks. However, mobile platforms offer new possibilities for machine learning on the basis of novel applications, enhanced capabilities and increased productivity. By addressing the issues and taking advantage of opportunities, we can create a smarter and more efficient mobility ecosystem (M Chen et al., 2019).

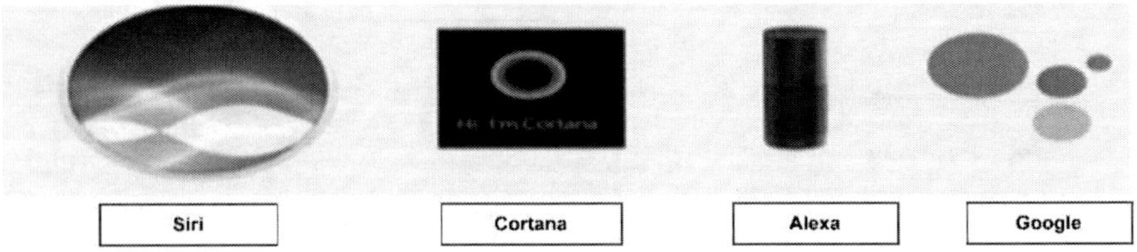

Figure 2. Evolution of Intelligent Mobile Assistants.

Table 2. Different types of virtual assistants

Made by	Apple	Microsoft	Amazon	Google
Wake – up word	"Hey Siri"	"Hey Cortana"	"Alexa"	"OK Google"
Which phones use it?	iPhone 45 + iPad 3+	Windows 10	Android, iOS, Fire OS, & PC	Android 4.1 or higher
Geofencing	Limited	Yes	No	Yes
Web search	Yes	Yes	Yes	Yes
Which search engine does it use?	Google Search Engine (Now)	Bing Search engine	Bing Search engine	Google Search engine
3rd-party app support	Yes	Yes	Yes	Yes
Search engine used	Google	Hard drive & Bing	Bing	Google

As time went on, the development of intelligent mobile assistants' IMAs was greatly improved. Although chatbots have been around since 1960, their popularity grew in the 1990s as a result of Internet development and more powerful computers. Although the original chatbots were limited in their functions, they contributed to building a foundation for developing more sophisticated support agents. In the second phase, voice assistants allowing consumers to communicate with devices by means of natural language were. Apple's original voice assistant, Siri, was brought to life by the company in 2007. Next came Amazon's Alexa, Google's Assistant, and Microsoft's Cortana as specified in Table 2. Voice assistants may be accessible on a variety of devices, where they are able to handle the management of Smart Home Devices, make calls, trigger alarms and answer questions. The current wave of intelligent machine assistants is driven by artificial intelligence algorithms which allow them to speak more natural language and carry out complex tasks. The LaMDA, developed by Google Artificial Intelligence, is one example of a next generation IMA which can generate text based on human quality. In future, Integrated Management Agencies could provide companionship, individual services, assistance with travel arrangements and the management of their time as well as health advice. In any case, the IMAs have a bright future ahead of them as they can be simplified, more efficient and improve our quality of life (Capponi et al., 2019).

Key Components of Intelligent Mobile Assistants

Intelligent Mobile Assistants is an Internet assistant that uses natural language processing and AI to offer a wide range of services and support for users on their cell phones (Felt et al., 2011).

Natural Language Processing NLP: Natural Language Processing, also known as NLP, is a subfield of Artificial Intelligence to study the interaction between humans and computers by way of their use of native languages. The interaction between a person and the machine is likely to be as follows in normal human language processing, a human talk to the machine.

- The machine captures the audio.
- Audio to text conversion takes place.
- Processing of the text's data.
- Data to audio conversion takes place.

What Is Natural Language Processing

Natural language processing, or NLP, is the use of algorithms to determine and extract rules from natural languages such as unintelligible language data is converted into a form that computers can understand When the text has been provided, the pc will utilize algorithms to extract which means related to every sentence and gather the crucial information from them.

The Techniques Applied in Natural Language Processing

The major techniques employed to complete the natural language processing tasks are synthesis analysis and semantic analysis. They are described in this way how they can be used.

Syntax

Syntax is the arrangement of words in a sentence that makes them sound grammatical. syntactic analysis is used to determine whether or not the Natural Language fits with grammar policies within NLP. Here's a set of syntax strategies you can use (Chowdhary K. R, 2020).

- Lemmatization
- Morphological Segmentation
- Word Segmentation
- Part-of-speech tagging
- Parsing
- Sentence breaking.

Sematics

The meaning to be conveyed by the wording is referred to as Semantics. One of the more complex factors in natural languages processing, which still needs to be further resolved, is linguistic analysis. In the semantic analysis, you'll find some techniques:

- Named entity recognition (NER)
- Word sense disambiguation
- Natural language generation.

Speech Recognition Technologies

Speech recognition technologies are playing an increasingly important role in intelligent mobile computing. The use of voice recognition in Intelligent Mobile Technologies provides several major advantages (Chen & Deng, 2021). Speech recognition allows users to communicate with their devices handsfree, which is especially helpful in situations when they have no hand and can't use it while on the road or working out. Improved accessibility: due to speech recognition, mobility devices can be used more easily by people who are disabled, for example blind or immobile. Using speech recognition can help users get more done by allowing them to combine and finish the work with no use of their hands. Customized user experience and speech recognition can be utilized to customize the user experience on mobile devices.

Computer Vision and Image Recognition

Computer vision and image recognition are the area of artificial intelligence which concerns the computer's ability to pick up and read sight information from our environment. Describes the task of image recognition as a more specialized one which is focused on identifying and categorising objects in images (Wiley & Lucas 2018). This branch of the computer vision is used for a number of purposes and branches as specified in Figure 3.

The process of identifying and validating people in photographs and videos as specified in Figure 4.

Object detection is a term used to identify and classify objects in photographs and videos as specified in Figure 5.

The classification of photographs is to place them in groups that have been established as specified in Figure 6.

To look at photographs of patients to identify conditions and monitor their progress in treatment as specified in Figure 7.

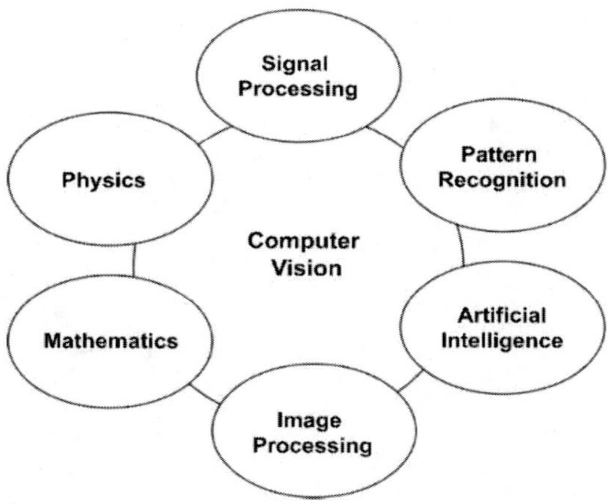

Figure 3. Branches of Computer Vision.

Figure 4. Face Recognition.

Figure 5. Object Detection.

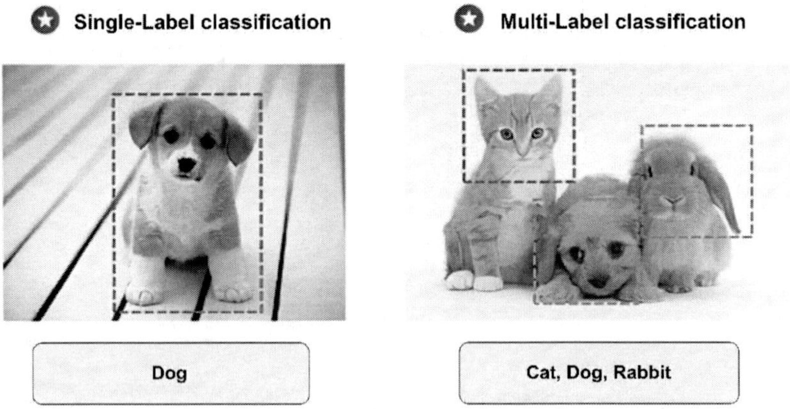

Figure 6. Image Classification.

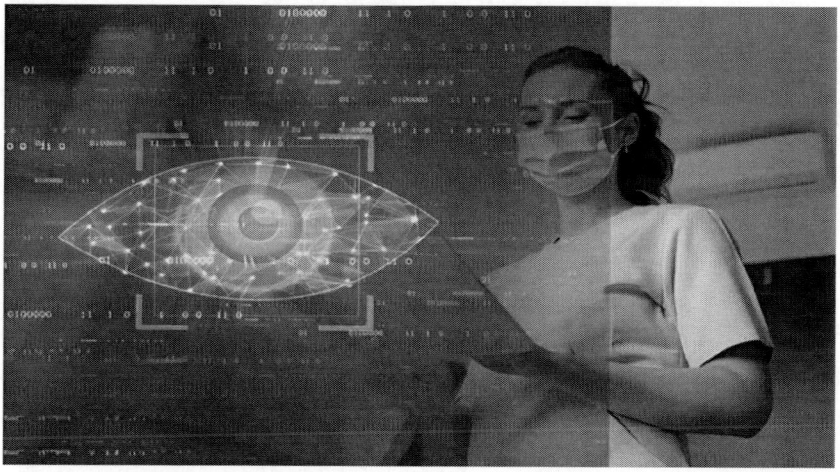

Figure 7. Medical Image Analysis.

Figure 8. Autonomous Driving.

Enabling self-driving automobiles to sense their environment and make judgments is known as autonomous driving as specified in Figure 8 (Zheng et al., 2007).

- Case study: Using computer vision to improve the driving of autonomous vehicles.

- Problem: Several sensors, like lidar, radar and cameras, are used by autonomous cars in order to sense their environment. However, these sensors may not work correctly in some cases due to difficult weather conditions or low visibility.
- Resolution: Computer vision is capable of increasing perception by providing self-driving cars with greater and accurate awareness of their surroundings. The computer vision algorithm, which allows real time tracking and identification of things such as humans, road signs or other vehicles, can be used.
- Findings: A safer, more reliable self-driving vehicle could be developed by computer vision. We can see steps in Figure 9. With computer vision, it is possible to provide autonomous cars with a more precise image of the environment that will help them avoid collisions and navigate safely in various settings.

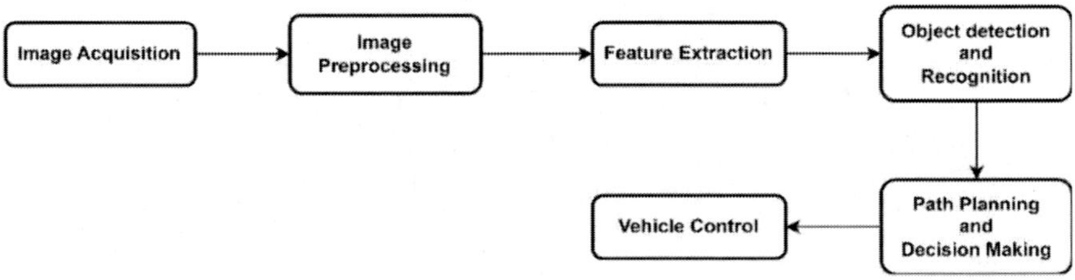

Figure 9. Flow Chart for Autonomous Driving Vehicles.

The advantages include increased recognition of objects, better understanding of the scene and the ability to withstand sensor failure. Computer vision is, for all intents and purposes, a promising method to improve the perception of autonomous vehicles. We'll be able to foresee that when computer vision algorithms advance further, they will play an even more important role in developing reliable and safe self-driving cars. Intelligent Mobile Assistants use artificial intelligence, speech recognition and natural language processing to provide dynamic, context aware interactions. With a view to ensuring an uninterrupted transition from ease of use to efficiency in the fast -evolving area of Intelligent Mobile Computing, Data Safety has been prioritised over security (Mao et al., 2017).

Machine Learning Applications for Mobile Devices

- Sentence recognition: Speech recognition using machine learning is possible. The technology that allows voice commands to be used to operate things and find information as specified in Figure 10.

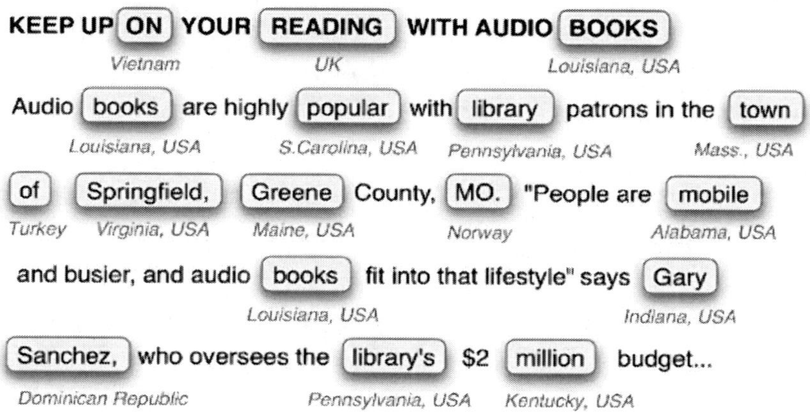

Figure 10. Sentence Recognition.

- Anomaly Detection: ML can be used to detect unusual patterns in data. This technology is used in apps such as fraud detection and predictive security. ML is making mobile apps more personalised, more intelligent, and more engaging, and it will probably keep doing so in the near future. Personalized recommendations represent a pivotal factor in delivering user-oriented experiences. Machine-driven targeted suggestions have redefined the way users connect to mobile applications, be it for entertainment, shopping, or content consumption.

Case Study: Personalized Recommendations at Amazon

Amazon is one of the largest online retailers in the world. Personalized recommendations play a key role in Amazon's success, helping customers find the right products and making their shopping experience more efficient and enjoyable (Gaber et al., 2015). Amazon uses a sophisticated recommendation engine. This engine examines an enormous amount of data, such as past purchases made by customers, browsing patterns, and product attributes, to find patterns and combinations. By using this information, the engine creates recommendations that are specific to each user's interests and personal requirements as specified in Figure 11.

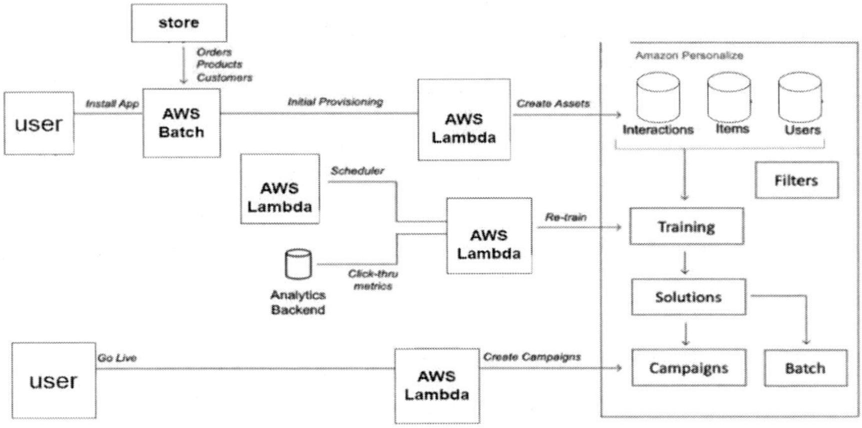

Figure 11. Recommendations at Amazon.

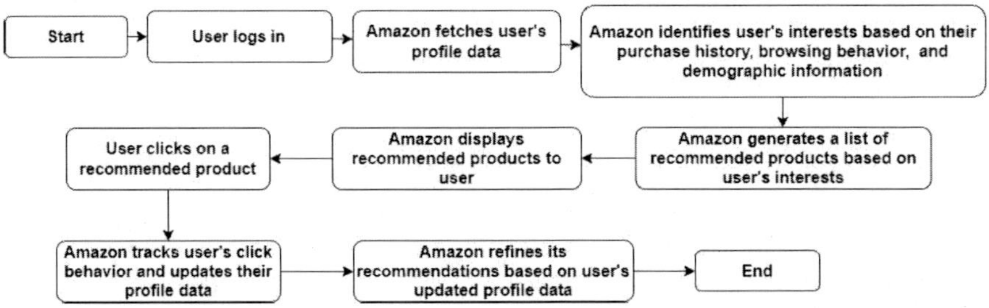

Figure 12. Clear Representations of Recommendations.

A range of touchpoints, such as product pages, search results, and email newsletters, are integrated with Amazon's tailored suggestions. Clear presentation of the recommendations draws customers' attention and influences their purchase decisions as specified in Figure 12.

Customer engagement, joy, and revenue have all grown vastly as a result of Amazon's tailored recommendations. According to studies, these tailored tips can raise average order values by 10%, rate of clicking by 30%, and rate of conversion by 20%. The success of Amazon's customized suggestions is evidence of machine learning's potential. This demonstrates the significance of data gathering and analysis, expert planning, and successful implementation of suggestions to maximise impact. Individuals tend to recognise content or products that align with their preferences, leading to increased involvement and enjoyment (Ray et al., 2017).

Predictive Text and Autocorrect

Mobile devices now have to contain predictive and self-correcting functions in order to improve transcription accuracy and speed. This section looks at the challenges and available technology for self-correction and predictive reading as specified in Figure 13.

Figure 13. Self-Correcting functions.

- Increased typing rate: Predictive text dramatically boosts typing speed by limiting the number of keystrokes needed to input a password.
- Greater Accuracy: Autocorrection improves the accuracy of user input and communications by reducing spelling errors and typos.
- Individual traits.: Machine learning enables these systems to adjust to the language, style, and of course, each user.

Challenges and Solutions

- Ambiguity: It can be tricky to tell the intended word. Advanced models, contextual embeddings, help address this challenge by considering the broader context of the sentence.
- Sensitivity to User Preferences:Striking the right balance between autocorrect interventions are crucial. Fine-tuning algorithms to be sensitive to individual user preferences for providing customization.

Adaptive User Interfaces

Adaptive user interfaces are a new design approach for digital experiences, particularly on mobile devices. These interfaces change based on the user's characteristics, preferences, and context as specified in Figure 14.

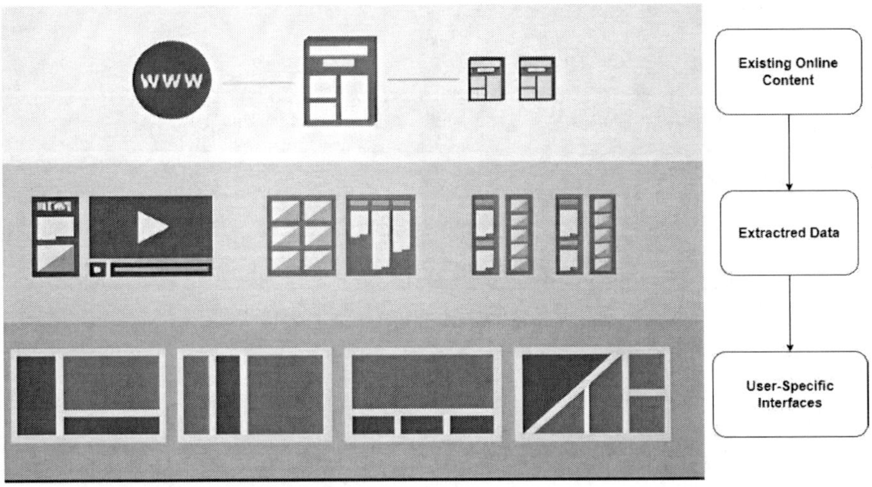

Figure 14. User Specific Interfaces.

Balancing Customization and Consistency

When delivering personalized experiences and maintaining a consistent brand or application identity. Careful design and user engagement strategies can help address this balance.

Data Privacy and Ethical Considerations

User data raises privacy concerns. Implementing transparent data processing policies, obtaining user consent, and preserving confidentiality procedures are essential to address ethical considerations.

Real-World Examples

- Facebook and other social media platforms actively adjust content displays based on user engagement patterns and interests.
- Amazon use adaptive interfaces to create app programs based on product recommendations, promotions, and even user browsing and purchase history.

Mobile consiAdaptive interfaces on mobile devices must meet the challenges of limited screen space, varying device capabilities. Machine learning models must be optimized for use on the device on to ensure real-time efficiency without excessive reliance on network connectivity.

Integration of Mobile Assistants with IoT

Mobileapps are revolutionizing to meet the growing demand for conversational commerce and services in the business world. Manufacturers are using the Internet of Things (IoT) to create better experience services. This increases the demand for IoT, further increasing the need for mobile apps as interactive interfaces (AI-Fuqaha et al., 2015).

Smart Homes and IoT Integration

Smart home systems have become increasingly popular over the last few decades as they increase comfort and quality of life. Wireless communication channels use a smartphone application to monitor and manage household tasks (AI Ameen et al., 2017).

To enable all of the above described activities and data management, the system is composed of the following components:

- Sensors to collect internal and external home data and measure home conditions. These sensors are connected to the home itself and to the attached-to-home devices.
- Processors for performing local and integrated actions. It may also be connected to the cloud for applications requiring extended resources.
- A collection of software components wrapped as APIs, allowing external applications execute it, given it follows the pre-defined parameters format. Such an API can process sensors data or manage necessary actions.
- Actuators to provision and execute commands in the server or other control devices. It translates the required activity to the command syntax; the device can execute.
- Database to store the processed data collected from the sensors. It will also be used for data analysis, data presentation and visualization as specified in Figure 15.

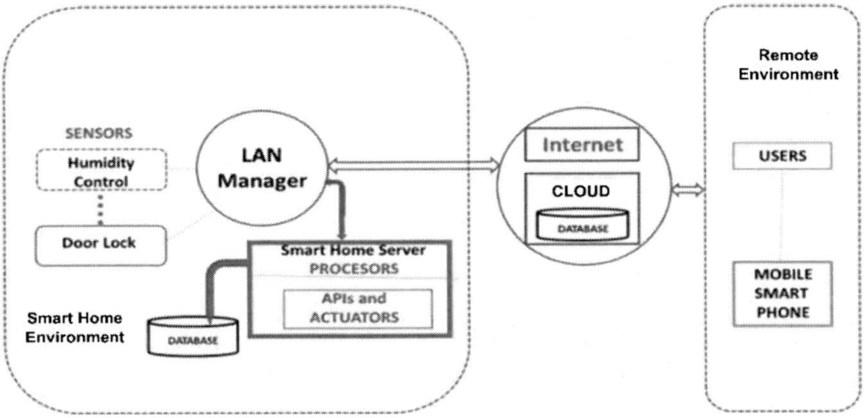

Figure 15. Database visualization.

Here is a case study on IoT Integration in Smart Homes (Rahmani et al., 2018).

Revolutionizing Home Living: IoT Integration in Smart Homes

- Background: The integration of Internet of Things (IoT) generation into clever houses has reshaped conventional dwelling spaces, allowing greater automation, connectivity, and comfort. This case observe explores the consequences and advantages of IoT integration in smart home environments.

- Overview: IoT integration in smart houses involves embedding intelligence into regular gadgets, facilitating conversation, and leveraging information-pushed insights to create interconnected ecosystems inside residential areas.
- Personalized Experiences: IoT integration enables the creation of personalized reports tailor-made to character preferences. By analysing person patterns and records accumulated from sensors, clever homes can adapt to occupants' behaviour, adjusting settings robotically for comfort, electricity performance, and comfort. Energy efficiency and cost One of the benefits of Integrated Internet of Things in a smart home is to improve electricity performance. Smart thermostats, for example, are capable of analysing the behaviour of occupants and changing their temperature accordingly so that they can save money in the long run by using less electricity (Baker et al., 2017).

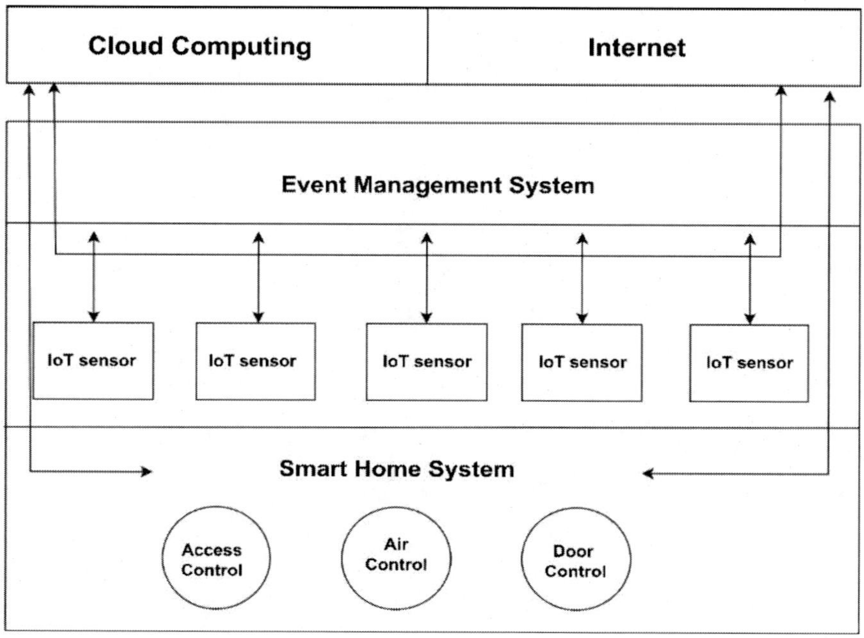

Figure 16. Event Management System.

- Aspirations of the future: As the Internet of Things becomes more widespread, there is also a prospect for exciting new services in the future of smart homes. Another anticipated improvement will be the development of a coherent and flexible environment for homes, thanks to intelligent analytics, artificial intelligence integration into home appliances as well as smooth communication with devices connected to Internet of Things (Goundar et al., 2021).
- It represents a revolutionary shift in residential living when Internet of Things technology is integrated into smart homes as the event management System specified in Figure 16. To improve the level of human comfort, it introduces a setting that allows devices to be connected, adjusted and adapted in response to user preferences (Khalid & Ameen, 2021).

Wearable Devices and Mobile Assistant Synergies

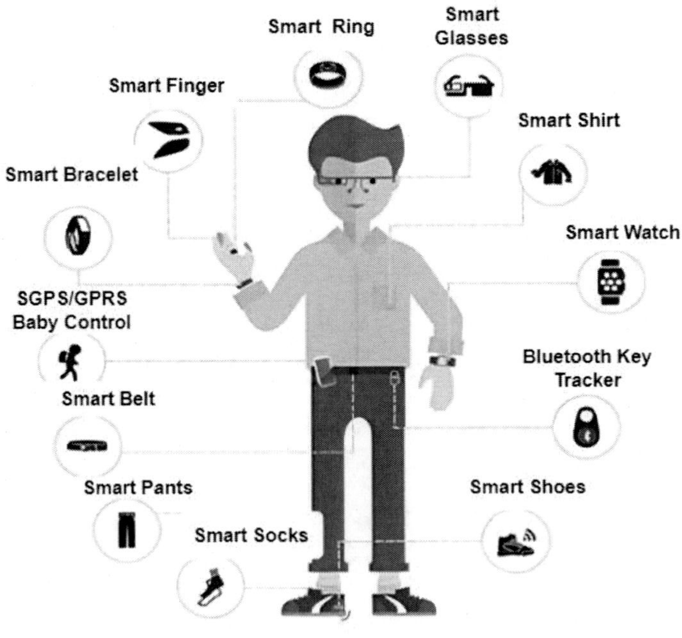

Figure 17. Wearable Devices and Mobile Assistants.

This integration empowers wearables to interact seamlessly with clever devices, imparting personalized user reports. Systems like CYCORE and EDoN exemplify how IoT-enabled wearables remodel affected person care, minimizing signs and symptoms and enabling early ailment detection (Nahavandi et al., 2015). This amalgamation redefines generation's position, promising superior functionalities and consumer-centric reports, paving the manner for an intuitive and interconnected future wherein IoT-pushed wearables revolutionize human-device interactions as specified in Figure 17.

Security and Privacy Considerations

Intelligent Mobile Assistant Systems (IMAS) have become popular for their wide range of features and services that help users in their daily tasks. However, the collection and storage of user data by IMAS raises concerns about security and privacy. IMAS gathers a variety of user data, including geographical data, usage trends, personal information, and even voice recordings. This information may be used to offer improved services, but there is also a risk that others will misuse it (Zhao et al., 2015).

There are viruses, data breaches, and unauthorized access to user information among the security weaknesses of Intelligent Virtual Assistant powered by Artificial Intelligence as specified in Figure 18. Through the use of these vulnerabilities, unauthorized access to user accounts may be obtained or personal data could be stolen. A major amount of data relating to users is collected and maintained by Imas, which raises privacy concerns. Concerns regarding the usage of their data, who can access it, and how long it will be kept may arise from users.

AI technology will help to protect user information in IMAs with the introduction of privacy safeguards such as data encryption, data minimization, access restrictions and educational material for users about the benefits and drawbacks associated with exchanging data. These safeguards shall ensure that only relevant information is gathered, that data are both transmitted and stored in an encrypted way during the transmission and retention process, user data access can be limited as well as users have been informed about possible risks related to sharing of their personal data.

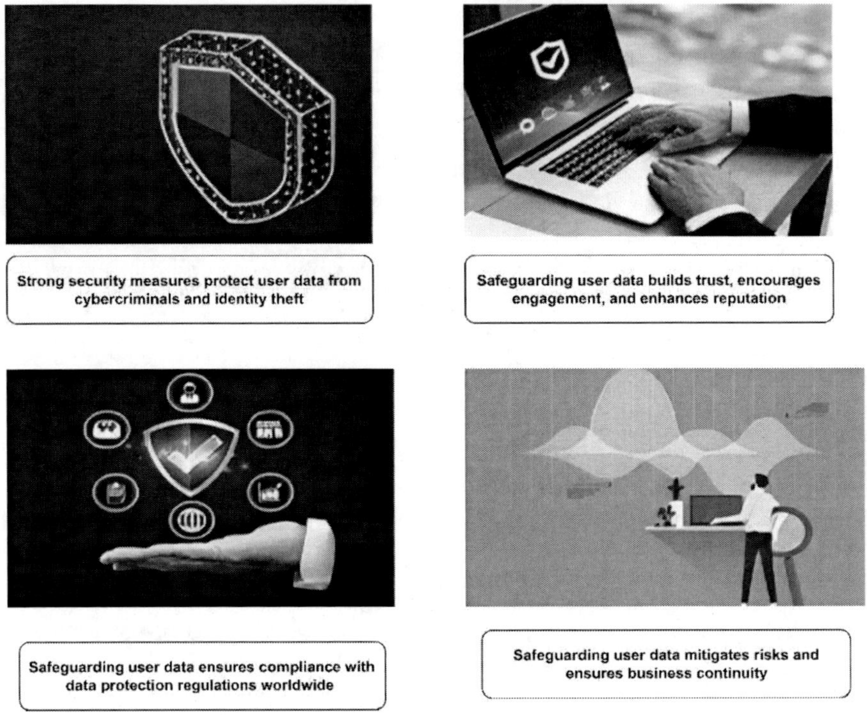

Figure 18. Steps In Safeguarding Users Data.

Ethical Implications of Machine Learning in Mobile Environments

Questions have arisen as to whether user data can be collected and used without explicit permission from apps based on machine learning. Apart from privacy, accountability, openness, prejudice and justice are all part of these issues.

- Privacy Concerns: Personal information, e.g., voice recordings, location, behaviour patterns, and biometrics, may be extracted from the user's data by ML algorithms. When using these data to identify features, preferences, and habits, a user profile can be created. However, since users do not know how or to what extent their information is being collected, it may be considered a breach of privacy to gather information without their consent or without explicit privacy policies (Char et al., 2020).

- Fairness and Bias: In particular, biases that can lead to unfair and discriminatory results are present in machine learning algorithms, which are used in artificial intelligence. The algorithms themselves, or the data they have been trained with, may be to blame for these biases. When a machine learning algorithm is applied to an application, it may disproportionately favor some set of applicants because of their age, gender or socioeconomic status. When using biased machine learning algorithms in mobile applications, they can have a significant impact on social networking, financial services and criminal justice. Inequitable outcomes may lead to an increase of current social disparities and undermine public confidence in such frameworks.
- Transparency and Accountability: Artificial intelligence plays a major role in addressing transparency and accountability issues. Complicated machine learning algorithms often make it difficult to understand how decisions are made and what information is being handled, which creates distrust and a sense of manipulation. The decentralised structure of mobile computing, making it difficult to identify and hold people accountable for the outputs of ML applications, is also hindering efforts in addressing ethical issues.
- Addressing Ethical Concerns: The following actions can be taken to address ethical concerns about machine learning (ML) in mobile environments: gathering only the records that are required; giving clear explanations for data usage and decision-making; getting user consent and granting them control over their data; putting bias detection and mitigation strategies into practice; setting up accountability mechanisms and guaranteeing auditability; and educating the public about the moral ramifications of ML in mobile environments. By taking into account those criteria, developers, legislators and consumers can cooperate to ensure that machine learning is ethically and responsibly used within an urban environment (La Polla et al., 2013).

Challenges and Future Prospects

Artificial intelligence and mobile computing are dynamic fields, and Intelligent Mobile Agents (IMAs) are no exception (Suna & El Fallah-

Seghrouchni, 2005). They've got a lot of opportunities and a lot of problems ahead of them. We'll go over each of these two:

- Limitations of resources: when mobile devices are equipped with battery life and computing power, they have a tendency to be limited. Creating smart agents that can respond well to those constraints is one of the main challenges.
- Security and privacy concerns: when communications between IMAs and servers are sensitive, there is a concern of security and privacy. Strict encryption and the protection of user data must be ensured.
- In combination with the Mobile Ecosystem: A major challenge is to be able to integrate seamless with various Mobile Platforms, Operating Systems and Applications. Infrastructure managers need to be able to adapt to a number of settings, in order to provide appropriate and effective support.
- Context awareness: Effective interpretation and adaptation of IMAs is required for mobile users' dynamic contexts. To understand user behaviour, preferences and environment is dependent upon improved contextual awareness.
- Upcoming prospects: The future of Intelligent Mobile Agents Systems looks promising, thanks to technology breakthroughs and an increasing focus on improving the user experience as a result of cell computing. Networks are going to be faster and more reliable as 5G technology continues to spread.

Getting Past Obstacles and Limitations

In order to overcome the obstacles and limits of intelligent mobile agents, a planned and iterative strategy will be needed. Some of the most important tactics are as follows (Wang et al., 2017).

- Optimise methods: in order to ensure the efficient functioning of IMAs, optimize strategies so as to take full advantage of low device resources. To this end, it may be possible to control the consumption of energy, improve algorithms and reduce memory use.

- NetworkDependency: Offline functionality: To enable IMAs to function and provide minimal support in situations where network availability is limited, create IMAs with offline capabilities.
- Strong Encryption: To protect data transfer between IMAs and servers, use strong encryption techniques. Create and implement safe storage practices for mobile devices, in accordance with the suggested user identification and authorisation standards.
- Understanding Context: Machine learning frameworks Invest in cutting edge models of machine learning that can adapt to user preferences, changing circumstances and behaviour.
- The development of interactions between humans and computers: Investigate novel and engaging ways for users to interact with IMAs by investigating advancements in HCI, such as augmented reality (AR) and virtual reality (VR).

Future Innovations and Trends in Intelligent Mobile Assistants

Revolutionising advancements for intelligent mobile assistants, particularly in the area of conversational AI, are expected to take place in the coming years. Better natural language processing (NLP) skills will be one of these developments, allowing for more complex and context-aware interactions (J Kang et al., 2018).

Conclusion

An important factor in the improved mobile agents' comprehension of natural language and models is machine learning. The incorporation of machine learning into mobile platforms enables the development of Intelligent Mobile Assistants (IMAs), which include features like computer vision and speech recognition. IMAs, which aim to improve user experience, are becoming more and more prevalent in wearable and smart homes. They do this by using adaptable interfaces, predictive text, and personalised recommendations. However, these advancements also have disadvantages, such as concerns about ethics, security, and privacy. Despite these challenges, IMAs seem to have a promising future as long as they continue to innovate and use machine learning to offer straightforward, morally sound, and intelligent mobile assistance. When everything is believed, machine learning-powered clever mobile assistants could totally transform the way.

References

Al Ameen, Moshaddique, Jingwei Liu, and Kyungsup Kwak. "Security and privacy issues in wireless sensor networks for healthcare applications." *Journal of Medical Systems* 36 (2012): 93-101.

Al-Fuqaha, Ala, Mohsen Guizani, Mehdi Mohammadi, Mohammed Aledhari, and Moussa Ayyash. "Internet of things: A survey on enabling technologies, protocols, and applications." *IEEE Communications Surveys & tutorials* 17, no. 4 (2015): 2347-2376.

Avanija, J., Gurram Sunitha, K. Reddy Madhavi, S. Sreenivasa Chakravarthi, and R. Hitesh Sai Vittal. "Prediction and Analysis of Cervical Cancer: An Ensemble Approach." In *2022 4th International Conference on Inventive Research in Computing Applications* (ICIRCA), pp. 1734-1739. *IEEE*, 2022.

Avanija, J., Suneetha Konduru, Vijetha Kura, Grande NagaJyothi, and Bhanu Prakash Dudi. "Designing a Fuzzy Q-Learning Power Energy System Using Reinforcement Learning." *International Journal of Fuzzy System Applications* (IJFSA) 11, no. 3 (2022): 1-12.

Baker, Stephanie B., Wei Xiang, and Ian Atkinson. "Internet of things for smart healthcare: Technologies, challenges, and opportunities." *IEEE Access* 5 (2017): 26521-26544.

Będkowski, Janusz. "Intelligent mobile assistant for spatial design support." *Automation in construction* 32 (2013): 177-186.

Capponi, Andrea, Claudio Fiandrino, Burak Kantarci, Luca Foschini, Dzmitry Kliazovich, and Pascal Bouvry. "A survey on mobile crowdsensing systems: Challenges, solutions, and opportunities." *IEEE Communications Surveys & tutorials* 21, no. 3 (2019): 2419-2465.

Carbonell, Jaime G., Ryszard S. Michalski, and Tom M. Mitchell. "An overview of machine learning." *Machine learning* (1983): 3-23.

Char, Danton S., Michael D. Abràmoff, and Chris Feudtner. "Identifying ethical considerations for machine learning healthcare applications." *The American Journal of Bioethics* 20, no. 11 (2020): 7-17.

Chen, Mingzhe, Ursula Challita, Walid Saad, Changchuan Yin, and Mérouane Debbah. "*Machine learning for wireless networks with artificial intelligence: A tutorial on neural networks.*" arXiv preprint arXiv:1710.02913 9 (2017).

Chowdhary, KR1442, and K. RChowdhary. "Natural language processing." *Fundamentals of artificial intelligence* (2020): 603-649.

Felt, Adrienne Porter, Matthew Finifter, Erika Chin, Steve Hanna, and David Wagner. "A survey of mobile malware in the wild." In *Proceedings of the 1st ACM workshop on Security and privacy in smartphones and mobile devices*, pp. 3-14. 2011.

Goundar, Sam, J. Avanija, Gurram Sunitha, K. Reddy Madhavi, and S. Bharath Bhushan, eds. Innovations in the industrial Internet of Things (IIoT) and smart factory. *IGI Global*, 2021.

Kang, Jiawen, Rong Yu, Xumin Huang, Maoqiang Wu, Sabita Maharjan, Shengli Xie, and Yan Zhang. "Blockchain for secure and efficient data sharing in vehicular edge computing and networks." *IEEE Internet of things journal* 6, no. 3 (2018): 4660-4670.

Khalid, Lawchak Fadhil, and Siddeeq Y. Ameen. "Secure Iot integration in daily lives: A review." *Journal of Information Technology and Informatics* 1, no. 1 (2021): 6-12.

La Polla, Mariantonietta, Fabio Martinelli, and Daniele Sgandurra. "A survey on security for mobile devices." *IEEE communications surveys & tutorials* 15, no. 1 (2012): 446-471.

Mao, Yuyi, Changsheng You, Jun Zhang, Kaibin Huang, and Khaled B. Letaief. "A survey on mobile edge computing: The communication perspective." *IEEE communications surveys & tutorials* 19, no. 4 (2017): 2322-2358.

Nahavandi, Darius, Roohallah Alizadehsani, Abbas Khosravi, and U. Rajendra Acharya. "Application of artificial intelligence in wearable devices: Opportunities and challenges." *Computer Methods and Programs in Biomedicine* 213 (2022): 106541.

Rahmani, Amir-Mohammad, Nanda Kumar Thanigaivelan, Tuan Nguyen Gia, Jose Granados, Behailu Negash, Pasi Liljeberg, and Hannu Tenhunen. "Smart e-health gateway: Bringing intelligence to internet-of-things based ubiquitous healthcare systems." In *2015 12th Annual IEEE consumer communications and networking conference (CCNC)*, pp. 826-834. IEEE, 2015.

Ray, Partha Pratim. "A survey on Internet of Things architectures." *Journal of King Saud University-Computer and Information Sciences* 30, no. 3 (2018): 291-319.

Sarker, Iqbal H., Mohammed Moshiul Hoque, Md Kafil Uddin, and Tawfeeq Alsanoosy. "Mobile data science and intelligent apps: concepts, ai-based modeling and research directions." *Mobile Networks and Applications* 26 (2021): 285-303.

Suna, Alexandru, and Amal El Fallah-Seghrouchni. "A mobile agent's platform: architecture, mobility and security elements." In *Programming Multi-Agent Systems: Second International Workshop ProMAS 2004*, New York, NY, USA, July 20, 2004, Selected Revised and Invited Papers 2, pp. 126-146. Springer Berlin Heidelberg, 2005.

Wang, Shuo, Xing Zhang, Yan Zhang, Lin Wang, Juwo Yang, and Wenbo Wang. "A survey on mobile edge networks: Convergence of computing, caching and communications." *IEEE Access* 5 (2017): 6757-6779.

Wiley, Victor, and Thomas Lucas. "Computer vision and image processing: a paper review." *International Journal of Artificial Intelligence Research* 2, no. 1 (2018): 29-36.

Zhao, Kao, Deqing Zou, Hai Jin, Zhangbiaoge Tian, Weizhong Qiang, and Weiqi Dai. "Privacy protection for perceptual applications on smartphones." In *2015 IEEE International Conference on Mobile Services*, pp. 174-181. IEEE, 2015.

Zheng, Nanning, George Loizou, Xiaoyi Jiang, Xuguang Lan, and Xuelong Li. "*Computer vision and pattern recognition*." (2007): 1265-1266.

Zhu, Hang, and Hongjie Wan. "Sound event detection based on convolutional neural networks with overlapping pooling structure." In *Journal of Physics: Conference Series*, vol. 1924, no. 1, p. 012008. IOP Publishing, 2021.

Chapter 8

Edge Computing Technology: Opportunities, Issues and Future Trends

Ch. Prathima[1,*]
J. Avanija[2]
Sam Goundar[3]
K. Reddy Madhavi[2]
Gurram Sunitha[2]
and Viswaksena Balaji[4]

[1]School of Computing, Mohan Babu University, Tirupati, Andhra Pradesh, India
[2]School of Computing, Mohan Babu University, Tirupati, Andhra Pradesh, India
[3]RMIT University, Hanoi, Vietnam
[4]University of Limerick, Limerick, Ireland

Abstract

A distributed computing paradigm known as "edge computing" moves data storage and processing closer to the location where the data is generated or consumed. In traditional cloud computing, devices or end users are not close to the centralized data centers where data processing and storage take place. In edge computing, the data-generating devices or sensors are located at or close to the network's edge, where processing and storage resources are located. Cutting down on latency and bandwidth needed to send data to distant data centers for processing is the main goal of edge computing. Faster response times and increased efficiency are made possible by edge computing, which processes data closer to the source and better utilization of network resources.

[*] Corresponding Author's Email: prathima.ch@vidyanikethan.edu.

In: The Future of Mobile Computing
Editors: Sam Goundar, J. Avanija and K. Reddy Madhavi
ISBN: 979-8-89113-715-8

Technologies encompass a wide range of tools, frameworks, and protocols that enable the deployment, management, and execution of computing resources at the network edge.

Keywords: distributed computing, cloud computing, storage, network, analytics

Introduction

The exponential growth of connected devices has led to the rise in popularity of edge computing. The Internet of Things (IoT), and the growing demand for real data distribution have all contributed to the rise in popularity of edge computing. Edge computing provides various benefits by distributing data at or close to the edge. These advantages include Decreased Latency Lower potential is achieved by reducing the amount of time that data must travel from the source to the processing point through edge computing. This is crucial for applications like autonomous vehicles, engineering automation, and augmented reality that call for responsiveness in real-time or almost real-time. Bandwidth Optimisation: By reducing the amount of data that must be transmitted to centralized cloud data centers, edge computing helps to conserve bandwidth. Edge devices can optimise bandwidth usage and lessen network congestion by filtering and optimizing data locally before sending it to the cloud through processing and analysis of statistics. Figure 1 specifies the architecture of edge computing. Enhanced Reliability: Distributed processing and storage among several edge devices, or nodes, are made possible by edge computing. This distributed architecture enhances reliability and fault tolerance since even if one edge node fails, others can continue to operate independently. It also improves resiliency by ensuring that critical services can still function in situations where network connectivity to the cloud is disrupted. Edge computing makes it possible to manage and store sensitive data locally, lowering the possibility of data breaches and guaranteeing compliance with Data Privacy and Security's data protection laws. This localized approach to data management provides an additional layer of privacy and security, as sensitive information doesn't have to traverse the network or reside in a centralized data center. Scalability: Edge computing allows for scalable deployment of computing resources by distributing them across various edge devices or nodes. This scalability is particularly advantageous in scenarios where the volume of data generated is vast or when processing requirements fluctuate rapidly.

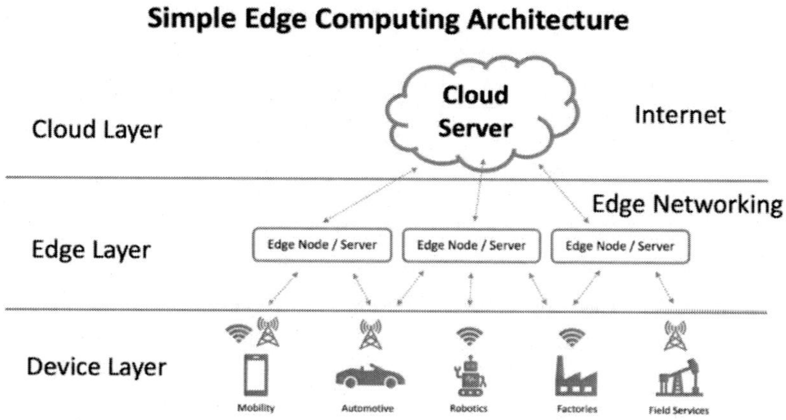

Figure 1. Simple Edge Computing Architecture.

Applications for edge computing can be found in many fields and industries. Smart Cities: Real-time monitoring and control of multiple urban systems, such as energy grids, waste management, and traffic management, are made possible by edge computing. Faster reaction times are made possible in urgent healthcare situations by edge computing. Manufacturing: In manufacturing facilities, edge computing facilitates process optimization, real-time quality control, and predictive maintenance. Retail: Real-time analytics for customer behavior analysis, inventory management, and personalized shopping experiences are made possible by edge computing. Edge computing is positioned to play a key role in enabling faster, more efficient, and decentralized data processing, ushering in a new era of intelligent and responsive applications, as technology develops, and the number of connected devices keeps growing.

Cloud computing and edge computing are two distinct paradigms in the field of computing that serve different purposes and address different needs. In terms of Infrastructure Location, the cloud computing infrastructure is centralized and located in data centers, typically operated by third-party service providers. Through the internet, users can access resources and services where the computing infrastructure is dispersed and located closer to the user or data source. It moves computation and storage power closer to the user device or data source, at the network's edge. Regarding Data

Dispensation and Storage, cloud computing relies heavily on remote data centers for processing and storing data. The cloud provider manages and maintains the infrastructure, and users rely on the provider's resources to run applications and store data whereas in edge computing, data processing and storage occur locally on edge devices or servers that are geographically distributed. Processing data closer to the source allows for faster processing, lower latency, and less bandwidth consumption. Regarding Processing, Both Potential and Actual Applications and services with low latency requirements or those that don't require real-time processing can benefit from cloud computing. Because of the data transmission to and from the remote data centers, there might be some latency. According to Lim et al., (2020), edge computing is intended for low-potential applications that need real processing. Edge computer shortens the time it takes to send data to the cloud and get a response, facilitating quicker decision-making and improved user experiences. In terms of Connectivity Dependency cloud computing, strong and reliable connectivity to the internet is essential for accessing cloud resources and services. Applications and data rely on network connectivity to function properly. Edge computing doesn't require constant internet access. Even in scenarios with restricted, erratic, or unpredictable internet connectivity, it can keep running and offer services. Regarding Allocation of Resources and Scalability Virtually infinite scalability is provided by cloud computing, enabling users to adjust their resource levels in response to demand. It provides a centralized platform for resource allocation and management across multiple users and applications. Edge computing typically offers limited scalability compared to the cloud due to the localized nature of resources. Scalability depends on the number and capacity of edge devices or servers deployed in different locations.

Edge networking (Zhao et al., 2019) refers to the infrastructure and technologies that enable the distribution of network resources and services provided to the network of the edge, typically near the end users or data sources. Its challenge is to reduce latency, improve performance, and increase the delivery of network services in distributed environments. Edge networking involves deploying network resources, such as routers, switches, and servers, closer to the end users or data sources. This proximity minimizes the distance data needs to travel, reducing latency and improving response times. It utilizes a distributed architecture where network resources are strategically placed at different locations, such as points of presence (PoPs), regional data centers, or even on the devices themselves. This decentralization enables faster data processing and efficient utilization of network resources. When using edge networking, data processing takes place on or close to the servers or edge devices. By processing information locally, edge networking lowers the requirement for sending massive amounts of data to be centralized data centers, increasing productivity and requiring less bandwidth. By processing data and running apps at the edge, it makes actual data possible. This is especially helpful for time-sensitive applications where quick decisions are essential, like Internet of Things devices, driverless cars, or industrial automation. By sending less data to centralized data centers or the cloud, it can also optimise the use of bandwidth. Only pertinent data is transmitted by processing and filtering data at the edge, which lowers operating expenses and bandwidth requirements. It frequently functions in tandem with edge computing. Edge computing focuses on localized data processing and storage, while edge networking ensures efficient and reliable network connectivity between edge devices, servers, and cloud services.

Methodologies

Edge technologies are referred to as various tools, frameworks, protocols, and devices that are utilized in edge computing (Cao et al., 2020) environments. These technologies enable the deployment, management, and execution of computing resources at the network edge. Here are some key edge technologies:

- Edge Devices: Physical devices that are situated at the edge of networks are known as edged devices. Examples of these devices include edge servers, gateways, routers, switches, and Internet of Things devices (Magesh, S., et al., 2020). To gather, process, and transmit data, these devices have sensors, processors, and storage capacities.
- Edge Computing Platforms: Edge computing platforms provide the software infrastructure for managing and orchestrating edge computing resources. These platforms enable the deployment, configuration, and monitoring of edge devices, as well as enable communication, analytics, and data processing between cloud and edge environments.
- Edge Analytics: Edge analytics involves processing and analyzing data at the edge devices in real-time or near-real-time. It encompasses

algorithms, machine learning models, and data processing techniques that enable intelligent insights and decision-making at the edge without relying on cloud-based processing.

- Edge Operating Systems: Edge operating systems are specifically designed for edge devices, providing lightweight, resource-efficient, and secure operating environments. These operating systems optimize power consumption, offer robust security features, and often support containerization and virtualization technologies for efficient execution of edge applications.
- Edge AI: The term "edge AI" refers to the incorporation of artificial intelligence (AI) technologies into edge devices, including machine learning (Chilukuri, Prathima et al., 2023) and deep learning. Edge AI gives edge devices the ability to process intelligent data locally, do predictive analytics, and make decisions without constantly relying on cloud connectivity.
- Edge Security: The main goals of edge security are to guard against cyberattacks, illegal access, and data breaches for edge devices, communications, and data. It includes secure protocols, encryption, access control methods, and secure boot procedures to guarantee the confidentiality and integrity of data processed at the edge.
- Fog Computing: Fog computing includes edge computing challenges by introducing fog nodes, which are sited between the edge and the cloud. Fog nodes provide additional computing and storage resources, enabling the execution of complex and resource-intensive applications at the edge.
- Edge-to-Cloud Integration: Edge computing often works in conjunction with cloud computing, necessitating protocols, APIs, and data synchronization mechanisms for seamless communication, data sharing, and workload offloading between edge devices and cloud infrastructure.

The edge computing technologies specified in Figure 2 collectively support the efficient and effective operation of edge computing architectures, enabling faster data processing, reduced latency, enhanced privacy and security, and real-time decision-making at the network edge.

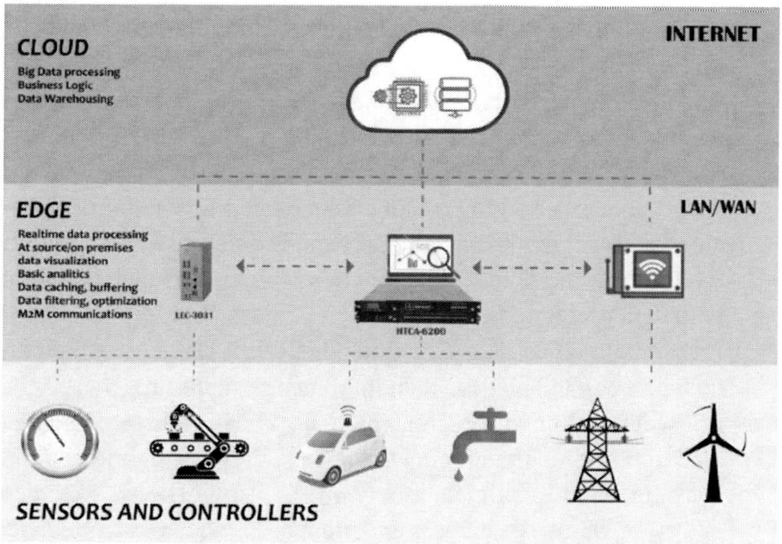

Figure 2. Edge Computing Technologies.

Challenges and Opportunities

Edge computing has numerous opportunities in a range of use cases and industries. A few of the most important chances (Zhang et al., 2022) associated with edge computing:

- Reduced Latency and Improved Responsiveness: Data processing closer to the source, edge computing allows for lower latency and quicker reaction times. This is especially useful for applications like augmented reality, gaming, industrial automation, and autonomous vehicles that need processing in real-time or almost real-time. Critical decisions can be made promptly without requiring a round-trip to a distant cloud server by processing data locally at the edge.
- Bandwidth Optimization and Cost Reduction: With edge computing, only the relevant data or processed results need to be transmitted to the data center. By filtering, aggregating, and analyzing data at the edge (Pierce), unnecessary data can be discarded, leading to optimized bandwidth usage and reduced network congestion. This can result in significant cost savings, especially for applications with

large volumes of data or in situations where network connectivity is limited or costly.

- Enhanced Privacy and Security: Data to be processed and analyzed locally, edge computing eliminates the need to send sensitive data to centralized cloud environments. By reducing the amount of sensitive data that is exposed to possible risks related to data transmission and cloud storage, this localized approach improves security and privacy. By limiting the data's geographic scope, it also makes compliance with data protection laws possible.
- Edge Intelligence and Real-time Analytics: Devices at the edge can now process and analyse data intelligently thanks to edge computing. Edge devices have the capability to extract valuable insights from data in real-time by utilising advanced analytics algorithms, machine learning, and artificial intelligence. Applications like anomaly detection, personalised user experiences, predictive maintenance, and contextual decision-making based on local data are made possible by EI.
- Offline Operation and Resilience: Edge computing can operate in offline or partially connected environments. This is especially useful in situations where there is no guarantee of constant cloud connectivity, such as remote locations or areas with intermittent network coverage. Edge devices can function independently, executing critical tasks and storing data until connectivity is restored, ensuring uninterrupted operation and improved resilience.
- Scalability and Distributed Architecture: Edge computing allows for distributed processing and storage capabilities across multiple edge devices or nodes. This distributed architecture provides scalability and flexibility, as additional devices can be easily added or removed from the network. It also improves fault tolerance, as a failure in one edge device or node does not disrupt the entire system.
- Edge-Cloud Collaboration and Hybrid Architectures: Edge computing complements cloud computing by enabling efficient collaboration between edge devices and cloud infrastructure. Hybrid architectures (Chilukuri, Prathima et al., 2023) that leverage both edge and cloud resources can be designed to balance computational requirements, storage needs, and network constraints. This enables workload offloading, data synchronization, and seamless integration between the edge and the cloud for optimal resource utilization.

Edge networking introduces certain challenges, such as managing a distributed network infrastructure, maintaining security across multiple locations, and coordinating data synchronization and consistency between edge devices and centralized systems. These opportunities (Xue H et al., 2020) offered by edge computing have the potential to revolutionize various industries, including manufacturing, healthcare, transportation, energy, retail, and smart cities. By harnessing the power of edge computing, organizations can unlock new levels of efficiency, responsiveness, and innovation in their operations and services.

The technology of edge computing offers many opportunities, but it also comes with a set of difficulties and an intriguing range of potential future developments. Its capacity to process and analyze data closer to the source opens up opportunities by lowering latency, facilitating real-time decision-making, and improving overall system performance. It makes it easier for AI and machine learning to be integrated at the edge, enabling uses like driverless cars, smart cities, and customized experiences.

However, several issues require attention. Scalability, connectivity, security, and data management pose challenges that need to be addressed. Managing a large number of distributed edge devices, ensuring robust connectivity, securing sensitive data, and optimizing resource utilization are critical aspects. Standardization, interoperability, and efficient orchestration and management systems are necessary for seamless integration and collaboration within the edge ecosystem. Looking ahead, future trends in edge computing include the integration of 5G networks, enabling ultra-low latency and high-bandwidth connectivity. Edge AI and machine learning will flourish, allowing real-time processing and decision-making on edge devices. The edge-to-cloud continuum will enable dynamic workload distribution, while edge security measures will strengthen to protect against cyber threats and preserve data privacy. The concept of Edge-as-a-Service will emerge, providing on-demand access to edge computing resources and capabilities. Federated edge computing and federated learning models will enable collaboration and knowledge sharing while preserving data privacy. Industry-specific edge solutions will continue to evolve, addressing the unique needs of various sectors.

Effective edge management and orchestration frameworks will be developed to handle the scale and complexity of edge deployments. These frameworks will enable centralized control, monitoring, and automation, optimizing resource allocation and ensuring seamless integration.

Present Issues of Edge Computing

Addressing issues in edge computing requires collaborative efforts from industry stakeholders, including standardization bodies, device manufacturers, network providers, and software developers (Akula CS et al., 2020). Some of the issues are scalability, connectivity, security, data management, standardization and interoperability, orchestration and management and energy efficiency.

Edge computing involves deploying numerous computing devices across a distributed network, which can pose challenges in terms of scalability. Managing a large number of edge devices and ensuring their seamless integration into the overall system can be complex. Connectivity: Edge computing relies on robust and reliable network connectivity between edge devices and centralized systems. In remote or rural areas with limited network infrastructure, maintaining consistent connectivity becomes a significant challenge.

Edge devices often process and store sensitive data, making them potential targets for cyberattacks. Securing edge devices against unauthorized access, data breaches, and malware attacks is crucial. Additionally, managing security updates and patches across a vast number of distributed devices can be challenging (Salman et al., 2020). Edge computing generates vast amounts of data, and managing this data efficiently poses challenges. Determining what data to process and store locally versus sending it to the cloud for analysis and storage requires careful consideration. Data governance, data privacy, and compliance with regulations add additional complexity to data management in edge computing. Resource constraints: Edge devices typically have limited processing power, memory, and storage capacities. Optimizing resource utilization and executing computationally intensive tasks within the constrained resources of edge devices can be a significant challenge.

The edge computing landscape is currently fragmented, with various vendors offering different edge solutions. Lack of standardized interfaces, protocols, and interoperability between edge devices, platforms, and cloud systems hinders seamless integration and limits the potential for collaboration and innovation. Managing a distributed edge infrastructure, monitoring device health, and ensuring smooth coordination and synchronization among edge devices require efficient orchestration and management systems. Developing robust management frameworks that can handle the scale and complexity of edge deployments is an ongoing challenge.

Many edge devices are resource-constrained and powered by batteries or renewable energy sources. Optimizing energy consumption and extending battery life in edge devices is critical to ensure their continuous operation and reduce environmental impact. Edge AI and machine learning: Deploying artificial intelligence (AI) and machine learning (ML) (Moustafa, 2021) models at the edge can enhance real-time decision-making and reduce dependence on cloud resources. However, running sophisticated AI/ML algorithms (Hamdan S et al., 2020) on resource-constrained edge devices poses computational challenges and requires efficient model optimization and deployment techniques.

Continuous and continued research and innovation will play a crucial role in overcoming these issues and unlocking the full potential of edge computing (Pan J and McElhannon 2020).

Future Trends

Edge computing has a bright future (Sonone et al., 2020), and a number of trends are anticipated to influence its advancement. The following are some major future trends for edge computing: Integration of 5G: The introduction of 5G networks, which offer extremely low latency and high bandwidth connectivity, will completely transform edge computing. With 5G integration, real-time data processing and analysis at the edge will be possible, supporting augmented reality, smart cities, and driverless cars, among other applications. The future scenarios and opportunities are specified in Table 1.

- Edge AI and Machine Learning: Edge computing will witness an increased integration of AI and machine learning capabilities. By deploying AI models (Chen CM et al., 2022) directly on pierce devices, real-time decision for data processing can be achieved without relying heavily on cloud resources. This trend will enable a wide range of applications, including real-time video analytics, predictive maintenance, and personalized user experiences.
- Edge-to-Cloud Continuum: The future will see a more centralized cloud systems and edge devices work together and integrate seamlessly (Deshpande S and Kulkarni N, 2021). The edge-to-cloud continuum will allow intelligent workload distribution, where data processing and storage can be dynamically allocated between the

edge and the cloud based on factors such as latency, bandwidth, and resource availability.

- Edge Security: As the number of connected edge devices increases, security will remain a critical concern. Future edge computing solutions will focus on enhancing security measures, including device authentication, encryption, secure bootstrapping, and real-time threat detection. Additionally, privacy-enhancing technologies, such as federated learning, will be employed to protect user data while enabling data-driven insights.
- Edge-as-a-Service (EaaS): The concept of Edge-as-a-Service will gain prominence, where organizations can access and utilize edge computing resources and capabilities on-demand, similar to the cloud computing (Perez J et al., 2022) model. This will enable businesses to leverage edge infrastructure without the need for significant upfront investments, facilitating rapid deployment and scalability.
- Federated Edge Computing: Federated learning and computing models will gain traction, enabling collaboration and knowledge sharing between multiple edge devices while maintaining data privacy. Federated edge computing allows distributed learning across multiple edge nodes, facilitating better model accuracy and efficiency.
- Industry-specific Edge Solutions: Edge computing will continue to be adopted across various industries, including healthcare, manufacturing, transportation, and retail. Industry-specific solutions will emerge, tailored to address the unique requirements and challenges of each sector. These solutions will improve operational efficiency and open up new business opportunities by providing optimised processing, analytics, and decision-making capabilities at the edge.
- Edge Management and Orchestration: As edge deployments grow in scale and complexity, efficient management and orchestration systems (Cui W, 2020) will become crucial. Future trends will focus on developing comprehensive management frameworks that enable centralized control, monitoring, and automation of edge resources, ensuring seamless integration, and optimizing resource allocation.

These trends highlight the ongoing evolution and maturation of edge computing, driven by advancements in connectivity, AI, security, and industry-specific requirements. As technology continues to advance, edge computing will play a pivotal role in enabling innovative applications and transforming various industries.

Table 1. Three scenarios for how the opportunity could play out in Future

Scenario Characteristics	Scenario 1 Hyperscaler-Telco Tie up	Scenario 2 Telco – Tie up	Scenario 3 Neutral hosts
Scenario based on...	Recent announcements	Network Sharing Through(5G) JVs and wholesale	Vapor's vision Equinix but deeper
Facilities Provided by...	Mainly telco (some neutral hosts)	Mainly telco (some neutral hosts)	Mainly neutral hosts (some telco)
Iaas provided by…	Mainly hyperscalers	Mainly telcos	Mainly hyperscalers and independents
PaaS provided by….	Mainly hyperscalers	MobileedgeX and other aggregators	Mainly hypersclers

Conclusion

Edge computing technology presents immense opportunities for transformative applications and improved system performance. Although challenges exist, ongoing advancements and collaborative efforts will overcome them. The future of edge computing is bright, driven by 5G integration, AI advancements, enhanced security measures, and industry-specific solutions. The continuous evolution of edge computing will empower businesses, industries, and society as a whole, revolutionizing the way we process, analyze, and leverage data.

References

Akula, Chandra Sekhar, Venkateswarlu Sunkari, and Ch Prathima. "High-Performance Computing Center Framework for Smart Farming." In *Proceedings of the International Conference on Computer Vision, High Performance Computing, Smart Devices and Networks: CHSN-2020*, pp. 157-162. Singapore: Springer Nature Singapore, 2022.

Cao, Keyan, Yefan Liu, Gongjie Meng, and Qimeng Sun. "An overview on edge computing research." *IEEE access* 8 (2020): 85714-85728.

Chen, Chien-Ming, Shehzad Ashraf Chaudhry, Kuo-Hui Yeh, and Muhammad Naveed Aman. "Security, Trust and Privacy for Cloud, Fog and Internet of Things." *Security and Communication Networks* 2022 (2022): 1-2.

Chilukuri, Prathima, K. Naveen Kumar Reddy, K. N. V. S. Divyanjali, L. Javali Royal, M. Hari Chandana, and D. Murali Krishna. "A Novel Model for Prediction of Next Word using Machine Learning." In *2023 7th International Conference on Intelligent Computing and Control Systems (ICICCS)*, pp. 393-400. IEEE, 2023.

Chilukuri, Prathima, S. Harshitha, P. Abhiram, S. Susanna, S. Vyshnavi, and B. Chalam Babu. "Analysing Of Image Quality Computation Models Through Convolutional Neural Network." In *2023 2nd International Conference on Vision Towards Emerging Trends in Communication and Networking Technologies (ViTECoN)*, pp. 1-7. IEEE, 2023.

Cui, Wei. "Research and Application of Edge Computing Based on Deep Learning." In *Journal of Physics: Conference Series*, vol. 1646, no. 1, p. 012016. IOP Publishing, 2020.

Deshpande, Sonali, and Nilima Kulkarni. "Recent Trends in Cloud Computing and Edge Computing." *Library Philosophy and Practice* (2021): 1-16.

Hamdan, Salam, Moussa Ayyash, and Sufyan Almajali. "Edge-computing architectures for internet of things applications: A survey." *Sensors* 20, no. 22 (2020): 6441.

Lim, Wei Yang Bryan, Nguyen Cong Luong, Dinh Thai Hoang, Yutao Jiao, Ying-Chang Liang, Qiang Yang, Dusit Niyato, and Chunyan Miao. "Federated learning in mobile edge networks: A comprehensive survey." *IEEE Communications Surveys & Tutorials* 22, no. 3 (2020): 2031-2063.

Magesh, S., J. Indumathi, R. RamMohan, V. Niveditha, and P. Prabha. "Concepts and contributions of edge computing in internet of things (IoT): A survey." *Int. J. Comput. Netw. Appl* 7 (2020): 146-156.

Moustafa, Nour. "A new distributed architecture for evaluating AI-based security systems at the edge: Network TON_IoT datasets." *Sustainable Cities and Society* 72 (2021): 102994.

Pan, Jianli, and James McElhannon. "Future edge cloud and edge computing for internet of things applications." *IEEE Internet of Things Journal* 5, no. 1 (2017): 439-449.

Pérez, Jorge, Jessica Díaz, Javier Berrocal, Ramón López-Viana, and Ángel González-Prieto. "Edge computing: A grounded theory study." *Computing* 104, no. 12 (2022): 2711-2747.

Salman, Ola, Imad Elhajj, Ayman Kayssi, and Ali Chehab. "Edge computing enabling the Internet of Things." In *2015 IEEE 2nd World Forum on Internet of Things (WF-IoT)*, pp. 603-608. IEEE, 2015.

Sonone, Swaroop S., Kavita Saini, Swapnali Jadhav, Mahipal Singh Sankhla, and Varad Nagar. "The future of edge computing." In *Advances in Computers*, vol. 127, pp. 333-358. Elsevier, 2022.

Xue, Huihui, Bi Huang, Mingming Qin, Hua Zhou, and Hongji Yang. "Edge computing for internet of things: A survey." In *2020 International Conferences on Internet of Things (iThings) and IEEE Green Computing and Communications (GreenCom) and IEEE Cyber, Physical and Social Computing (CPSCom) and IEEE Smart Data (SmartData) and IEEE Congress on Cybermatics (Cybermatics)*, pp. 755-760. IEEE, 2020.

Zhang, Yongqiang, Hongchang Yu, Wanzhen Zhou, and Menghua Man. "Application and Research of IoT Architecture for End-Net-Cloud Edge Computing." *Electronics* 12, no. 1 (2022): 1.

Zhao, Yongli, Wei Wang, Yajie Li, Carlos Colman Meixner, Massimo Tornatore, and Jie Zhang. "Edge computing and networking: A survey on infrastructures and applications." *IEEE Access* 7 (2019): 101213-101230.

Chapter 9

Sustainable Mobile Technologies: Eco-Friendly Innovations for the Future

K. Reddy Madhavi[1]
Chevuru Nandini[2,*]
Chinnakotla Jagannath[2]
J. Avanija[1]
P. Dhanalakshmi[1]
and Viswaksena Balaji[3]

[1]Department of AI and ML, School of Computing, Mohan Babu University, Tirupati, A.P, India
[2]Department of CSE, Sree Vidyanikethan Engineering College, Tirupati, A.P, India
[3]University of Limerick, Limerick, Ireland

Abstract

"Sustainable Mobile Technologies: Eco-Friendly Innovations for the Future" explores the evolving landscape of mobile technologies with a focus on environmentally conscious innovations. As the demand for mobile devices and services continues to rise, the ecological impact becomes a critical concern. This abstract highlight cutting-edge solutions, including energy-efficient designs, eco-friendly materials, and recycling initiatives, paving the way for a greener mobile industry. Emphasizing the integration of renewable energy sources, reduced electronic waste, and lifecycle sustainability, the chapter advocates for a

* Corresponding Author's Email: nandinichevuru999@gmail.com.

In: The Future of Mobile Computing
Editors: Sam Goundar, J. Avanija and K. Reddy Madhavi
ISBN: 979-8-89113-715-8

holistic approach towards eco-friendly mobile technologies. By examining current trends and future prospects, this research contributes to a more sustainable and responsible technological future, aligning with global efforts to address climate change and promote a circular economy in the realm of mobile technology.

Keywords: sustainable mobile tech, eco-friendly innovations, recycled materials, energy efficiency, circular economy, renewable energy

Introduction

The way we live our daily lives has been completely transformed by modern mobile technologies, which have brought about revolutionary changes in communication, entertainment and information access. Undoubtedly, the use of smartphones, tablets and other mobile devices has improved connectivity and convenience as well as brought about other benefits. Despite its significant contributions to global connectivity, the mobile industry is increasingly being criticized for its environmental impacts. Mobile technologies are important in promoting sustainable practices and minimizing possible environmental damage.

- Manufacturing and Raw Materials Extraction
- Electronic Waste(e-waste)
- Energy Consumption
- Resource Depletion
- Network Infrastructure
- Biodiversity and Habitat Disruption
- Consumer Behavior

The environmental impact of a mobile device increases in various stages of its life. The production of energy, the extraction of raw materials, disposing of electronic waste and usage of devices also have serious impacts on the environment based on how mobile technologies affect it. Mining regions that produce rare minerals like lithium and coltan that are used in cell phone manufacture have caused conflicts and environmental degradation. Also, energy-intensive industrial processes as well as their carbon footprint influence green house (Almalki, Faris A, Saeed H. Alsamhi, Radhya Sahal, et al., 2020). gas emissions. In this situation, it is evident that the extensive usage of mobile devices has a negative effect on the environment in Figure 1. Major problems of efficient disposal and recycling of electronic waste are energy consumption by data centers enabling cloud services, manufacturing electronic parts and discarding outdated devices. The more technology evolves, the worse the e-waste situation becomes as products have shorter life cycles and people upgrade their gadgets more often.

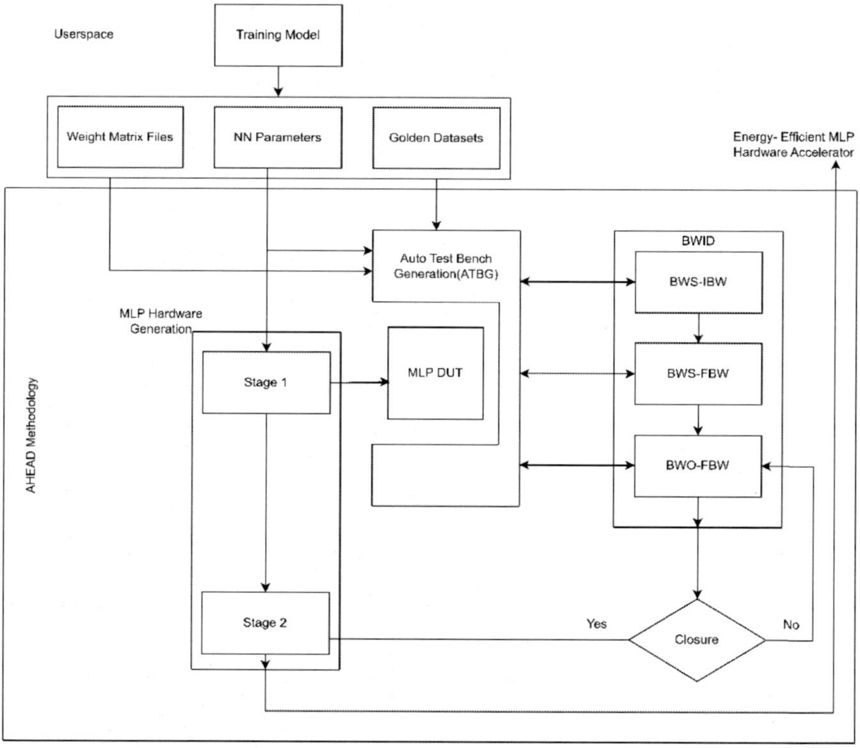

Figure 1. Implementation of the AHEAD methodology.

To address these environmental issues, the mobile sector is starting to realize the increasing desire for sustainable solutions. Mobile device manufacturers, legislators and consumers need to collaborate in order to develop strategies to minimize the negative impact of these gadgets on the environment. Industry can take steps at various points in the life cycle of products from energy efficient manufacturing techniques, ecological design, and ethical sourcing of raw materials in order to reduce its impact on nature. The conversation explores the effect of mobile technologies on the environment and underscores the need for the mobile sector to adopt sustainable business approaches. As we move through this digital age, if we want a lasting existence for our planet, we have to strike a balance between technological progress and environmental responsibility. In the following sections, possible solutions will be tackled as well as specific areas touching on how mobile technology affects the environment.

Energy-Efficient Hardware Designs

Advances in Low-Power Processors for Mobile Devices

The development of low-voltage electronic devices is important for the electricity generation of more powerful and energy-efficient electronic devices, smartphones, tablets and other devices (Lee et al., 2021). The ongoing need for mobile devices to have greater power, better performance, and longer battery life is what is driving these advancements.

Process Technology Advancements: Shrinking Process Nodes and FinFET Technology.

- Advanced Power Management: Dynamic Voltage and Frequency Scaling (DVFS) and Adaptive Voltage Scaling (AVS)
- Low-Power Memory Technologies: LPDDR (Low Power Double Rate Data) memory, Developments in low-power memory technology, including LPDDR, can save energy by lowering the amount of power used by the device's memory subsystem.
- AI-Based Power Management: AI-Driven Power Optimization, AI algorithms are used to forecast and dynamically control power use. The device's power profile can be modified by these algorithms in response to user activity and consumption patterns.
- Energy-Efficient Display Technologies: OLED and AMOLED Displays: Mobile devices can use less energy overall by utilizing energy-saving devices like OLED and AMOLED.
- Sensor Hub Integration: Dedicated sensor processing: Some mobile CPUs are equipped with a dedicated sensor hub, which efficiently handles sensor data and frees up the primary processor.

Energy-Efficient Displays and Batteries

Sensors and automation capabilities are built into energy-efficient batteries and displays (Piguet and Christian, 2018), enabling homes to maximize energy use and drastically lower their carbon footprint while also extending the life of their devices, improving user experiences, and addressing environmental concerns.

Energy-Efficient displays include OLED Technology, Power-Efficient Backlighting, Low-Power Display Technologies, Adaptive Brightness and Refresh Rate. Lithium-Ion Batteries, Solid-State Batteries, Advanced Battery Management Systems (BMS), Optimized Power Consumption, Fast Charging Technologies can be used as energy efficient batteries. Ultimately, information science, engineering, and design are all involved in the complex process of creating energy-efficient batteries and displays.

Sustainable Materials in Mobile Manufacturing

Businesses are starting to include sustainable materials (Zhang et al., 2020) into their production processes as they become more conscious of the environmental impact of their products in Figure 2. The IT sector has concentrated on the usage of fixed devices in the creation of mobile devices.

These are a few eco-friendly materials that can be put to good use or utilized to make portable electronics.

Recycled Metals, Bioplastics, Recycled Plastic, Sustainable Wood, Bio-based Materials, Recycled Paper Packaging, Modular Design, Fair Trade Materials.

Renewable Energy Integration in Mobile Devices

- Solar-Powered Mobile Devices: Solar power (Page and Tom, 2015) gadgets employ solar panels to turn sunlight into electricity, allowing users to charge their electronics with clean energy in Figure 3. This technology may be appealing to people who wish to lessen their environmental effect and depend less on conventional energy sources. These are some crucial things to think about when utilizing mobile devices that run on solar power.

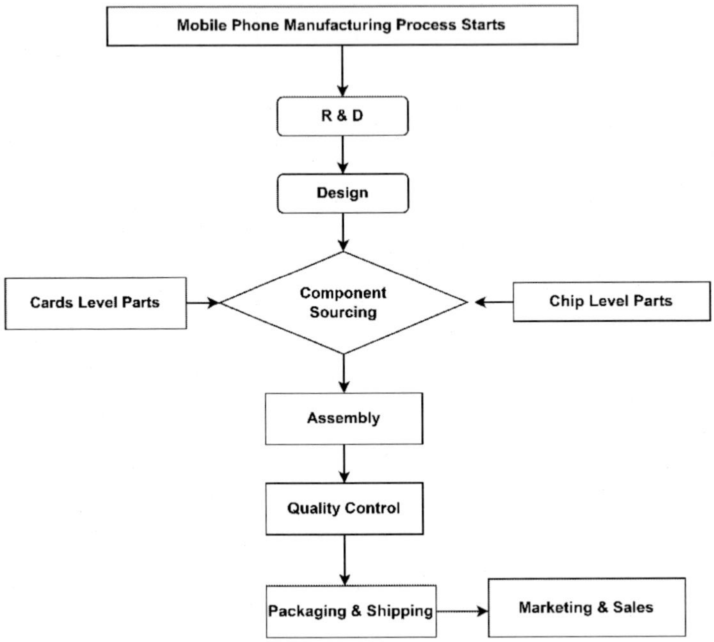

Figure 2. Mobile phone manufacturing.

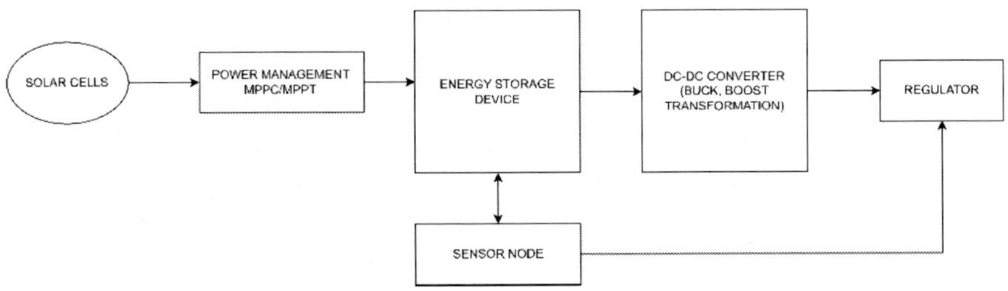

Figure 3. Solar energy harvesting system.

- Solar Panels: Type and Efficiency, one crucial factor to take into account is the solar panels' efficiency. More electricity can be produced in fewer locations via more efficient panels.
- Device Types: Mobile phones, some cell phones with solar charging features can use solar energy to charge mobile devices. Power Banks, A solar powered power bank is a compact device that can be used to store solar energy for later use. This becomes an easy way to pay them on the go.

- Charging Speed and Storage: Charging Speed, generally speaking, solar charging will take longer than traditional devices. Factors such as solar energy intensity and panel efficiency affect charging speed. Battery storage, some devices are equipped with batteries that can use solar energy when the sun shines. This provides more reliable power.
- Durability and Weather Resistance: Information, because solar products can be exposed to many types of environments, they must be strong and weatherproof.
- User Behavior and Adaptation: Sunlight Availability, the availability of sunlight affects the performance of solar panels. Users will be able to update their payment options. For example, to get the best payout, placc thc house in direct sunlight.
- Environmental Impact: Sustainability, Solar energy technology contributes to sustainability by reducing dependence on non-renewable energy sources.

Kinetic and Piezoelectric Charging Technologies

Two advanced methods of converting electricity into electrical energy (Jiju et al., 2014) are kinetic charging and piezoelectric charging. Now let's look at these one by one. The process of converting mechanical energy or kinetic energy into electrical energy is called kinetic energy load. These systems are often used by devices that can record movement (such as the movements of the human body or other systems) and convert it into electricity. Also, to convert kinetic energy into electricity, kinetic energy (Malla et al., 2016) chargers usually use electromagnetic induction, piezoelectric materials or other means. Fitness monitors, technology and some consumer electronics often use kinetic energy to charge products. The main advantage of kinetic charging is that it produces electricity from an external source and the limitation is kinetic charging frequently produces very little energy compared to other charging techniques

The foundation of piezoelectric charging is the piezoelectric effect (Elmannai et al., 2023) the capacity of some materials to produce an electric charge when mechanical stress is applied. Quartz, Rochelle salt, and lead zirconate titanate (PZT) are examples of common piezoelectric materials. These substances were picked because they can produce a voltage under mechanical stress. Applications: Piezoelectric charging finds use in a number of industries, such as pressure sensors, self-powered sensors in Internet of Things devices, and energy harvesting from vibrations in industrial environments. The conversion of mechanical energy to electrical energy by piezoelectric charging has the potential to be very effective.

The drawback of using this technique will be difficulties producing significant power for high-energy devices, much like kinetic charging.

The Role of Wireless Charging in Sustainability

Because wireless charging solves a number of the financial and environmental issues that come with using conventional charging techniques, it contributes significantly to sustainability. The following are a few ways that wireless charging supports sustainability:

- Energy Efficiency: Systems for wireless (Zhou et al., 2019) charging can be made to be extremely effective, reducing the amount of energy lost during charging. In order to promote sustainable behaviours and lower overall energy usage, this efficiency is essential.
- Reduced E-Waste: By eliminating the need for throwaway wires and connectors, wireless charging reduces the amount of electronic garbage (e-waste) that is produced.
- Increased Product Lifespan: Device failure can frequently be attributed to physical connector wear and tear, such as that seen in USB ports. By doing away with the necessity for physical connections, wireless charging may extend the life of electronics and lower the frequency of replacements.
- Clean Energy Integration: A more sustainable charging ecosystem is facilitated by wireless charging infrastructure that is fueled by clean, renewable energy sources.
- Flexibility and Convenience: There is greater freedom in where and how gadgets can be charged when using wireless charging.

Green Mobile Networks and Connectivity

Energy-Efficient Cellular Infrastructure

In the telecommunicationssector, energy-efficient cellular infrastructure is essential since it minimises operational expenses and the impact on the environment while meeting the growing demand for mobile connection (Ismail et al., 2014; Antonopoulos et al., 2015).

- Network Optimization: Load Balancing and Dynamic Resource Allocation
- Green Base Stations: Renewable Energy Sources and Energy Storage
- Small Cells and HetNets (Heterogeneous Networks): Deploy microcells in densely populated areas to reduce stress on large macrocells and improve energy efficiency
- Energy-Efficient Antennas: Smart Antennas and Massive MIMO
- Energy-Efficient Protocols: LTE-A and 5G Standards and Network Function Virtualization (NFV) and Software-Defined Networking (SDN).
- Energy-Efficient Hardware: Low-Power Components and Energy Harvesting
- Public Awareness and Education: Educate consumers about how mobile phones impact the environment and promote responsible use.

Combining these technologies can help create a more secure and energy-efficient cellular infrastructure.

Eco-Friendly Data Centers for Mobile Services

Here are many eco-friendly travel and transportation apps (Pathak et al., 2022) that help users choose eco-friendly options, reduce carbon footprint, and promote green initiatives as specified in Table 1.

Before utilizing any program, it's a good idea to check evaluations and updates to make sure it fulfills your sustainability objectives and offers reliable information and updates.

Table 1. Eco-friendly travel and transportation apps

Name of the app	Purpose	Advantage
Blablacar	An app that matches drivers with open seats with passengers travelling in the same route for carpooling.	Promotes resource efficiency by lowering the number of individual autos on the road.
Uber and Lyft (Shared Rides)	Ride-sharing apps that facilitate shared rides in an effort to cut down on the number of individual trips and encourage the economical use of automobiles	Lower emissions per passenger by reducing the number of vehicles on the road.
Citymapper	The goal is to give consumers up-to-date information about public transit so they may select the route that is both safest and most environmentally friendly.	Encourage public transportation use and lessen reliance on private automobiles
Bikemap	finds and plans bike routes for riders to enjoy or commute on.	Cycling encourages an eco-friendly and sustainable form of transportation.
Plug and Play	Assist owners of electric vehicles (EVs) in scheduling lengthy trips and locating charging facilities.	Lower the risk of osteoporosis and encourage the usage of electric vehicles.

Optimizing Network Protocols for Sustainability

One of the most important ways to lessen the environmental impact of digital infrastructure is through network protocol optimization for sustainability (Zhang et al., 2014). Here are a few tactics and things to think about when creating more sustainable network protocols.

- Energy Efficiency: Low Power Modes and Dynamic Scaling
- Data Compression: Efficient Compression Algorithms
- Minimize Round Trips: HTTP/2 and HTTP/3
- Content Delivery Networks (CDNs): Edge Computing
- Caching: Client-Side and Server-Side Caching
- Quality of Service (QoS): Adaptive Bitrate Streaming
- Protocol Optimization: TCP Optimization
- Efficient Routing: Routing Algorithms
- Network Virtualization: Network Function Virtualization (NFV)
- Monitoring and Analytics: Energy Monitoring Tools.

Eco-Friendly Mobile Design Principles

Modular and Repairable Mobile Devices

Smartphones and other handheld electronic devices (Maskeliūnas et al., 2020) that are built with easily replaceable or upgradeable parts by technicians or consumers are referred to as modular and repairable mobile devices. Here are some key aspects of modular and repairable mobile devices:

In Modularity, these devices are constructed with modular components, meaning that different parts of the devices (such as the battery, camera, processor, etc.) are separate and can be replaced individually. The Ease of Repair, Repairability (Amend et al., 2022) is a central focus in the design of these devices. Manufactures aim to make it easy for users or third-party technicians to access and replace faculty components. The Sustainable Design in the primary goal of modular and repairable design is to reduce electronic waste. By Challenges and Barriers, while the concept of modular and repairable devices is admirable, there are challenges in implementation.

Several initiatives and companies have embraced the concept of modular and repairable mobile devices, but the widespread adoption of these principles in the mainstream consumer electronics market is still evolving.

Sustainable Packaging and Product Lifecycle

Sustainable packaging (Vila et al., 2015) and product lifestyle are critical components of environmentally responsible business practices.

Sustainable Packaging

Sustainable packaging refers to the use of materials and design techniques that have a reduced environmental impact, both in terms of the production and disposal of packaging material. Material Selection in Usage of renewable and biodegradable materials and Recyclability and recycled content. And also Design Efficiency in the Minimization of packaging material and Lightweight packaging to reduce transportation-related emissions. Biodegradability and Compostability in selecting materials that can break down naturally without harming the environment. In Circular Economy, Approach Encouraging the recycling and reuse of packaging materials. Innovation can Exploring new technologies and materials for sustainable packaging.

Product Lifecycle

The product lifecycle represents the stages a product goes through from its inception to its disposal. In Raw Material Extraction, Sourcing materials with minimal environmental impact and considering ethical sourcing practices. Manufacturing in Energy-efficient production processes and Minimizing waste during manufacturing. Distribution and Transportation will Reducing transportation-related emissions And Efficient supply chain management. Product Use in Energy efficiency during use and promoting proper use and maintenance to extend product life. By integrating sustainable packaging with a thoughtful approach to the entire product lifecycle, businesses can contribute significantly to environmental conversation and meet the growing demand for eco-friendly products.

Extended Product Longevity through Upgradability

Extending product longevity (Jensen et al., 2021) through upgradability is a strategic approach that aligns with sustainability goals and customer preferences. Here are some key points to consider when aiming to enhance product longevity through upgradability:

Utilize Modular Design in Component Separation and Standardized Interfaces. In Software Updates, Firmware and Software Compatibility Develop products with the capability to receive software updates. Regular updates can improve functionality, security, and performance, contributing to a longer useful life for the product. User-Friendly Upgrade Processes Can Clear Instructions and Tool-Less Design. Then Environmental Impact in Sustainable Materials and Reduced E-Waste. customer Incentives can Upgrade Programs

Mobile Apps for Environmental Awareness

Sustainable Lifestyle Apps

Now-a-days there were several apps designed to help individuals adopt and maintain a sustainable lifestyle (Brauer et al., 2016; Hoffmann et al., 2022) as specified in Table 2.

Table 2. Sustainable lifestyle apps

Substainable lifestyle	Purpose	Availability
Ecosia	An eco-friendly search engine that uses its profits to plant trees. Users can track the number of trees they've contributed to by using the search engine.	iOS, Android, Web
Good On You	Helps users discover and support ethical and sustainable fashion brands. It provides ratings based on environmental and social performance.	
Too Good to Go	Aims to reduce food waste by connecting users with restaurants, cafes, and grocery stores that have surplus food available at discounted prices.	iOS, Android
Oroeco	Allows users to track and reduce their carbon footprint. It provides tips and challenges to help individuals make sustainable choices in their daily lives.	Web (Mobile version available)

Table 3. Carbon footprint tracking and reduction apps

Source	Name of the App	Usage
Carbon Footprint Calculator Apps	PAWPRINT	By entering data about daily activities including transportation, energy use, and garbage generation, this software assists users in estimating their carbon footprint. It then offers suggestions for cutting carbon emissions.
Sustainable Transportation Apps	C02 Fit	This app focuses on tracking and reducing carbon emissions related to transportation
	Ecolife	It helps users track their carbon footprint related to commuting and travel.
Energy Usage Tracking Apps	JouleBug	It provides challenges and rewards for reducing energy consumption, waste, and water usage
	Enerfy	This app assists users in tracking and optimising their household energy consumption. It offers information on how much electricity is used and makes recommendations for lowering energy waste

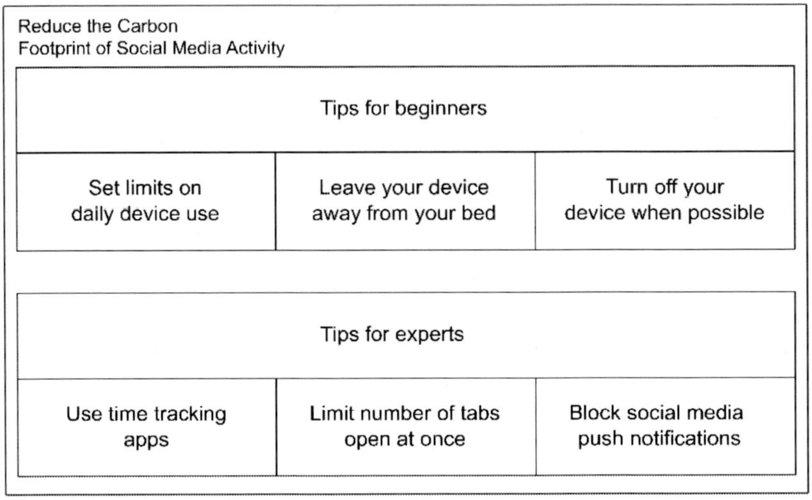

Figure 4. Reduce the carbon footprint of social media.

There are several apps designed to help individuals and organizations track and reduce their carbon footprint in Figure 4. These apps often provide information on energy usage, transportation habits, and lifestyle (Shabir et al., 2022) choices that contribute to carbon emissions as specified in Table 3.

Table 4. Eco-friendly transportation and travel apps

Name of the app	Purpose	Advantage
Blablacar	An app that matches drivers with open seats with passengers travelling in the same route for carpooling.	Promotes resource efficiency by lowering the number of individual autos on the road.
Uber and Lyft (Shared Rides)	Ride-sharing apps that facilitate shared rides in an effort to cut down on the number of individual trips and encourage the economical use of automobiles	Lower emissions per passenger by reducing the number of vehicles on the road.
Citymapper	The goal is to give consumers up-to-date information about public transit so they may select the route that is both safest and most environmentally friendly.	Encourage public transportation use and lessen reliance on private automobiles
Bikemap	finds and plans bike routes for riders to enjoy or commute on.	Encourages cycling, an eco-friendly and sustainable form of transportation.

Eco-Friendly Transportation and Travel Apps

Numerous environmentally (Namoun et al., 2021) friendly travel and transportation apps are available to assist users in choosing ecologically friendly options, lowering their carbon footprint, and supporting green initiatives as specified in Table 4.

Case Studies: Successful Implementations

Examples of Mobile Manufacturers Embracing Sustainability

Many mobile device makers are currently working to incorporate sustainability into different facets of their business operations. Here are a few instances from that era.

- Apple: When it comes to sustainability (Ghoreishi et al., 2020) efforts, Apple has been a pioneer. The corporation has made progress in utilising more recyclable materials in its gadgets and has pledged to running its global corporate operations entirely on renewable energy.
- Samsung: Samsung has pledged to use eco-friendly materials in its products.
- Google: Google has been making investments in environmental initiatives, such as using recycled materials in its hardware products. Like Sony, Nokia, OnePlus, ... etc.

Impact Assessment on Carbon Footprint Reduction

Evaluating the changes in greenhouse gas emissions brought about by particular actions or efforts is necessary to determine the impact of reducing one's carbon footprint (Luo et al., 2022). The following are essential actions and things to think about while performing a thorough impact assessment. Define Scope and Boundaries in Clearly state what your assessment's parameters are in Figure 5. Identify Baseline Emissions by Determine the current greenhouse gas emissions baseline. Set Reduction Targets in Set quantifiable, time-bound, and precise reduction goals. Implement Carbon Reduction Measures in Determine and put into action strategies to cut carbon emissions. Monitor and Collect Data in a reliable monitoring system to gather emissions data during the reduction efforts (Goundar et al., 2021). Quantify Reductions in the direct and indirect reductions in greenhouse gas emissions brought about by the actions put in place. Evaluate Co-benefits and Trade-off, The additional benefits of carbon reduction initiatives, such as financial savings, increased resource efficiency, and higher brand recognition for the company. Determine any trade-offs or unforeseen repercussions that might result from the actions taken. Report and Communicate Results can Write a thorough report on the impact assessment that includes the methodology, sources of data, and findings. Finally, External Verification For reliability and transparency, consider external verification or certification by a third party, depending on the scope and significance of mitigation efforts.

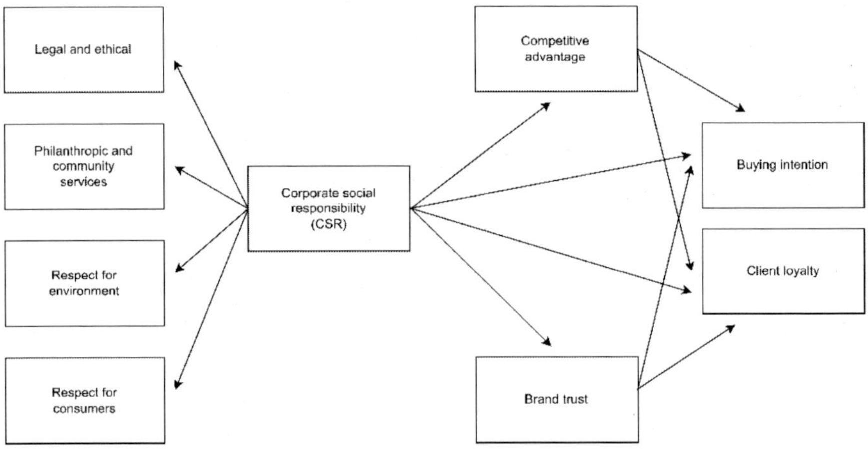

Figure 5. Conceptual model.

Challenges and Future Prospects

Overcoming Obstacles in Sustainable Mobile Technology

Overcoming the barriers to sustainability (Greve et al., 2022) mobility technology requires a multifaceted approach that takes into account social, economic and environmental issues. Here are some key challenges and solutions:

Energy consumption:

- Obstacle: The huge energy demand of mobile devices and networks increases carbon emissions.
- Solution: Design and use energy-saving devices such as battery-powered devices and low-energy devices.
- Obstacle: Technology develops very quickly and makes products very efficient, therefore the waste produced by electronic products is also decreasing.
- Solution: Create durable mobile devices that allow customization (Wang et al., 2012) and reconfiguration.
- Social Impact and Equity:
- Obstacle: Access to sustainable mobile technology is not evenly distributed, leading to digital divides and social inequalities.
- Solution: Implement policies that ensure affordable access to sustainable technology for all socio-economic groups.

Regulatory Challenges:

- Obstacle: Inconsistent or inadequate regulations may hinder the adoption of sustainable practices in the mobile technology sector.
- Solution: Advocate for and support the development of comprehensive regulations that promote sustainability in the mobile industry.

Behavioral Change:

- Obstacle: Consumer behaviors, such as frequent device upgrades, can contribute to environmental issues.
- Solution: Promote consumer awareness about the environmental impact of their choices.

Emerging Innovations and Trends in Green Mobile Technologies

Now-a-days several trends and innovations are emerging in the field of green mobile technologies, focused on making mobile devices and their associated infrastructure more environmentally friendly. Here are some key trends and innovations in green mobile technologies

- Energy-efficient hardware in Low-power processors and Advanced battery technologies.
- Renewable energy sources in Solar-powered charging and Wireless charging.
- Energy-efficient communication protocols in 5G and beyond.
- Energy-efficient software and applications can Optimized software and Cloud computing.
- Smart city initiatives can Integrated transportation systems and Environmental monitoring.
- User awareness and engagement in green certifications and Energy-saving features. Electronic waste management recycling programs and circular economy.
- Eco-friendly materials in Sustainable materials and Modular design.

Corporate Social Responsibility in the Mobile Industry

Initiatives by Mobile Companies for Environmental Sustainability

Mobile companies have increasingly recognized the importance of environmental sustainability (Alinikula and Petteri, 2013) and have taken various initiatives to reduce their carbon footprint, promote recycling, and adopt more eco-friendly practices. Energy Efficiency in Devices, this includes optimizing hardware and software to consume less power, thereby extending battery life. Sustainable Materials using recycled plastics, bio-based materials, and reducing the use of harmful substances. Eco-Friendly Packaging can use recycled materials, lowering package sizes, and implementing more environmentally (Mohamed et al., 2007) friendly packaging techniques, businesses are attempting to reduce the amount of trash that comes with packing.

Programs for Recycling E-Waste in Mobile service providers regularly run campaigns to encourage customers to recycle their old equipment. Adoption of Renewable Energy, many cellular companies have committed to operating their operations solely on renewable energy. Cutting Carbon Emissions Companies want to minimize their overall carbon footprint. Extended Product Lifecycles in Mobile companies are designing their products with durability in mind, hoping to persuade customers to retain their devices longer.

Promotion of Sustainable Practices in Sustainable practices and environmental awareness are actively promoted by numerous mobile companies. Collaboration with Environmental Organizations, some businesses support conservation efforts, tree planting campaigns, and other programs aimed at protecting natural resources by working with NGOs and environmental organizations. Certifications and Standards to make sure their goods fulfil tight environmental requirements; mobile companies are more and more pursuing certifications like EPEAT (Electronic Product Environmental Assessment Tool) and complying with RoHS (Restriction of Hazardous Substances) standards.

The Role of Regulation in Promoting Green Practices

By creating a framework that directs and incentivizes companies and individuals to adopt ecologically sustainable behaviours, regulation plays a critical role in promoting green practices. Setting Standards and Requirements in Businesses are required by regulations to comply with minimal environmental standards and criteria. Incentives and Subsidies in Governments frequently employ rules to establish financial rewards and subsidies for companies that implement environmentally friendly practices. Fines and penalties are Regulations, on the other hand, have the authority to impose fines and penalties for disregard for the environment. Market access and certification in a company may be required by law to comply with specific environmental standards in order to be certified or enter a given market. Information disclosure in Businesses may be required by regulations to provide environmental information. Research and support in the government can encourage the development of green technologies through regulations. Public education and awareness in the regulatory procedure will incorporate requirements that will motivate firms to adhere to security measures in addition to public education and awareness campaigns.

Conclusion

In summary, we need to be concerned about how mobile technology affects the environment. Increased resource consumption, energy waste production, and carbon emissions are the outcomes of the mobile industry's growth. We need to talk about the effects of mobile device manufacture, use, and disposal on the environment as we depend on them for communication, entertainment, and production. In order to lessen adverse consequences in the mobile business, stable solutions are crucial. In order to implement good environmental practices, decrease e-waste, and promote the development and use of sustainable materials, businesses, regulators, and consumers must work together in this area. By including business cycle ideas like recycling and maintenance, this should increase the lifespan of mobile devices. Additionally, the carbon footprint of the technology can be reduced by using green energy in data centers and production processes. The first step to encourage change is acknowledging the environment (Peng et al., 2021) issues associated with mobile devices. It is imperative for the mobile industry to proactively seek out sustainable solutions to guarantee that technological progress does not impede environmental preservation. For a more sustainable and responsible future in the digital age, environmental factors must be incorporated into the design, manufacture, and disposal of mobile devices.

References

Alinikula, Petteri. "Sustainability as an Innovation Catalyst for Mobile Phones." In ISPIM Conference Proceedings, p. 1. *The International Society for Professional Innovation Management (ISPIM)*, 2013.

Almalki, Faris A., Saeed H. Alsamhi, Radhya Sahal, Jahan Hassan, Ammar Hawbani, N. S. Rajput, Abdu Saif, Jeff Morgan, and John Breslin. "Green IoT for eco-friendly and sustainable smart cities: future directions and opportunities." *Mobile Networks and Applications* 28, no. 1 (2023): 178-202.

Amend, Clara, Ferdinand Revellio, Isabell Tenner, and Stefan Schaltegger. "The potential of modular product design on repair behavior and user experience–Evidence from the smartphone industry." *Journal of Cleaner Production* 367 (2022): 132770.

Antonopoulos, Angelos, Elli Kartsakli, Alexandra Bousia, Luis Alonso, and Christos Verikoukis. "Energy-efficient infrastructure sharing in multi-operator mobile networks." *IEEE Communications Magazine* 53, no. 5 (2015): 242-249.

Brauer, Benjamin, Carolin Ebermann, Björn Hildebrandt, Gerrit Remané, and Lutz M. Kolbe. "Green by app: The contribution of mobile applications to environmental sustainability." (2016).

Elmannai, Wafa, Khaled Elleithy, Andrew Anthony Benz, Alberto Carmine DeAngelis, and Nick Weaver. "An Enhanced Piezoelectric-Generated Power Technique for Qi Wireless Charging." *Clean Technologies* 5, no. 1 (2023): 94-115.

Ghoreishi, Malahat, and Ari Happonen. "Key enablers for deploying artificial intelligence for circular economy embracing sustainable product design: Three case studies." *In AIP conference proceedings*, vol. 2233, no. 1. AIP Publishing, 2020.

Goundar, Sam, J. Avanija, Gurram Sunitha, K. Reddy Madhavi, and S. Bharath Bhushan, eds. *Innovations in the industrial Internet of Things (IIoT) and smart factory*. IGI Global, 2021.

Greve, Maike, Alfred Benedikt Brendel, Nils van Osten, and Lutz M. Kolbe. "Overcoming the barriers of mobile health that hamper sustainability in low-resource environments." *Journal of Public Health* 30, no. 1 (2022): 49-62.

Hoffmann, Stefan, Wassili Lasarov, and Hanna Reimers. "Carbon footprint tracking apps. What drives consumers' adoption intention?" *Technology in Society* 69 (2022): 101956.

Ismail, Muhammad, Weihua Zhuang, Erchin Serpedin, and Khalid Qaraqe. "A survey on green mobile networking: From the perspectives of network operators and mobile users." *IEEE Communications Surveys & Tutorials* 17, no. 3 (2014): 1535-1556.

Jensen, Peter Byrial, Linda Nhu Laursen, and Louise Møller Haase. "Barriers to product longevity: A review of business, product development and user perspectives." *Journal of Cleaner Production* 313 (2021): 127951.

Jiju, K., P. Ramesh, P. Brijesh, and B. Sreekumari. "Development of Android based on-line monitoring and control system for Renewable Energy Sources." In *2014 International Conference on Computer, Communications, and Control Technology (I4CT)*, pp. 372-375. IEEE, 2014.

Lee, Jinsu, and Hoi-Jun Yoo. "An overview of energy-efficient hardware accelerators for on-device deep-neural-network training." *IEEE Open Journal of the Solid-State Circuits Society* 1 (2021): 115-128.

Luo, Xiaoyu, Mengyu Ren, Jiahong Zhao, Zitao Wang, Jian Ge, and Weijun Gao. "Life cycle assessment for carbon emission impact analysis for the renovation of old residential areas." *Journal of Cleaner Production* 367 (2022): 132930.

Malla, Siva Ganesh, D. Jaya Deepu, D. Pavan Kumar, and Jagan Mohana Rao Malla. "Solar powered mobile phone: An innovative experiment." *In 2016 International Conference on Signal Processing, Communication, Power and Embedded System (SCOPES)*, pp. 1015-1020. IEEE, 2016.

Maskeliūnas, Rytis, Audrius Kulikajevas, Tomas Blažauskas, Robertas Damaševičius, and Jakub Swacha. "An interactive serious mobile game for supporting the learning of programming in javascript in the context of eco-friendly city management." *Computers* 9, no. 4 (2020): 102.

Mohamed, Mudzamir Bin, and Norfaiezah Binti Sawandi. "Corporate Social Responsibility (CSR) activities in mobile telecommunication industry: case study of Malaysia.*" In European Critical Accounting Conference,* pp. 1-26. 2007.

Namoun, Abdallah, Ali Tufail, Nikolay Mehandjiev, Ahmed Alrehaili, Javad Akhlaghinia, and Evtim Peytchev. "An eco-friendly multimodal route guidance system for urban areas using multi-agent technology." *Applied Sciences* 11, no. 5 (2021): 2057.

Page, Tom. "An Approach to the Management of the Sustainable Issues in Mobile Phone Design and Manufacturing." *Journal on Management* 10, no. 2 (2015).

Pathak, Prakash Kumar, Sachin Kumar, Hirdesh Sharma, and Devanshu Dube. "Green Computing and Eco-Friendly Computing System." *Journal Of Algebraic Statistics* 13, no. 3 (2022): 5526-5530.

Peng, Hui, Neng Shen, Huanqin Ying, and Qunwei Wang. "Can environmental regulation directly promote green innovation behavior? ——based on situation of industrial agglomeration." *Journal of Cleaner Production* 314 (2021): 128044.

Piguet, Christian, ed. *Low-power electronics design.* CRC press, 2018.

Shabir, Habiba, Matthew D'Costa, Zain Mohiaddin, Zaeem Moti, Hamza Rashid, Daria Sadowska, Benyamin Alam, and Benita Cox. "The barriers and facilitators to the use of lifestyle apps: a systematic review of qualitative studies." *European journal of investigation in health, psychology and education* 12, no. 2 (2022): 144-165.

Vila, C., José Vicente Abellán-Nebot, J. C. Albiñana, and G. Hernández. "An approach to sustainable product lifecycle management (Green PLM)." *Procedia engineering* 132 (2015): 585-592.

Wang, Xiaofei, Athanasios V. Vasilakos, Min Chen, Yunhao Liu, and Ted Taekyoung Kwon. "A survey of green mobile networks: Opportunities and challenges." *Mobile Networks and Applications* 17 (2012): 4-20.

Zhang, Wu, Haizeng Li, Mohamed Al-Hussein, and Abdulhakem Y. Elezzabi. "Electrochromic battery displays with energy retrieval functions using solution-processable colloidal vanadium oxide nanoparticles." *Advanced Optical Materials* 8, no. 2 (2020): 1901224.

Zhang, Xiaoxia, Zhongming Zheng, Qinghua Shen, Jing Liu, Xuemin Sherman Shen, and Liang-Liang Xie. "Optimizing network sustainability and efficiency in green cellular networks." *IEEE transactions on wireless communications* 13, no. 2 (2014): 1129-1139.

Zhou, Pengzhan, Cong Wang, and Yuanyuan Yang. "Self-sustainable sensor networks with multi-source energy harvesting and wireless charging." *In IEEE INFOCOM 2019-IEEE Conference on Computer Communications*, pp. 1828-1836. IEEE, 2019.

Chapter 10

The Application of Mobile Computing in a Smart City

N. Ashokkumar[1,*]
M. Bharathi[1]
P. Nagarajan[2]
Kavitha Thandapani[3]
S. Deepa Nivethika[4]
and N. Swetha[5]
[1]Mohan Babu University, Tirupati, A.P, India
[2]SRM Institute of Science and Technology, Vadapalani Campus, Chennai, T.N, India
[3]Vel Tech Rangarajan Dr. Sagunthala R&D Institute of Science and Technology, Chennai, T.N, India
[4]Vellore Institute of Technology, Chennai, T.N, India
[5]Sethu Institute of Technology, Virudhunagar, Madurai, T.N, India

Abstract

When we talk about mobile computing, we are referring to the collection of information technology systems, products, services, and operational strategies and processes that make it possible for end users to access computation, information. The word "mobile" may also be used to refer to access in a fixed location via the use of equipment that users are able to move about as required but that stays stationary while it is performing its function. It is common practice to refer to this method of operation as nomadic computing. Currently, mobile computer technology can be found almost anywhere. A wide variety of specialized vertical markets,

* Corresponding Author's Email: ashoknoc@gmail.com.

In: The Future of Mobile Computing
Editors: Sam Goundar, J. Avanija and K. Reddy Madhavi
ISBN: 979-8-89113-715-8

as well as commercial and consumer markets, industrial and entertainment sectors, and other industries, may all benefit from its uses. Desktop computers provide a greater number of hardware configuration options and a higher level of processing capability. Despite this, the great majority of end consumers gravitate toward mobile devices as their preferred option. One of the most major advantages of mobile computing is its convenience, since it gives users the ability to access information and computational resources whenever and wherever they want.

Introduction

Mobile computing systems are typically comprised of a mobile device, which may be a laptop computer, tablet, or smartphone, in addition to a wireless network connection that is based on Wi-Fi or cellular wireless technologies, such as 5G. The majority of the time, a mobile computing system is comprised of these two components. Each and every one of these components is essential for the system to operate in an appropriate manner. It is not necessary to be connected to a network in order to access the data that is stored locally on mobile devices since these devices are equipped with the potential to save data locally.

In most cases, mobile computers are able to provide access to both wireless and wired technologies. As a result of the collaborative nature of work in the current day, it is very vital to have access to shared network resources. These resources may include mobile cloud-based services. Integrated rechargeable batteries are what provide power to mobile devices. These batteries are embedded into the gadget itself. The majority of these batteries are able to function on an alternating current (AC) power source when they are used from a fixed location.

There is a wide variety of mobile computing devices available for use in vertical and specialized applications, in addition to laptops, tablets, and smartphones. A variety of applications, including medical, surveillance, security, telemetry, and control, are included in this category. The selection of the device is determined by the application. As an example, laptops are particularly well-suited for the production of material, whilst tablets are often selected for the consumption of information. The screens on smartphones are quite tiny, and they use screen-based keyboards. Smartphones are able to perform the functions of pocket-sized computers and communication devices.

Mobile Computing Is Utilized for What Reasons?

There is a possibility that mobile computing will be used in every facet of life, including the business world and the consumer world.

The users are able to be free from the need to be connected to a power source for extended periods of time. Traveling professionals who wish to maintain their connection to their jobs while they are on the go will find this to be an attractive situation. Those who work from home, who may not have access to all of the connection and power choices that they would have in an office environment, might also benefit from this.

Mobile computing is used by consumers in a variety of ways, including the following among others:

1. access to the internet
2. communicating while on the go
3. navigating the web
4. Programs for mobile devices
5. streaming media for entertainment purposes

Applications and devices designed for mobile usage have the capability to collect data from users in a broad range of different environments and conditions. Some examples of wearable technology that can collect data from users in novel environments include those that are used in the fitness and health industries. As an illustration of how this kind of technology operates, two examples are smartwatches and Fitbits.

Additionally, mobile computing enables the internet of things (IoT) to become a reality. The Internet of Things (IoT) is comprised of non-traditional computers, sensors, and other devices that are able to connect with one another and communicate without the influence of a human being.

How Many Different Kinds of Mobile Computing Are There?

There are several different components that are included under the umbrella of mobile computing. These components include infrastructure, hardware, and software technologies. For your convenience, the following is a summary of the several components that comprise mobile computing:

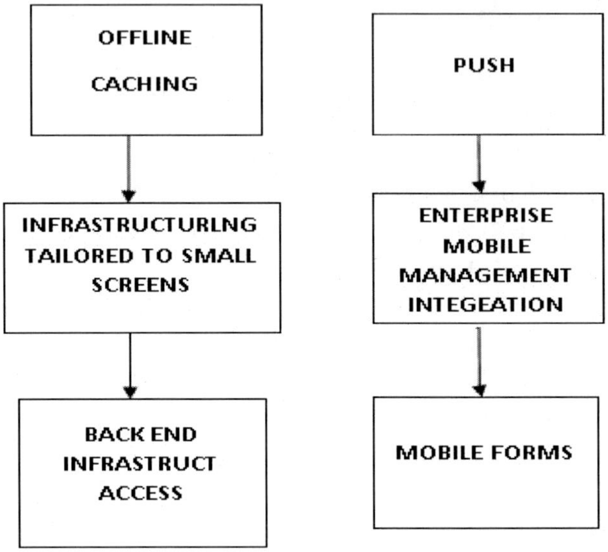

Figure 1. Companies may quickly create push-notification mobile apps using low-code.

An infrastructure that can be moved around. The infrastructure of a network is comprised of the many technical components that make it possible for devices to communicate with one another. The mobile hardware infrastructure is comprised of a number of different components, including wireless information formats, wireless protocols, and wireless networks.

Hardware that can be moved around. Mobile hardware refers to any accompanying gear that users engage with in addition to the mobile device itself. Gear for mobile devices includes both the mobile device itself and any accompanying gear. Mobile phones, laptops, tablets, and wearable computers, together with the chargers and peripherals that accompany them, might fall under this category.

For mobile devices, software. Mobile apps are software programs that are built to run on mobile devices. The phrase "mobile applications" refers to these programs. Mobile operating systems (OSes) and user-facing apps, such as mobile browsers and digital commerce applications, are included in this category of applications. Creation of push-notifications using mobile apps is specified in Figure 1.

There are many various kinds of mobile computing, and some examples include the following:

- Utilization by buyers. A wide variety of activities, such as communication, entertainment, banking, bill paying, and monitoring health and fitness, may be performed by consumers using mobile devices such as computers, smartphones, wearables, and tablets.
- Perform tasks from a remote location. Laptops and tablets are the methods of choice for workers when it comes to working together and communicating. The staff members who are responsible for delivery utilize mobile devices in order to get information on logistics and administration, as well as to check that the items were delivered to the correct place. The members of the field service workforce make use of mobile devices for the purposes of field service administration, tracking, and support skills and capabilities.
- Applications in both the commercial and consumer sectors Devices that are part of the Internet of Things are able to link with other pieces of technology without the need for human intervention. Self-driving cars, for example, make use of sensors, onboard computers, and other connected devices in order to create a link with geographic information systems (GIS), weather, and other systems in order to travel on the road in a safe way. Additionally, supply chain management systems make use of sophisticated sensors in order to monitor the movement of products while they are in transit. This allows for effective tracking of those items.

The Importance of Computing in the Context of Smart Cities

Heat islands, traffic congestion, energy consumption, and industrial waste are some of the problems that have arisen as a result of the increasing urbanization of the globe (Rao 2012; Zhong 2017; Rizwan 2008). These problems have been brought about by the expanding urbanization of the world at an alarming rate. These difficulties have a significant impact on the lives of those who live in metropolitan areas, and they are quite detrimental. All of these experiments are being conducted with the intention of fostering sustainable development and alleviating urban problems. Monitoring sensors are installed in a number of different trash cans and information systems by the Copenhagen Municipality (State of Green Denmark 2018). This is done with the intention of achieving the highest possible level of efficiency in the management of waste operations. According to Hwang and Choe (2013), Meters are capable of measuring energy consumption. These meters are able to provide a real-time report on the quantity of power, water, and natural gas that is being used. When it comes to the creation of smart cities, there are a number of information and communications technologies (ICT) that are absolutely necessary.

According to Cisco (2017), the number of devices that are linked to the Internet will approach or perhaps surpass 50 billion by the year 2020. The transmission system of the smart city is defined as the communication network, which is responsible for delivering data from sensors to computer platforms. Networks that are dependable, scalable, and possess high speeds, including both wired and wireless networks, provide the essential infrastructure for the transfer of such data. In order to discover city-related events that need processing and action, computing platforms provide assistance for the administration and analysis of relevant city data in a larger context so that they may be identified. Numerous smart-city sensors are continually producing a substantial amount of data, which is continuously created. One that is constantly updated to reflect changes in traffic patterns and congestion. Over the course of the last several years, a variety of methods and technologies that make use of information and communication technology have been created in order to monitor and predict UHI. One example is the Heat Health Watch Warning System that was established in France (Casanueva et al., 2019). This system was designed to monitor heat waves that might potentially lead to a significant rise in death rates. The key technology of smart city is specified in Figure 2.

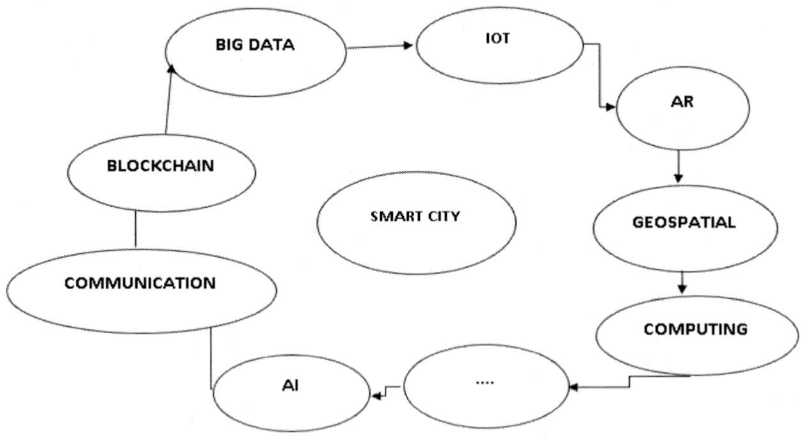

Figure 2. Key smart-city technologies.

Computing on Mobile Devices for Smart Cities Two

Methodology

The three main elements that make up mobile computing are as follows: (1) communication, (2) hardware, and (3) software. When it comes to wireless networks, data flow, and protocols, the communication idea is more specifically referring to these things. There are many different kinds of mobile devices that may be considered hardware. The software that is used in mobile computing is comprised of the programs that are installed in the hardware of mobile devices. These applications include specialized software for the industry, apps for data collecting, and web browsers (Laurila et al., 2012). Mobile devices, in contrast to purpose-oriented Internet of Things (IoT) devices, are equipped with sensors that may serve several purposes. A few examples of these sensors include microphones, accelerometers, gyroscopes, and global positioning system receivers.

A consequence of the meteoric rise in the number of users and the widespread use of technologies related to electronic smartphones. As mobile computing continues to advance, it is also becoming a contributor to the offloading of jobs that are traditionally performed by computers. The application layer of mobile computing is experiencing a wide range of challenges as a consequence of the properties that it has. Consequently, this is a consequence of the fact that mobile technologies are gaining an increasing amount of prevalence.

Challenges, Motivations, and Opportunities

The conditions of the wireless network, it is reasonable to anticipate that there will be inconsistencies in communication and changes in operating state. This necessitates that mobile devices switch modes in order to accommodate particular circumstances. The security flaws that are already present in these kinds of networks are made more worse, which further diminishes the dependability of mobile computing.

The integrated rise of smart-city applications is being made possible by the fast development of mobile computing and apps for smartphones. Mobile computing has the potential to assist in addressing the following difficulties that are associated with smart-city computing:

1. Address user needs across various places. Mobile computing chains smart city computing with mobility and flexibility. This support may help end users and policymakers satisfy diverse computing demands. Location-based and higher education services are application use cases (Gikas and Grant 2013). These services take use of smart devices' mobility to gather and consume data (Raja et al., 2018). According to Zheng and Ni (2010), mobile computing may also integrate smart gadgets into smart settings. This smart city idea covers a large area with plenty of room for mobile computing infrastructure and flexibility in execution.
2. Mobile cloud computing and dynamic offloading are interactive smart devices in smart environments (Huang et al., 2012). Current research covers these topics. The combination of cloud and mobile computing has been envisioned since 2009. It combines mobile computing's mobility with cloud computing's elastic processing.

Study of the Case

Heat Island in Cities (UHI)

Typically, three scales that are used to measure UHI: the border UHI, the canopy UHI, and the surface UHI. In order to determine the boundary UHI, the height of the rooftop is measured in relation to the atmosphere. In general, it is used for the purpose of investigating the UHI impact at the mesoscale, A microscale research is the most appropriate setting for conducting an evaluation of canopy UHI, and the data from weather stations are often used to produce the assessment. The UHI computer architecture is specified in Figure 3. It is at the surface level of the Earth that surface UHI is detected. Remotely sensed data were used by researchers in order to investigate the changes and consequences of the urban heat island (UHI) over a long or short period of time (Earl et al., 2016).

Challenges and Opportunities at UHI

The scientific problems that were discussed previously in this essay are directly responsible for these concerns that have arisen. The course of a number of years, cloud computing has been used for the goal of allocating computer resources in order to assist auto-scalable modeling and detection in a number of different study disciplines. According to Yang et al., 2017a, this strategy has shown itself to be an alternative that is not only effective but also cost-efficient. There is a cloud computing platform known as the Google Earth Engine that offers processing resources that are naturally parallel. By making use of a considerably big collection of data acquired from observations of the Earth, it also makes it feasible to monitor and assess changes in the environment of the Earth on a global scale, as stated by Moore and Hansen (2011). This is accomplished by using the data that is gathered from the observations of the Earth.

The capabilities of conventional architectures, which are unable to meet the supplies of the Internet of Things. Santamouris (2015) carried out an analysis to determine the extent of heat islands and the characteristics that they possess in one hundred various cities and areas. Based on the results of this inquiry, it was discovered that out of the 43 percent of station measurements, only one was based on an urban station, and the other was based on a rural station (Meulen 2017). Gartner predicts that by the year 2020, there will be as many as 20.4 billion Internet of Things devices that are connected to one another via the use of machine-to-machine communication technologies.

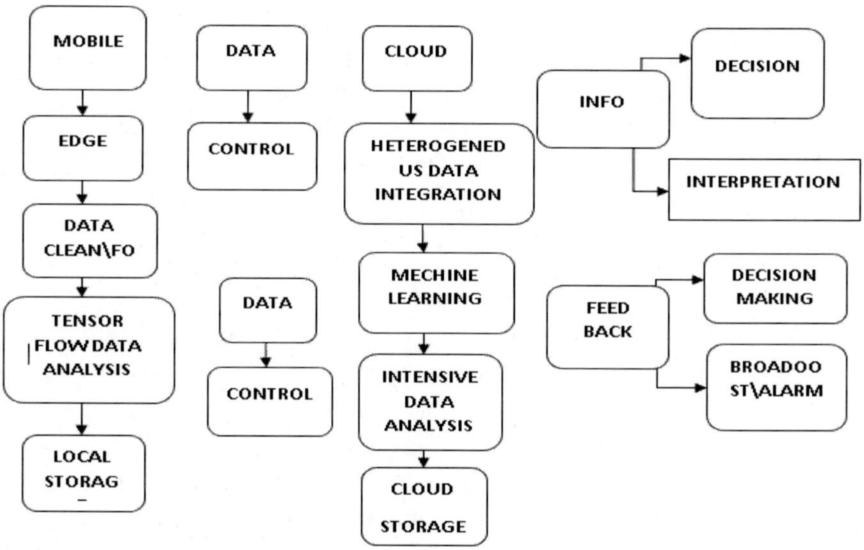

Figure 3. Overall UHI computer architecture.

Data and Model in Smart Cities

When it comes to producing information that can assist decision-making, smart cities need many data sources and models that can be relied upon. In situations when a large number of intelligent devices and sensors are involved, the difficulty of the situation increases significantly. In this part, five sample applications for smart cities are presented, together with the data involved, the models that correspond to them, and the computational needs that are necessary for them.

Transport and Traffic Management

In terms of activities that are associated with urban life, transport is one of the most significant factors. Sensors put in cars that are used for traffic or monitors that are placed along roads are responsible for the generation and collection of traffic data. Data that document people's routine mobility in cities are referred to as commuting data. The data collected from geo-tagged social networks includes postings (such as blogs and tweets) that are tagged with geoinformation and are collected from social networks. Road segments and junctions are the two types of data that are represented by road network data. Intelligent transportation systems make use of a variety of models, including agent-based traffic management models, cognitive rationality-based executive models, and mixed-ranked logit models.

Smart City Technology

Components that are used in the development of smart cities include software solutions, user interfaces, communication networks, and devices that are linked to the internet of things (IoT). The Internet of Things, on the other hand, may be considered their principal source of dependence. The Internet of Things (IoT) is a network of interconnected devices, for example autos, sensors, or home appliances, that are able to communicate with one another and exchange information. Examples of these types of devices include connected devices. Sensors and gadgets connected to the Internet of Things are the ones responsible for gathering and transmitting data, which is after that saved either in the cloud or on other servers. The convergence of the physical and digital aspects of the city is made possible by the connectivity of these devices and the use of data analytics. This results in an improvement in the efficiency of both the public and commercial sectors, which in turn enables economic gains and improves the lives of citizens.

Sometimes, the Internet of Things devices have processing capabilities that are referred to as edge computing. Through the use of edge computing, it is possible to guarantee that the communication network is only exposed to the information that is the most significant and relevant.

Within a computer system, the protection, monitoring, and control of network traffic are all essential functions that need the implementation of a firewall security system. In order to guarantee the safety of the data that is continuously sent inside a smart city network, firewalls are installed to prevent anyone getting into the Internet of Things without permission network or the data of the city.

Other smart city technologies include:

- APIs, which stand for application programming interfaces
- AI stands for artificial intelligence.
- computed in the cloud
- control panels
- learning via machine (ML)
- M2M stands for machine to machine.
- a network of mesh.

Devices and Sensors

Data is collected from physical assets, machinery, and equipment via a broad variety of devices and sensors that are a part of the Industrial Internet of Things (IIoT) networks. A wide variety of sensors and devices, such as temperature sensors, pressure sensors, motion sensors, actuators, and others, may be included in this category.

Edge Computing

When it comes to processing and analysing the data at the network's edge, which is located closer to the user to the source, edge computing is an essential component of an Industrial Internet of Things (IIoT) system. By reducing latency, improving real-time decision-making, and minimising data transfer to the cloud, edge computing helps to enhance the overall experience.

Future Urban Computing for Smart Cities

At this point, with increased connectivity to the cloud, the network's periphery is increasingly serving as a mobile computing system. This is as a result of the fast development of 5G networks as well as the increased integration with cloud computing. There have been a number of instances in which the phrase "mobile cloud computing" has been used in the field of mobile computing. The whole computer network will be pushed to a new decentralised computing stage, and the process of developing smart cities will be hastened as a consequence of the interaction between how mobile computing and cloud computing can be used to handle data on demand. Both of these developments will occur simultaneously.

As the number of mobile devices endures to rise, it will become more obvious that there is a need for interaction with neighbouring edge applications. When combined with enhanced dispensation, computing, and power capacities, as well as the decentralised nature of mobile computing, edge computing is anticipated to deliver meaningfully enhanced throughput, enhanced performance, and real-time responses. This is accomplished by bringing computing and data closer to the user, as well as by tailoring the dispensation requirements of each individual user. Computing at the edge and computing on mobile devices are both capable of managing localised data for the purpose of facilitating rapid response for a certain range of area sizes. Nevertheless, centralised cloud computing is also being driven by the growing amount of data generated in metropolitan areas and the geo-analysis of data across cities.

The purpose of detecting, recording, sharing, and analysing a wide range of human-related activities, a number of different devices will link to the cloud-based Internet inside the smart city. Computing on the cloud, when combined with the assistance of algorithms that are powered by artificial intelligence, will provide businesses, governments, and individual citizens with more intelligent solutions.

Internet of Things for Smart Cities

The concept of smart cities is a product of the pervasive digitalization that has been made possible by the supporting technology that has made it feasible for this to happen. The efforts that are being conducted to construct smart cities are centred upon the Internet of Things (IoT), which is fundamental to the concept. According to projections, the internet will have over 75 billion connected devices by the year 2025. This will result in an increase in the number of apps that are being created. When it comes to smart cities, the IoT makes it feasible for sensors to collect and send the city status data to a central cloud. This information contains information on the city's present condition. This information may then be mined or analysed with the intention of obtaining patterns and making decisions according to those patterns.

Built-in Workflow

Mobile Computing for Quick Responses Close to Home

Mobile computing is the initial gate through which data enters the workflow at the beginning of the process. Only lightweight preparatory tasks, such as data cleansing and reorganization, may be carried out at the mobile computing stage. This is because mobile computers, in general, have a limited capacity, and because of limits such as battery life, they are unable to function properly. On the other hand, in-situ monitoring, when combined with a basic comprehension of the data, has the potential to cut down on time delay for tasks that do not need a great deal of calculation but rather merely the capacity to make straightforward judgments. When an unexpected amount of heat is detected, for instance, alerts that have been set up on a mobile device with a temperature threshold that is limited may be activated in a responsive manner.

Edge Computing Prepares Data and Controls Microcontrollers

In addition to the collection of data at the edge and the transmission of the raw data to the cloud, as is the case with mobile computing, computing at the edge offers additional possibilities for greater data preparation. These capabilities are in addition to the fact that the data is collected at the edge.

It may take a considerable amount of time to upload everything in its raw form to the cloud due to the growing volume of data, and the tremendous load that is imposed upon the central cluster may cause it to surpass the limit of the computing capabilities available provides observations with a resolution of seconds. These observations are supplied by the data. Through the collection of data from networks consisting of hundreds of sensors, this study keeps track of local temperatures as well as other environmental characteristics. The high-velocity data transfers that take place inside the network, on the other hand, have the potential to generate traffic congestion owing to the restricted bandwidth that is available.

Cloud Computing for Processing and Analyzing Huge Amounts of Data

The data that is transmitted from sensors is sent via the edges to the center for improved management. This is made possible by the fact that the virtual storage system is capable of expanding itself automatically. Both mobile and edge devices are unable to process the data that the cloud is able to manage, and the cloud is also able to speed up the processing beyond what a standalone server is capable of accomplishing (Goundar et al., 2021). This is because the cloud has a large computational capacity.

One of the most important problems is the heterogeneity of the data, and the enormous amount of labor involved in cleaning the data needs a substantial amount of processing capacity. According to Botta et al., (2014), the cloud, which is a centralized computing resource pool, provides adequate capacity for any job of this kind. The UHI study is influenced by a wide variety of elements, as was previously noted. Making modifications to the composition will need making changes to the parameters of the model. The amount of time spent constructing the model and the amount of human error that occurs during the process of transferring the experimental setting are advantages.

Conclusion

The tremendous reduction in the size of Using sensing and communication tools in cities has made it possible to conceive of the possibility of creating innovative technical networks for smart city applications. Therefore, the development of smart cities has become feasible as a result of this. The goal of urban computing is to enhance the operational intelligence of smart city services while simultaneously bringing about changes to the lives of city residents and the environs in which they live. This is the objective of urban computing.

With the intention of analyzing, highlighting, and reporting on the most recent initiatives that have been made in the area of urban computing that are aimed toward the smart city paradigm, the objective of this article was to research, highlight, and report on such endeavors. We highlighted four primary use cases of urban computing systems; these use cases were given within the architecture of intelligent cities. In addition to that, a number of possible challenges that may arise in the course of future research were identified. In conclusion, we come to the awareness that although urban computing has the potential to give various benefits in smart cities, the confluence of these paradigms leads to the formation of specific recent studies issues that will need to be solved in the future.

References

Casanueva Vicente, Ana, Annakatrin Burgstall, Sven Kotlarski, Alessandro Messeri, Marco Morabito, Andreas D. Flouris, Lars Nybo, Christoph Spirig, and Cornelia Schwierz. "*Overview of existing heat-health warning systems in Europe*." (2019).

González-Gil, Arturo, Roberto Palacin, P. Batty, and J. P. Powell. "A systems approach to reduce urban rail energy consumption." *Energy Conversion and Management* 80 (2014): 509-524.

Graham, Steve, and Simon Marvin. *Telecommunications and the city: Electronic spaces, urban places*. Routledge, 2002.

Giannaros, T. M., D. Melas, I. A. Daglis, and I. Keramitsoglou. "Development of an operational modeling system for urban heat islands: an application to Athens, Greece." *Natural Hazards and Earth System Sciences* 14, no. 2 (2014): 347-358.

Goundar, Sam, J. Avanija, Gurram Sunitha, K. Reddy Madhavi, and S. Bharath Bhushan, eds. Innovations in the industrial Internet of Things (IIoT) and smart factory. IGI Global, 2021.

Hwang, Jong-Sung, and Young Han Choe. "Smart Cities Seoul: a case study." *ITU-T technology watch report* (2013): 1-20.

Hoffiman, J. "Where do we need shade? Mapping urban heat islands in Richmond, Virginia." *Retrieved May* 1 (2018): 2019.

Ashokkumar, N., V. Arun, S. Prabhu, V. Kalaimagal, Dhamodharan Srinivasan, and B. Shanthi. "Design and Implementation of IoT based Energy Efficient Smart Metering System for Domestic Applications." In *2023 9th International Conference on*

Advanced Computing and Communication Systems (ICACCS), vol. 1, pp. 1208-1212. IEEE, 2023.

Li, Yangfan, Yi Li, Yan Zhou, Yalou Shi, and Xiaodong Zhu. "Investigation of a coupling model of coordination between urbanization and the environment." *Journal of environmental management* 98 (2012): 127-133.

Morán, Alberto Jáñez, Paolo Profaizer, María Herrando Zapater, María Andérez Valdavida, and Ignacio Zabalza Bribián. "Information and Communications Technologies (ICTs) for energy efficiency in buildings: Review and analysis of results from EU pilot projects." *Energy and buildings* 127 (2016): 128-137.

Mitchell, Shane, Nicola Villa, Martin Stewart-Weeks, and Anne Lange. "The internet of everything for cities." *Connecting People, Process, Data, and Things to Improve the 'Livability' of Cities and Communities, Cisco* (2013): 1-21.

Petkova, Elisaveta P., Jan K. Vink, Radley M. Horton, Antonio Gasparrini, Daniel A. Bader, Joe D. Francis, and Patrick L. Kinney. "Towards more comprehensive projections of urban heat-related mortality: estimates for New York City under multiple population, adaptation, and climate scenarios." *Environmental health perspectives* 125, no. 1 (2017): 47-55.

Rao, Amudapuram Mohan, and Kalaga Ramachandra Rao. "Measuring urban traffic congestion-a review." *International Journal for Traffic & Transport Engineering* 2, no. 4 (2012).

Rizwan, Ahmed Memon, Leung YC Dennis, and L. I. U. Chunho. "A review on the generation, determination and mitigation of Urban Heat Island." *Journal of environmental sciences* 20, no. 1 (2008): 120-128.

Pappa, C. Kanmani, N. Ashokkumar, P. Nagarajan, and Kavitha Thandapani. "Bluetooth based Garage Door Opening System." In *2023 5th International Conference on Smart Systems and Inventive Technology (ICSSIT)*, pp. 131-134. IEEE, 2023.

Zhong, Shi, Yun Qian, Chun Zhao, Ruby Leung, Hailong Wang, Ben Yang, Jiwen Fan, Huiping Yan, Xiu-Qun Yang, and Dongqing Liu. "Urbanization-induced urban heat island and aerosol effects on climate extremes in the Yangtze River Delta region of China." *Atmospheric Chemistry and Physics* 17, no. 8 (2017): 5439-5457.

Chapter 11

Privacy and Security in Mobile Computing: Strategies for Safeguarding User Data

Tangudu Naresh[1,*]
Dasari Reventh Raj[2]
Baratam Pravallika[2]
Yajjala Vineela[2]
Bommali Santhoshkumar[2]
and Giri Deekshith[2]
[1]Department of IT, Aditya Institute of Technology and Management, Tekkali, A.P, India
[2]Aditya Institute of Technology and Management, Tekkali, A.P, India

Abstract

In the contemporary fabric of daily life, mobile computing has seamlessly woven itself into diverse scenarios, each posing distinct security challenges that call for inventive solutions. This summary explores the intricate landscape of security threats across various mobile applications, pinpoints significant challenges, and proposes robust strategies to shield user data from potential breaches. Our security spans a spectrum of use cases, from personal communication to mobile banking and enterprise mobility, each introducing its own set of security intricacies. As we unravel the complexities, we illuminate the dynamic threads encountered by mobile users—ranging from the proliferation of evil apps to vulnerabilities in wireless communication channels. The spectrum of challenges discussed encompasses traditional concerns like data breaches and phishing attacks, extending to emerging problems like

[*] Corresponding Author's Email: itsajs@gmail.com.

In: The Future of Mobile Computing
Editors: Sam Goundar, J. Avanija and K. Reddy Madhavi
ISBN: 979-8-89113-715-8

IOT devices combined with malware that is becoming more fluid. Throughout, we underscore the imperative for adaptive security measures capable of evolving alongside the ever-changing nature of these challenges. Proposed solutions encompass deploying sophisticated authentication mechanisms, fortified data transmission protocols, and proactive real-time threat detection systems. Delving into artificial intelligence and machine learning, we explore how these technologies can fortify mobile security by anticipating and pre-empting potential threats. Exploring the intricate challenges in safeguarding user privacy, the discussion encompasses issues like invasive data collection by applications and the susceptibility of sensitive information during wireless transmissions.

Keywords: data privacy, data breaches, encryption protocols, user-centric approach, authentication mechanism

Introduction

Safeguarding confidential data, including personal information, health records, and financial transactions, is paramount in contemporary mobile computing systems. Due in large part to the increasing adoption of mobile devices such as smartphones, tablets, and wearables, network applications and services have proliferated along with the Internet's dramatic growth. Although this development has greatly improved accessibility and connectedness, it has also raised more worries about security and privacy. In an era where personal data is consistently gathered and shared, individuals face heightened risks such as identity theft, cyber-attacks, and privacy breaches. As our dependence on technology grows, it becomes imperative for individuals, organizations, and governments to implement robust measures to protect sensitive information.

Strategies like employing strong passwords, utilizing encryption, keeping software regularly updated, and carefully managing access to personal data are vital. Preserving privacy and security is not only essential for safeguarding personal and professional aspects of life but also for upholding social and political freedoms in an increasingly interconnected world. The continuous growth of the Internet and mobile technologies has created a dynamic environment where the exchange of information is constant. This interconnectedness, while offering unprecedented access and convenience, also exposes individuals to potential threats like identity theft, cyber-attacks, and invasions of privacy. Recognizing this, it becomes imperative for individuals, organizations, and governments to proactively implement comprehensive strategies to fortify the confidentiality data (Mollah M. Band Azad M. A. K, 2017; Imielinski T et al., 1996; Hammouri Q et al., 2016).

Consequence of Privacy and Reliability of Data in Mobile Computing

Privacy holds significant importance within the realm of mobile computing as it affords individuals a sense of control over their personal information. By enabling users to manage the disclosure of their data, privacy empowers them to make informed decisions about what particulars are shared and with whom. This autonomy becomes particularly vital in a digital environment where personal information is frequently gathered and processed. Additionally, upholding privacy establishes a foundation of trust between users and technology providers. When individuals have confidence that their data is handled responsibly, it fosters a positive relationship, encouraging more open engagement with digital platforms. Sensitive data protection places a high priority on security evaluation of security measures like privacy, data vacancy, and correctitude by acting as barriers against unauthorized access. Because mobile devices frequently hold a lot of personal information, strong security measures are essential to avoid data breaches and unauthorized use. Aside from preventing malware, phishing scams, and other malicious activities that could jeopardize the security and functionality of mobile devices, security is also essential in eliminating other cyber threats. It encompasses broader dimensions such as upholding user confidence and adhering to the ethical responsibility of technology providers.

The assurance of privacy and security instills confidence in users, motivating them to embrace and integrate new technologies. Moreover, prioritizing privacy and security aligns with the ethical obligations of technology providers to prioritize the well-being and rights of individuals, fostering a digital landscape founded on trust and responsible practices. When the client uses the website normally the website consists of confidential data, and reliable data when the attacker is involved then he misuses the sensitive data then there is a cause of data leakage, and then the leakage data is collected by the attacker in the system as specified in Figure 1 (Haris M et al., … 2014).

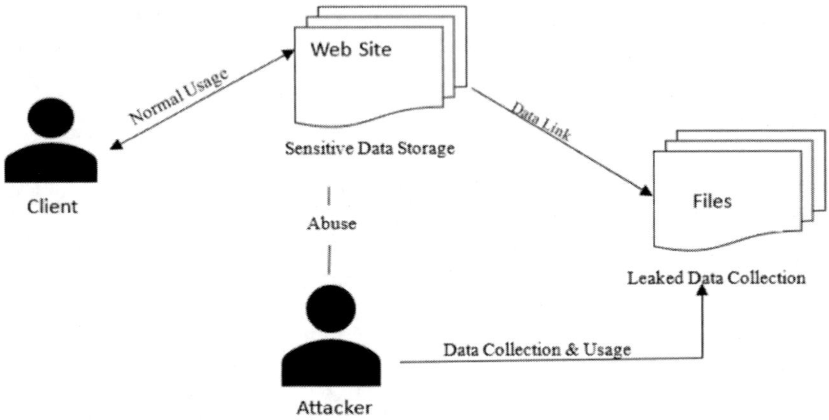

Figure 1. Data Leakage Flow Diagram.

Outline of Wireless Mobility

The landscape of nomadic computing has transformed the way we engage with information and technology, offering unprecedented flexibility and connectivity. Essentially, mobile computing revolves around the utilization of portable devices like smartphones, tablets, and wearables, allowing users to access data, applications, and services while on the move. This fundamental change has redefined how people work, communicate, and consume content. The widespread use of mobile devices is made possible by advanced hardware, diverse operating systems, and an extensive array of mobile applications. Critical elements of mobile computing encompass wireless communication technologies such as 4G and 5G, facilitating seamless connectivity. Mobile applications, spanning from productivity tools to entertainment, play a crucial part in improving user presence. The integration of cloud computing has further enhanced the capabilities of mobile devices, enabling storage, processing, and collaboration in the cloud. Despite the evident advantages of mobile computing in terms of convenience and accessibility, persistent challenges include security, privacy concerns, and the imperative for effective power management. The continuous progression of mobile technologies, coupled with ongoing innovations, ensures that the mobile computing landscape remains dynamic and influential, shaping digital experiences for individuals and businesses on a global scale.

The prevalence of mobile devices owes its ubiquity to advanced hardware, diverse operating systems, and a vast ecosystem of mobile applications. These applications, ranging from productivity tools to entertainment, are instrumental in elevating user experiences and meeting diverse needs. The advent of wireless communication technologies, exemplified by the evolution from 4G to the now ubiquitous 5G, has further facilitated seamless connectivity, ensuring that individuals can stay connected anytime, anywhere. Moreover, the integration of cloud computing has significantly expanded the capabilities of mobile devices. This advancement enables storage, processing, and collaboration in the cloud, reducing reliance on local device resources and enhancing overall efficiency. As individuals increasingly leverage the cloud for various tasks, the boundaries of what is achievable on mobile devices continue to expand (Ghadi B et al., … 2021; Bilogrevic I et al., ... 2011).

Definition and Scope

Mobile computing is the utilization of portable computing devices, including smartphones, tablets, and wearable technologies, enabling users to access and interact with information and applications seamlessly while on the move. This paradigm extends far beyond the limitations of traditional fixed computing environments, granting users the freedom to connect, communicate, and execute various tasks from virtually any location. The expansive scope of mobile computing encompasses diverse activities, ranging from wireless communication and the utilization of mobile applications to the seamless integration of cloud services (Mollah M et al., … 2017; Ghadi S et al., 2021).

This transformative shift in computing has brought about a revolution in how individuals approach work, socialization, and engagement with digital content. The emphasis lies on flexibility, convenience, and the immediate availability of information in real-time. Whether for professional tasks, staying connected with friends and family, or consuming digital media, Today, everyone relies heavily on portable computing. The rise of nomadic computing has transformed wireless infrastructure mobility and scope, exerting a significant influence on various facets of personal and professional life on a global scale. It is a paradigm that transcends the confines of traditional computing setups, providing users with the ability to harness the power of computing wherever they go. As technology advances further, the impact of mobile computing is expected to grow, reshaping the way we navigate the digital landscape and enhancing the possibilities for connectivity, productivity, and convenience. Mobile computing stands as a dynamic force, continuously shaping and redefining the digital experiences of individuals worldwide. At its essence, mobile computing revolves around the utilization of compact and portable devices equipped with both computing capabilities and wireless communication features. These devices, including smartphones, tablets, and wearables, have seamlessly integrated into our daily routines, providing a wide array of applications and services that cater to diverse needs. The extensive scope of mobile computing encompasses various activities and functionalities, with wireless communication technologies like 4G and 5G forming the backbone to facilitate smooth connectivity and immediate access to data. Mobile applications designed for a spectrum of tasks, from productivity tools to entertainment, significantly contribute to the adaptability and versatility of mobile computing. The incorporation of cloud services further enhances the capabilities of these devices, enabling collaborative work, data storage, and synchronization across multiple platforms. The transformative impact of mobile computing is evident across different aspects of life. In the business realm, it facilitates remote work, improves communication, and provides efficient access to crucial information. On a social level, it fosters global connections and real-time interactions, while the educational landscape benefits from e-learning platforms and educational apps. Furthermore, new and developing technologies like virtual reality (VR) and augmented reality (AR) are expanding the potential of mobile computing and adding new aspects to user experiences. Despite its numerous advantages, challenges in terms of security, privacy, and the need for efficient power management remain key focal points in the ongoing evolution of mobile computing. As technology advances, the trajectory of mobile computing is poised for growth, influencing and reshaping how individuals, businesses, and societies engage with the digital world. The dynamic and ever-evolving landscape of mobile computing reflects an ongoing redefinition of how we connect and interact in our increasingly mobile-centric world. At its essence, mobile computing revolves around the utilization of compact and portable devices equipped with both computing capabilities and wireless communication features. These devices, including smartphones, tablets, and wearables, have seamlessly integrated into our daily routines, providing a wide array of applications and services that cater to diverse needs. The extensive scope of mobile computing encompasses various activities and functionalities, with wireless communication technologies like 4G and 5G forming the backbone to facilitate smooth connectivity and immediate access to data. Mobile applications designed for a spectrum of tasks, from productivity tools to entertainment, significantly contribute to the adaptability and versatility of mobile computing. The incorporation of cloud services further enhances the capabilities of these devices, enabling collaborative work, data storage, and synchronization across multiple platforms. The transformative impact of mobile computing is evident across different aspects of life. In the business realm, it facilitates remote work, improves communication, and provides efficient access to crucial information. On a social level, it fosters global connections and real-time interactions, while the educational landscape benefits from e-learning platforms and educational apps. Moreover, the scope of mobile computing continues to broaden with the introduction of popular technology such as Actual presence (AP) and Supplementary Presences (SP) introducing new dimensions to buyers' experiences. Despite its numerous advantages, challenges in terms of security, privacy, and the need for efficient power management remain key focal points in the ongoing evolution of mobile computing. As technology advances, the trajectory of mobile computing is poised for growth, influencing and reshaping how individuals, businesses, and societies engage with the digital world. The dynamic and ever-evolving landscape of mobile computing reflects an ongoing redefinition of how we connect and interact in our increasingly mobile-centric world (Mollah M et al., 2017; Ghadi S et al., 2021; Imielinski T and Korth H, 1996).

Evolution of Mobile Devices

The evolution of mobile devices traces a transformative journey through technological leaps and consumer-driven innovation, revolutionizing how we communicate, work, and engage with information. It began with the advent of the first commercial mobile phone, the Motorola DynaTAC 8000X, in 1983. These devices, albeit bulky and limited to voice calls, marked the inception of mobile communication. They swiftly evolved with the introduction of digital cellular networks, paving the way for better call quality and basic text messaging. The Nokia Communicator and BlackBerry devices of the late 1990s and early 2000s heralded a new era, offering email access and rudimentary web browsing, albeit on smaller screens and with physical keyboards. However, the mobile landscape experienced a seismic shift with the debut of the iPhone in 2007. Apple's innovative touchscreen interface, coupled with the App Store, transformed the concept of mobile devices. It popularized the idea of smartphones as multipurpose tools, not just for communication but also for entertainment, productivity, and a myriad of other applications. Simultaneously, Google's introduction of the Android operating system in 2008 opened the floodgates for a diverse range of smartphones, fueling competition and innovation across the industry. Technological advancements propelled smartphones into the realm of sophistication. The integration of high-resolution cameras, faster processors, sharper displays, and longer-lasting batteries became standard features, enhancing user experiences. Moreover, the evolution of network connectivity from 4G to the advent of 5G promised lightning-fast internet speeds, lower latency, and expanded possibilities for IoT applications, augmented reality, and more immersive experiences.

Phones evolved to be sleeker, with larger screens dominating the landscape. The emergence of foldable phones introduced new possibilities, enabling users to enjoy the benefits of larger displays without sacrificing portability. This shift in design sparked curiosity and opened avenues for multitasking and diverse user interactions. Today, mobile devices serve as more than mere communication tools. They've become indispensable companions, integrating artificial intelligence for voice assistants, personalized recommendations, and security features. With these devices at the forefront of our connected lives, the evolution of mobile technology continues to push boundaries, promising a future where these devices seamlessly intertwine with our daily routines and technological innovations. Form factors also transformed. Phones evolved to be sleeker, with larger screens dominating the landscape. The emergence of foldable phones introduced new possibilities, enabling users to enjoy the benefits of larger displays without sacrificing portability. This shift in design sparked curiosity and opened avenues for multitasking and diverse user interactions. Today, mobile devices serve as more than mere communication tools. They've become indispensable companions, integrating artificial intelligence for voice assistants, personalized recommendations, and security features. The form factor of mobile devices has undergone significant changes over time, with smartphones becoming sleeker and more portable while incorporating larger screens. The emergence of foldable phones has introduced new possibilities, allowing users to enjoy the benefits of larger displays without sacrificing portability. This shift in design has sparked curiosity and opened avenues for multitasking and diverse user interactions. Today, mobile devices have become indispensable companions, integrating artificial intelligence for voice assistants, personalized recommendations, and security features. As mobile technology, these are expected to sell innovations that open a venue for multitasking and diverse user interactions. Today, mobile devices have become indispensable companions, integrating artificial intelligence for voice assistants, personalized recommendations, and security features. As mobile technology continues to evolve, these devices are expected to seamlessly intertwine with our daily routines and technological innovations (Edmondson J et al., 2014).

The Ubiquity of Portable Computing

The broad adoption of mobile computing in our everyday lives and its profound consequences, fueled by the explosive growth of smartphones, tablets, and related devices, has brought significant data privacy implications. Gathering and using location data is a major challenge in this environment. In the context of ubiquitous mobile computing, existing techniques grapple with practical security limitations due to the sheer volume of devices and data. Challenges include the accurate collection of crucial data and effective analysis of security risks. Mobile devices come equipped with sensors capable of tracking a user's GPS location, serving purposes such as location-based services, weather apps, and local search functionalities. However, this same data can be exploited by third-party apps or service providers to monitor a user's movements without explicit consent. The transfer and storage of personal data on mobile devices presents another significant obstacle. Sensitive information could end up in the wrong hands if mobile devices are lost or stolen frequently as described in Figure 2. Additionally, the security vulnerabilities of mobile networks, susceptible to interception and hacking, add another layer of concern.

In response to these privacy challenges, manufacturers of mobile devices and app developers have implemented various measures, including encryption, two-factor authentication, and giving users control over permissions. Governments and regulatory bodies have also taken proactive steps by establishing privacy laws and regulations aimed at safeguarding consumer privacy. While the ubiquity of mobile computing has undoubtedly enriched our daily experiences, it has simultaneously introduced novel challenges in safeguarding our data. It becomes paramount for technology companies, governments, and individuals alike to stay vigilant and undertake proactive measures to uphold data privacy standards in the era of mobile technology (Haris M et al., 2014; Fahmair M et al., 2005).

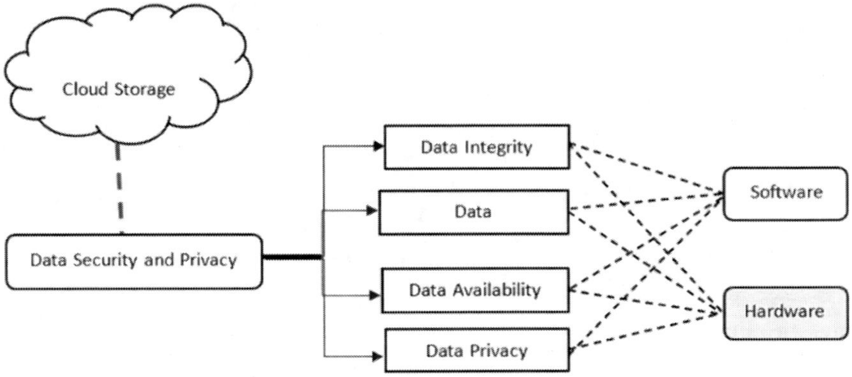

Figure 2. Data Security and Privacy in Cloud Computing.

Evolving Threats and Vulnerabilities in Mobile Landscape

The rapid growth of the mobile landscape has made it a prime target for cybercriminals because it is an easy avenue to access sensitive information. The mobile landscape is a dynamic ecosystem, constantly evolving with new technologies, features, and unfortunately threats. The following are some evolving threats and vulnerabilities in the mobile landscape:

- Malware attacks:

Malicious links, fake advertisements, or malicious software can all be downloaded concurrently with other apps. Passwords and sensitive data can be stolen by this malware. Malicious software created expressly to target mobile devices, like smartphones and tablets, is known as mobile malware. Phishing emails, unofficial app stores, and even advertising networks can all be used to distribute malware.

- Phishing attacks:

Phishing attacks are used by cybercriminals to trick users into divulging their personal information by using fake emails, texts, and pop-up ads.

- Device loss and theft:

Mobile devices are frequently lost or stolen, and if they contain sensitive data that is not protected, it can lead to data breaches.

- Unprotected Wi-Fi Networks:

Due to the general lack of security on public Wi-Fi networks, it is simple for hackers to intercept unencrypted data being transferred, including sensitive information like login passwords and personal emails.

- Outdated Software:

The use of older software increases the chances of cybercriminals exploiting vulnerabilities and gaining access to sensitive data. To solve these evolving threats, users should keep their mobile devices, applications, and software updated and avoid risky websites and downloads. They should also enable encryption and device login passcodes or biometrics to protect the data on the device. Moreover, users are advised to be cautious when hacking into local wireless networks and virtual private networks (VPNs) to record all of their mobile communications. They should also be careful while opening emails, links, and attachments from unknown sources. Finally, they should enable two-factor authentication (Weichbroth P and Lysik L, 2020; Khan J et al., 2015).

Congregation of Data and Tracking

Data collection and tracking play a crucial role in mobile computing. The following are some ways in which data collection and tracking can be utilized in mobile computing:

- Location tracking: Applications that provide location-based services can track a user's location using GPS data.
- Customized advice: Tailored recommendations can be generated according to the user's interests and activity by monitoring their browser history and app usage.
- Usage analytics:

Applications can track usage analytics to understand user behavior, identify bottlenecks, and improve user experience.

- Social network integration: Applications can use social network integration to collect data on user demographics, preferences, and behavior to provide more personalized services.
- Real-time data collection: Mobile devices can collect real-time data from sensors and send it to servers for analysis.

The gathering and tracking of data in mobile computing offer significant advantages across various applications such as traffic management, weather forecasting, and health monitoring. This process not only facilitates innovative services and enhances user experiences but also provides valuable insights for businesses and organizations. However, a critical challenge associated with data collection lies in ensuring user consent and transparency. While users typically grant implicit approval for data collection through app permissions and terms of service agreements, there is often a lack of clarity regarding the extent and nature of the information being collected. This opacity raises legitimate concerns about the potential misuse or unauthorized access to personal data, underscoring the necessity for more transparent and informative consent mechanisms (Bilogrevic I et al., 2011).

Personally Identifiable Information Exposure

The primary issue here is the accidental or unlawful disclosure of private user information (PII), which includes names, addresses, and bank account information. This exposure can manifest through various channels, encompassing data breaches, third-party access, social engineering, location tracking, andan ignorance on the part of users regarding privacy regulations. Data breaches pose a significant threat, potentially granting unauthorized entry to extensive repositories of personal data. Inadequate security measures, app vulnerabilities, or deliberate cyberattacks can compromise databases or systems, leading to identity theft, financial fraud, or other malicious activities exploiting the exposed information, affecting individuals on a large scale. Moreover, mobile apps often receive permissions that surpass what is necessary for their functionalities. This can inadvertently result in third-party access, allowing apps to potentially expose sensitive information. Inadequate security measures or careless data-sharing practices increase the risk of personal information exposure, underscoring the importance of more stringent controls and ethical data handling. Social engineering and phishing tactics introduce additional risks by manipulating human vulnerabilities and coaxing individuals into disclosing sensitive data or login credentials, thereby compromising personal information security. Continuous tracking of location data, even with user consent, introduces potential exposure risks. Unauthorized access or misuse of this data can impinge on privacy, compromise safety, or lead to intrusive tracking and profiling. It's crucial to find a balance between user privacy and functionality. Strengthening cybersecurity measures, putting in place reliable encryption protocols, carrying out frequent security audits, and abiding by strict data protection laws are essential in the face of these obstacles. Giving users detailed information about data practices, guaranteeing comprehensive and unambiguous privacy policies, granting fine-grained control over permissions, and promoting digital literacy to identify and counteract possible risks are all equally important. Achieving a secure mobile computing environment demands a comprehensive approach that prioritizes both technological fortification and user education to effectively safeguard personal information as specified in Figure 1 (Bilogrevic I et al., 2011).

Privacy and Security Challenges in Mobile Computing

It includes a variety of problems that put information on mobile devices at risk for availability, confidentiality, and integrity. These are a few significant security issues facing mobile computing:

Unauthorized Access:

- Challenge: The risk of unauthorized individuals gaining access to mobile devices, either through physical theft or by exploiting vulnerabilities in authentication mechanisms.
- Impact: Unauthorized access can lead to data breaches, identity theft, and misuse of sensitive information.

Information Breakage:

- Challenge: Inadequate protection of data during storage, transmission, or processing, leading to unintentional exposure or leakage of sensitive information.
- Impact: Exposure of personal or confidential data can result in privacy violations and compromise the security of individuals and organizations.

Malicious Apps:

- Challenge: The presence of malicious applications that may be downloaded or installed, posing threats such as data theft, unauthorized access, or the exploitation of device vulnerabilities.
- Impact: Malicious apps can compromise the security and functionality of mobile devices, leading to various forms of cyberattacks.

Network Security:

- Challenge: Hazards related to man-in-the-middle attacks, eavesdropping on mobile communications, and unsecured Wi-Fi networks.
- Impact: Unauthorized interception of data during transmission can result in data compromise, financial loss, or exposure to sensitive information.

Device Loss and Theft:

- Challenge: The risk of sensitive data exposure and unauthorized access arises from the possible loss or theft of mobile devices.
- Impact: Loss or theft can result in data breaches, identity theft, and potential misuse of personal or corporate information.

Insufficient Encryption:

- Challenge: Inadequate use of encryption to protect data stored on the device, leaving it vulnerable to unauthorized access.
- Impact: Without encryption, sensitive data becomes susceptible to theft or unauthorized viewing.

Insecure Authentication:

- Challenge: Weak or easily bypassed authentication methods, such as simple passwords or lack of multi-factor authentication.
- Impact: Unauthorized users have an easier time accessing mobile devices and the accounts connected to them when authentication procedures are weak.

Phishing Attacks:

- Challenge: Attempts to trick users into providing sensitive information through deceptive emails, messages, or fake websites.
- Impact: Financial loss, identity theft, and illegal access are all possible outcomes of successful phishing attempts.

Outdated Programs and Updates:

- Challenge: Devices left open to known exploits due to incomplete or delayed software updates and security patches.
- Impact: Unpatched devices are more susceptible to security vulnerabilities and may become targets for cyberattacks.

Biometric Security Concerns:

- Challenge: Utilizing biostatistics authentication techniques, like face detection or smudge, comes with several risks, including possible vulnerabilities and consequences for privacy.
- Impact: Biometric data theft or spoofing can compromise the effectiveness of biometric security measures.

Addressing these security challenges requires a comprehensive approach involving secure coding practices, regular software updates, user education, and the implementation of advanced security technologies.

The overwhelming obstacles that mobile technology presents for information validation are about 13%, secured data is about 9% from malware attacks, The trusted is about 9% of outdated programs and updates, The privacy from phishing attacks is about 13%, the information is breakage due to design ie. is about 4%, various attacks such as the insufficient encryption,

Insecurity of authentication. The energy consumption is about 9% from unauthorized access and data security as stated in Figure 3. As the mobile computing landscape evolves, staying vigilant and proactive in mitigating security risks is essential for ensuring the safety and privacy of users and their data (Kohlenberg T et al., 2010; Khera G. B, 2015).

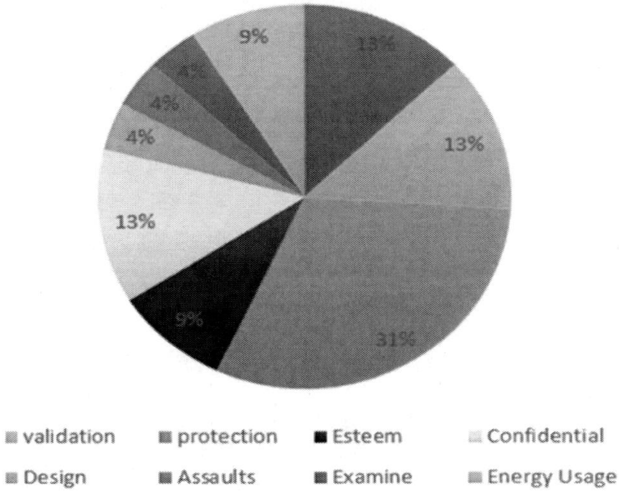

Figure 3. Data Preservation Challenges.

Device Security

Securing devices within the realm of mobile computing is a crucial facet, involving a range of measures dedicated to protecting the integrity, confidentiality, and accessibility of stored data. It is essential to establish strong device security to safeguard sensitive information and counter various potential threats. Key practices include implementing robust authentication methods like screen locks, PINs, passwords, and biometric recognition to prevent unauthorized access. Security policy enforcement and centralized control are made possible in large part by mobile device management (MDM) systems. A thorough security posture also greatly benefits from using virtual private networks (VPNs) on public Wi-Fi, stressing secure network connections, and adopting safe browsing practices. Consistent updates for both operating systems and applications are of paramount importance in maintaining device security. These updates often bring patches to address identified vulnerabilities, closing potential entry points for cyber threats. Regularly applying these updates ensures that the device remains fortified against evolving security risks, reducing the likelihood of exploitation by attackers attempting to breach the system's defenses. Effective device security also involves careful management of app permissions. Users should scrutinize and limit permissions granted to apps, allowing access only to necessary data and functions. The vetting processes implemented by app stores, coupled with user diligence in downloading apps from reputable sources, play a crucial role in minimizing security risks associated with apps. In summary, securing devices in the context of mobile computing necessitates a comprehensive strategy, incorporating multiple layers of protection to counter the dynamic landscape of potential threats (Fife E et al., 2019).

Network Security

In the realm of mobile computing, network security is a crucial focus aimed at ensuring the protection of communication channels and data transfers between mobile devices and other networks. This emphasis is vital because insecure connections can expose data to risks such as eavesdropping, manipulation, or hijacking. Given that mobile devices often utilize cellular networks, securing these connections becomes paramount. The use of encrypted protocols, like HTTPS, is recommended to safeguard sensitive data during transmission. Strengthening authentication mechanisms, such as Only authorized users can access network resources thanks to the improved verification process provided by implementing two-factor authentication. Virtual Private Networks (VPNs) play a crucial role, especially when utilizing public Wi-Fi networks. VPNs create encrypted tunnels for data traffic, providing protection against potential interception and masking the user's IP address by screening incoming and outgoing data, firewalls serve as barriers that stop hackers and other potential threats from infiltrating a system or network. IDSs monitor network traffic, alerting users or administrators about any suspicious activities that might indicate potential security breaches. This enables proactive responses to mitigate risks. In essence, a holistic approach to network security in mobile computing involves a combination of encryption, secure authentication, vigilant monitoring, and proactive measures to stay ahead of emerging threats (Kohlenberg T et al., 2010; Khera G. B, 2015).

App Security

Securing applications is a foundational element in the realm of mobile computing, involving a set of practices dedicated to strengthening the integrity and privacy of both applications and user data. In our interactions with mobile apps, which often involve entrusting sensitive information such as banking details, personal communication, and location data, breaches in security can have severe consequences, including identity theft, financial loss, and privacy violations. Therefore, comprehending and implementing best practices for app security is essential to ensure secure mobile usage. Authentication and authorization mechanisms embedded within apps play a critical role in app security. Robust authentication protocols, including multi-factor authentication and effective password management, play a key role in securely verifying user identities. Efficient authorization minimizes the possibility of unauthorized access by guaranteeing that users can only access the functionalities for which they have been expressly granted permission. The use of data encryption becomes essential for safeguarding private information kept in applications. It is ensured that even in the case of a breach, the exposed data is unintelligible to unauthorized parties by using encryption techniques for both data in transit and at rest. Employing secure communication protocols like HTTPS during data transmission between the app and servers further mitigates the risk of data interception or tampering. Prudent management of app permissions and user privacy is crucial. App developers should request only essential permissions from users, accompanied by transparent explanations of why those permissions are necessary. Respecting user privacy by limiting access to sensitive device features and data helps minimize potential risks associated with excessive permissions, fostering a trustworthy relationship between users and the app.

Regular updates and effective patch management constitute crucial aspects of app security. Timely release of updates, incorporating security patches to address newly discovered vulnerabilities, is vital in protecting against potential exploits. Encouraging users to install updates ensures they benefit from the latest security enhancements, safeguarding against emerging threats and strengthening the overall security posture of the app as specified in Figure 4. Relying on reputable app stores for app vetting and review processes, coupled with user caution in app selection and download, collectively contributes to a more secure mobile app environment (Xi k et al., 2011).

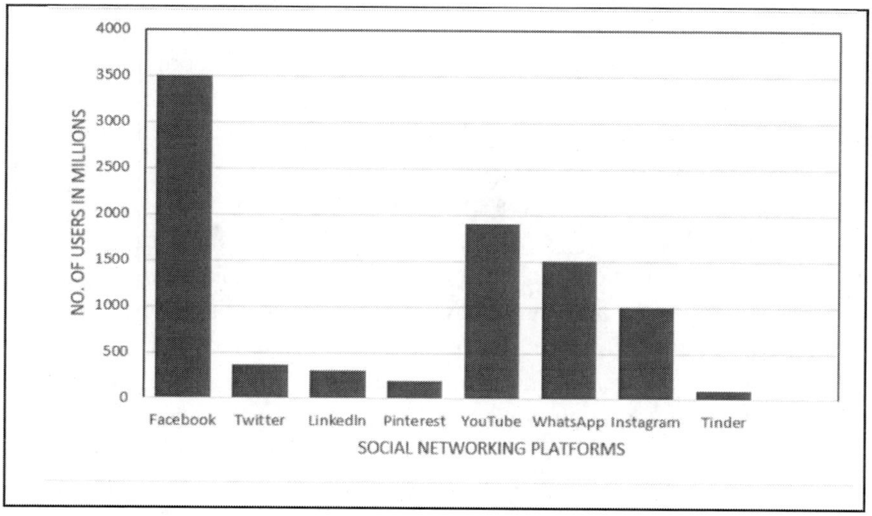

Figure 4. Online Social Networks Security & Privacy.

Employing secure communication protocols like HTTPS during data transmission between the app and servers further mitigates the risk of data interception or tampering. Prudent management of app permissions and user privacy is crucial. While the users use the app many malware attacks will be profound. Most frequently used apps will have security issues from the above plot graph people used Facebook i.e., is 3500 users are thereafter that YouTube takes a vital role in the app security ie. in between 1500 and 2500. For Instagram, the users are about 1000. After the graph results may change because of the updation of the features in the apps in future emerging days. It all depends upon the user's involvement in social networking (Koyuncu M and Pusatli T, 2019).

Authentication Security

Ensuring the security of access to mobile devices, apps, and sensitive data relies heavily on authentication security, forming the foundation for permitting entry exclusively to authorized individuals. The forefront of this security aspect emphasizes the necessity of implementing robust and varied verification techniques. The four main components of authentication are passwords, passphrases, PINs, and biometrics. By utilizing distinct biological traits, biometric techniques like fingerprint or facial recognition provide an additional degree of security. Multi-factor authentication (MFA) plays a pivotal role in elevating authentication security by combining various authentication factors. By requiring users to provide two or more forms of authentication, such as something they know (like a password) and something they have (like a token or a fingerprint), this approach greatly improves the verification process and lowers the risks associated with relying solely on passwords. Token-based authentication, utilizing cryptographic tokens or keys, contributes an additional layer of security. These tokens, often generated through authenticator apps or stored on devices, offer time-sensitive or one-time-use verification, particularly fortifying authentication processes in multifaceted or remote authentication scenarios. Modern security frameworks emphasize continuous monitoring and adaptive authentication mechanisms. These systems observe user behavior and contextual factors during login attempts, adjusting security measures based on detected anomalies or potential threats. This adaptive approach fortifies authentication processes in response to evolving risks. The protection of biometric data is a critical consideration in authentication security. Biometric data must be encrypted and stored securely to guard against misuse and unauthorized access, maintain user privacy, and stop any breaches involving extremely personal identifiers. By integrating these multifaceted authentication approaches and protective measures, mobile computing environments enhance their defenses against unauthorized access attempts and evolving security threats (Xi k et al., 2011).

Case Studies

Case Study 1: Unauthorized Access to Corporate Devices

- Challenge:

Employees are experiencing unauthorized access to company-issued mobile devices, compromising sensitive corporate data.

- Existing Solution:

Basic PIN or password protection has been implemented, but it proves insufficient against sophisticated attacks.

- Proposed Solution:

Enhance security with biometric authentication (fingerprint or facial recognition) and enforce strong, unique passwords. Introduce Mobile Device Management (MDM) solutions for centralized control and monitoring, allowing remote device management and data wiping in case of loss or theft.

Case Study 2: Data Leakage via Insecure Wi-Fi

- Challenge:

Sensitive data is being leaked as employees connect to unsecured public Wi-Fi networks.

- Existing Solution:

Encouraging the use of VPNs helps secure data in transit, but there is room for improvement.

- Proposed Solution:

Develop a comprehensive policy promoting secure Wi-Fi practices, implement automatic VPN connections, and utilize secure, encrypted communication protocols (like HTTPS). Conduct periodic security awareness training for employees regarding the risks associated with insecure Wi-Fi networks.

Case Study 3: Malicious Apps Exploiting Device Vulnerabilities

- Challenge:

Malicious apps are exploiting vulnerabilities in the mobile operating system, posing risks to device security.

- Existing Solution:

Regular app store vetting and security patches are in place, but the threat landscape is evolving.

- Proposed Solution:

Enhance app store security measures by implementing advanced threat detection algorithms. Conduct regular security audits of app permissions and behavior. Promote user education on recognizing and avoiding potentially harmful apps through awareness campaigns and tutorials.

Case Study 4: Phishing Attacks on Corporate Emails

- Challenge:

Employees are falling victim to phishing attacks through corporate email accounts, posing a risk to sensitive information.

- Existing Solution:

Email filters and employee training are implemented, but more proactive measures are needed.

- Proposed Solution:

Implement advanced email security protocols, such as DMARC, DKIM, and SPF. Conduct regular phishing simulations to identify vulnerable individuals and provide targeted training. Enhance user awareness by regularly communicating the latest phishing trends and tactics.

Case Study 5: Device Loss and Unauthorized Access

- Challenge:

Devices are lost or stolen, leading to potential unauthorized access and data exposure.

- Existing Solution:

Remote wipe and device tracking are employed, but additional security measures are necessary.

- Proposed Solution:

Enhance remote wipe capabilities, implement geofencing to trigger additional security measures when devices leave predefined areas, and enforce strong authentication for unlocking devices. Educate users on reporting lost or stolen devices promptly.

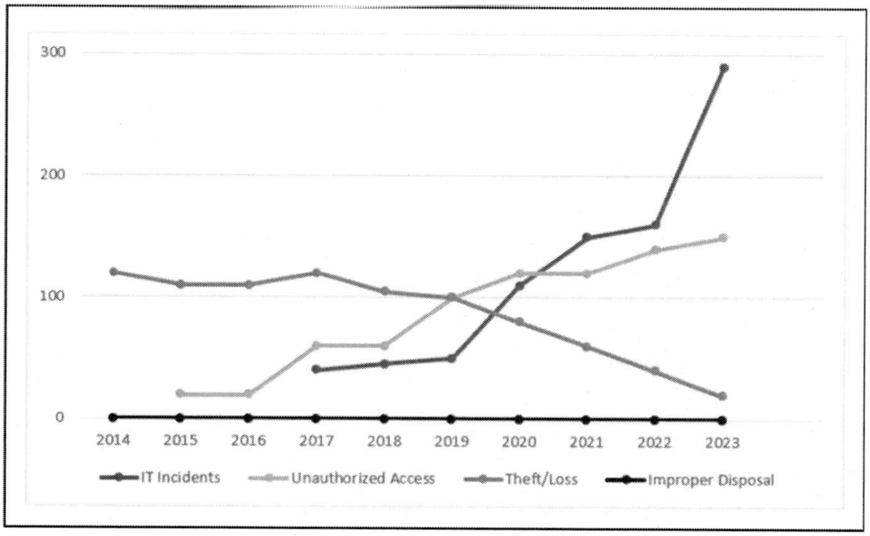

Figure 5. Data Security and Encryption.

Figure 5 shows a noticeable increase in hacking/IT incidents and unauthorized access occurrences in recent years, but a decrease in theft/loss and improper disposal incidents.

Case Study 6: Inadequate Encryption of Sensitive Data

- Challenge:

There's a lack of encryption for sensitive data stored on mobile devices.

- Existing Solution:

Basic device encryption is in place but might not cover all sensitive data.

- Proposed Solution:

While sensitive data is in transit or at rest, use end-to-end encryption. Encourage people to utilize safe storage options, like secure cloud storage or external drives with hardware encryption. Verify that encryption policies are being followed by conducting routine audits (Haris M et al., 2014).

Case Study 7: Weak Authentication Methods

- Challenge:

Weak authentication methods are in use, making unauthorized access easier as specified in Figure 6.

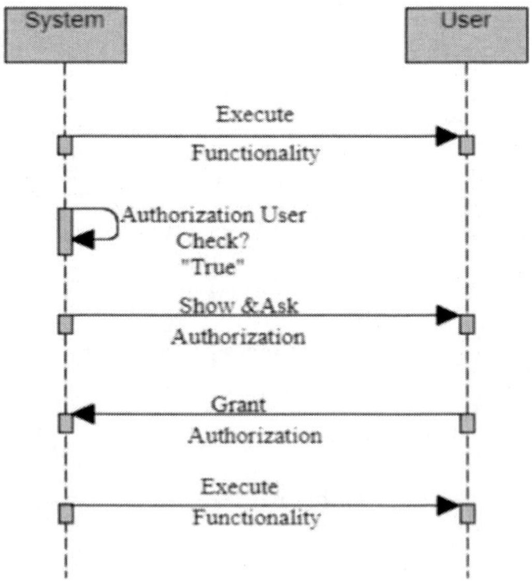

Figure 6. Cause for Weak Authentication Process.

- Existing Solution:

Password policies are in place, but their effectiveness can be limited.

- Proposed Solution:

Due to weak authentication purposes, double-check Authorization is proposed to overcome the problem by showing and asking permission from the system, and granting permission to the system by executing the functionality (Xi K et al., 2011).

Case Study 8: Outdated Software and Patching

- Challenge:

Devices are running outdated software with unpatched vulnerabilities.

- Existing Solution:

Automated updates are in place, but there's a need for a more proactive approach.

- Proposed Solution

Establish a proactive software update policy that ensures timely deployment of security patches. Conduct regular security audits to identify devices with outdated software and implement automated reminders for users to update their devices (Khan J et al., 2015).

Case Study 9: Biometric Data Vulnerabilities

- Challenge:

Concerns arise regarding the security of biometric authentication data.

- Existing Solution:

Biometric encryption is in place, but potential vulnerabilities need attention.

- Proposed Solution:

Investigate cutting-edge biometric encryption techniques, like homomorphic encryption, to protect biometric templates. To improve security, establish a procedure for routinely updating biometric templates. Test biometric systems thoroughly to find and fix any potential vulnerabilities (Koyuncu M and Pusatli, 2019; Yang W et al., 2018; Xi K et al., 2011).

Case Study 10: Insider Threats to Data Privacy

- Challenge:

Insider threats pose a risk to data privacy, with employees compromising sensitive information.

- Existing Solution:

Access controls and monitoring are implemented, but the system can be strengthened.

- Proposed Solution:

Implement a comprehensive insider threat detection system that analyses user behavior for anomalies and potential malicious intent. Conduct regular audits of user access to identify and address potential insider threats. Continually train staff members on privacy, stressing the value of handling data responsibly and the repercussions of unauthorized access (Yang W et al., 2018).

These proposed solutions address the specific challenges in each case study, aiming to create a more robust and comprehensive security posture in the context of mobile computing. Implementation, user adherence, and continuous monitoring and improvement procedures are.

Notable Privacy and Security Breaches

- The Cambridge Analytica/Facebook Scandal (2018): lack of authorization or knowledge, 87 million users' private data on Facebook had been gathered for political advertising purposes.
- Data Breach at Equifax (2017): financial reporting agency the credit bureau suffered from a data breach that exposed 147 million people's personal information, including names, social welfare figures, dates of time of their birth, and other information.
- Yahoo breaches of data in 2013 and 2014: Two significant data breaches at Yahoo exposed the accounts of billions of users, allowing passwords that are encrypted, telephone numbers, email addresses, and identities to be seized.
- Data Breach at Capital One in 2019: The personal data of more than 100 million Capital One consumers, including address information, scorecards, and social security numbers, has been accessed by an unauthorized hacker.
- Supply Chain Attack by SolarWinds (2020): The software supply chain was breached by a sophisticated cyberattack that affected numerous organizations, including government agencies. The malicious code was added by the attackers to the SolarWinds Orion software updates.
- Attack by Cybersecurity Incident (2021): A ransomware attack subjected a cyber threat aimed towards critical infrastructure, specifically the fuel supply, demonstrating the vulnerability of critical systems to such situations.
- Cyberattack on JBS Meat Processing (2021): A ransomware attack caused operational disruptions in North America and Australia for JBS, a prominent meat processing company worldwide (Noor T. H et al., 2018; Xi k et al., 2011).

The privacy breaches for sensitive and non-sensitive data at Equifax (2017) the non-sensitive data is 0.8. The data breach in Yahoo is because of the encryption of passwords, it's a combination of sensitive and non-sensitive the sensitivity is released below 0.2 and non-sensitive data is about 0.8. The attack by Colonial Pipeline Ransomware and JBS Meat Processing is breached. The notable data is released below which is non-sensitive, it is the highest value is specified in Figure 7.

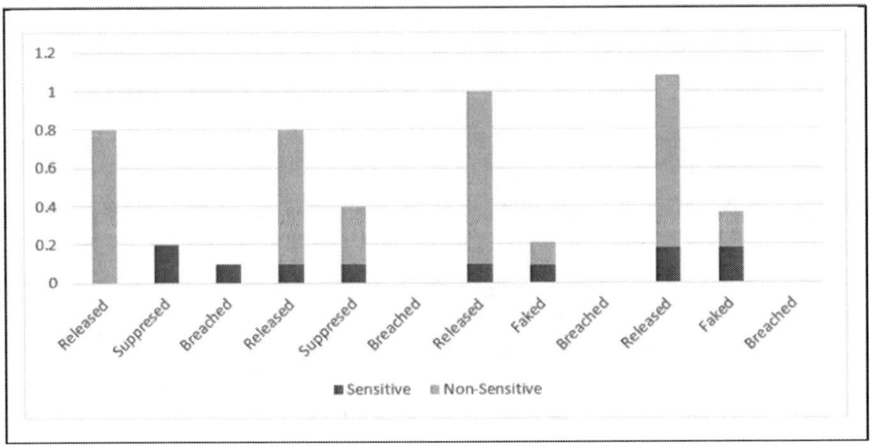

Figure 7. Privacy Breaches Comparisons.

Successful Implementation of Security Measures

Effective security measures must be put in place in the modern digital landscape to protect important assets and maintain the privacy, availability, and integrity of data. To identify potential threats and vulnerabilities and enable organizations to prioritize risks based on their potential impact, the first step is to conduct a thorough risk assessment. Developing and implementing thorough security policies and procedures, along with continual employee awareness and training programs to guarantee comprehension and compliance, are essential steps in strengthening security. Access control plays a crucial role, requiring the adoption of strong procedures to restrict system and data access to individuals who are authorized, by the least privilege principle. One essential component of security is encryption; companies encrypt sensitive data while it's in transit and at rest by using robust employing strong algorithms and key management practices. The deployment of firewalls and intrusion prevention systems assists in monitoring and controlling network traffic, while regular software updates and patch management ensure that all systems are equipped with the latest security patches. Continuous security awareness training remains essential to educate and utilize powerful algorithms and important management techniques. Network traffic monitoring and control are aided by the installation of firewalls and intrusion prevention systems, and all systems are kept up to date on security patches through patch management and routine software updates. To teach staff members about new security threats and best practices, ongoing security awareness training is still crucial. For a prompt and efficient response to security incidents, it is also essential to create and test an incident response plan regularly. Network segmentation is implemented to isolate various network segments, thereby reducing the possible impact of a security breach. Assessing the efficacy of security controls and quickly identifying incidents are made possible by routine security audits and monitoring. A strong plan for backup and recovery that includes frequent reduced downtime in the event of data loss, recovery planning, and data backups is crucial. To ensure compliance with security standards and guidelines, organizations should assess and monitor the security practices of third-party vendors as described in Figure 7. Physical security measures are also used to protect vital infrastructure, such as data centers, by limiting access and preventing unwanted entry. Organizations can strengthen their defenses against cyberattacks and create a secure computing environment that protects sensitive data and overall operational integrity by incorporating these measures into a comprehensive security strategy (Barth et al., 2019).

User Awareness and Education

Educating users about privacy and security in mobile computing is crucial for fostering a proactive and informed approach to protecting sensitive information on smartphones and tablets. As the reliance on mobile devices grows for various activities, it becomes essential to ensure that users are well-versed in potential risks and the best practices to mitigate them.

These are some of the main components of this important educational project: ...

- Targeted advertising: Create targeted campaigns tailored to diverse demographics and user groups, addressing their unique needs and concerns related to mobile privacy and security. Engaging educational experiences: Make the learning process for mobile security engaging and fun by incorporating interactive techniques like games, role-playing, and seminars.
- Plain language: makes sure a wider audience can easily understand complex concepts by avoiding technical language and presenting them in clear, concise terms.

- Employ a variety of channels: Various platforms, such as social media, PSAs, and collaborations with educational institutions and neighborhood associations, can be used to spread awareness.
- Fundamental hygiene procedures: Provide users with basic knowledge about safe password creation, two-factor authentication, controlling app permissions, and making sure apps and devices are updated regularly.
- Recognizing risks: Help users recognize common mobile security threats, such as malware, phishing scams, and unsecured public Wi-Fi networks.
- Awareness of data Privacy: Describe ideas such as data tracking, data sharing policies, and online data user rights.
- Enabling wise decision-making: Educate users so they can make wise choices about the online services they want to use, the apps they download, and the permissions they grant.

Best Practices and Strategies

To remain ahead of the constantly changing landscape of cybersecurity threats, organizations need to take a proactive approach. A fundamental understanding of potential threats and vulnerabilities is provided by regular risk assessments, which facilitate the deployment of focused security measures and the strategic allocation of resources. This ongoing process ensures that organizations are well-prepared to face emerging challenges in the dynamic landscape of cyber threats.

Security policies and procedures act as the backbone of an organization's defense strategy. These comprehensive guidelines cover critical aspects such as data handling, access controls, and incident response protocols. The regular updating and effective communication of these policies are paramount, fostering a culture of security and keeping employees well-informed about their roles in maintaining a secure environment. Human error remains a persistent challenge in cybersecurity, making continuous employee training and awareness programs essential. Companies enable their staff to be watchful guardians against possible cyberattacks by providing them with training on the most recent threats and social engineering techniques. Through this approach, a knowledgeable workforce turns into a valuable asset in the group's endeavor to foil phishing scams and other online attacks. It is essential to implement access control by applying the least privilege principle into practice, the risk of illegal entry and possible data breaches diminishes because only authorized people have access to personally identifiable information. Individuals must be given the minimum amount of access required to complete their tasks, based on this principle.

The safeguarding of confidential data can be greatly enhanced by the use of data encryption. Organizations add an extra layer of protection by encrypting data both in transit and at rest. This makes it much harder for unauthorized parties to access and misuse critical data, even in the unlikely event that they do. A preventative measure against online attacks is the regular updating of software. Hackers frequently take advantage of security holes in out-of-date software, so companies can lower the chance of exploitation and improve the overall robustness of their systems by installing security patches as soon as possible. Firewalls and intrusion prevention systems are crucial because they are the first line of protection against unauthorized access and potential cyber threats. Continuous testing and updates are necessary to effectively lessen the effects of security incidents. An incident response plan that incorporates lessons gained guarantees the readiness and applicability of the strategy. To minimize the possible consequences of a security breach, network segmentation is essential in limiting the lateral movement of attackers within a network. Organizations can add an extra layer of active protection to their cybersecurity posture by using continuous monitoring to identify and address security issues in real-time.

Regular data backups enable the maintenance of company continuity in the event of data loss. By reducing downtime and potential losses through backup system testing and data recovery plan definition, a business can become more resilient to unanticipated events. It becomes essential to evaluate and keep an eye on the security policies of outside vendors and service providers, especially when outsourcing specific tasks. This ensures that the entire supply chain adheres to robust security standards, preventing potential vulnerabilities from entering the organization through external partners Physical security measures, including controlled access to data centers and other critical infrastructure, are integral components of a holistic security strategy. By preventing unauthorized physical access, organizations add an extra layer of protection to sensitive information and equipment. Staying informed about relevant laws and regulations is crucial for legal compliance. Adhering to industry standards and regulations helps organizations maintain a strong security posture and avoid potential legal consequences.

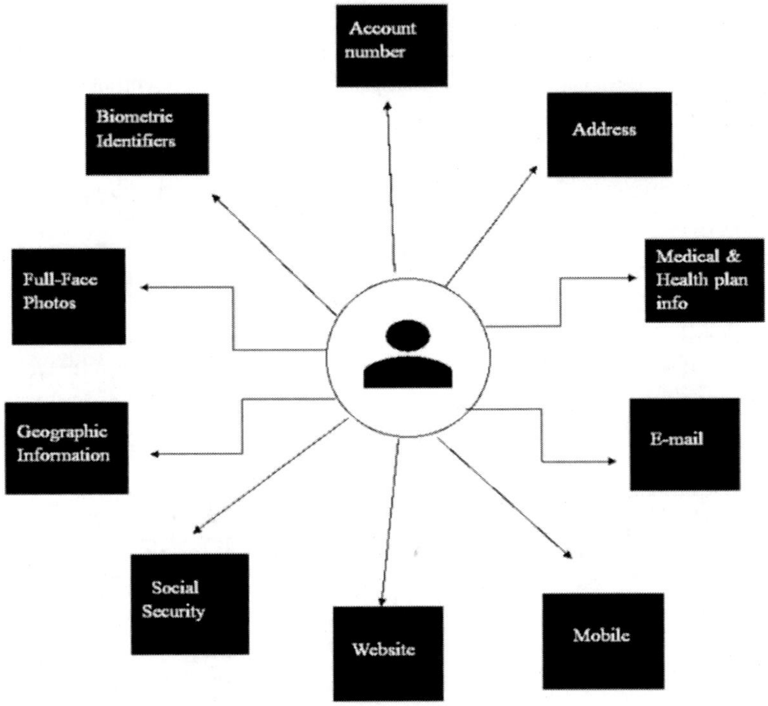

Figure 8. Data Privacy Protection Strategies.

Frequent security audits offer important information about how well security controls are being applied. Organizations stay proactive in responding to emerging threats and upholding a strong cybersecurity posture by assessing and correcting areas that could require improvement. Employees at all levels should be encouraged to prioritize and actively engage in maintaining a secure environment to foster a culture of security awareness. Open communication about security concerns creates a more resilient organization, where each individual understands their role in the collective effort to uphold cybersecurity. Implementing multi-factor authentication adds protection for user accounts, making it significantly more challenging for malicious actors to gain unauthorized access.

Endpoint security is critical because cyber attacks frequently target endpoints, which include computers and mobile devices. The overall security of an organization's digital infrastructure is influenced by regular monitoring and making sure security software is up to date. It is crucial for businesses using cloud services to adhere to standard practices for protecting their data and apps online. The benefits of cloud computing can be reached without sacrificing security thanks to appropriate configuration, strict access rules, and strong encryption. Working together with the larger cybersecurity community is a proactive way to remain up to date on the newest trends and potential dangers. Participating in knowledge-sharing programs and interacting with experts can improve an organization's capacity to adjust and address the always-changing cyber risk environment (Weichbroth P and Lysik L, 2020).

Data privacy and protecting personal data is a wide-ranging topic with numerous aspects as specified in Figure 8. By putting strong security measures in place to prevent sensitive data from being lost, compromised, or tampered with, the risk of an attack can be reduced. Protecting the privacy of private information is the primary objective in the field that deals with confidentiality. such as account number, Address, medical, E-mail, Website, Social security, geographical, information, photos, etc.

Privacy by Design

Privacy by Design represents a forward-thinking strategy that places a premium on integrating privacy considerations right from the inception of the design and development process, rather than dealing with privacy issues as an afterthought. This proactive approach involves identifying and mitigating potential privacy risks at the early stages, allowing organizations to construct more resilient and privacy-aware systems. In this framework, privacy is not an opt-in choice but is ingrained by default, relieving individuals from the need to take extra steps to protect their privacy. The core concept revolves around incorporating privacy considerations at every phase, encompassing the conceptualization, design, development, and deployment of systems and services. Integrating privacy into the design process enables the early detection and resolution of potential privacy concerns before they escalate into significant problems. The principle insists that privacy measures should not compromise the intended purpose or functionality of technology. The overarching objective is to achieve both robust privacy protections and full functionality, striking a balance without sacrificing one for the other. To safeguard data throughout its lifecycle, robust security measures are implemented, thwarting unauthorized access and potential data breaches. Providing transparent visibility into privacy practices establishes trust and enables individuals to make informed decisions about their personal information. Granting individuals control over their data is crucial, and organizations should honor user preferences regarding the handling of their data, offering mechanisms for users to opt in or opt out of specific data processing activities.

Unlike the zero-sum mentality that sees the success of one party as the loss of another, Privacy by Design strives for mutually beneficial solutions that serve the needs of individuals and companies. This cooperative strategy creates a win-win situation and promotes benefits for both parties. In this strategy, constant observation, evaluation, and adjustment to changing privacy hazards and laws are essential. Organizations are better equipped to adapt to evolving privacy challenges when they stay focused throughout the whole lifecycle. Privacy is prioritized by this user-centric approach, which also helps to design technologies that are both user-friendly and privacy-conscious. Privacy by Design ultimately aims to strike a balance that benefits both individuals and enterprises by balancing strong privacy protections with technical improvements (Gupta B et al., 2018).

Continuous Monitoring and Updates

Continuous monitoring and regular updates stand as essential pillars in the domain of mobile computing, forming a dual foundation for upholding the security, functionality, and overall well-being of devices. The practice of continuous monitoring involves the ongoing scrutiny of diverse aspects of a device's functioning, encompassing network traffic analysis, device health metrics, behavioral patterns, and comprehensive logging of security events. This real-time observation facilitates the swift identification of anomalies or security threats, enabling rapid response and effective mitigation. Network traffic analysis plays a key role in detecting unusual patterns that might indicate unauthorized access or potential data breaches while monitoring device health ensures optimal performance and a seamless user experience. Behavioral analysis contributes to identifying irregular activities, offering valuable insights into potential security risks such as malware. Simultaneously, continuous monitoring includes vulnerability scanning to proactively address known weaknesses (Barth S et al., 2019).

However, regular upgrades are essential to keeping mobile devices current and resilient. These updates include bug fixes for improved stability, feature improvements for better general use, and security upgrades to strengthen defenses against new threats. Regular updates also address compatibility issues, ensuring seamless integration with the latest applications and services.

Moreover, they contribute to compliance with industry standards and regulations about privacy and security. Of particular significance are firmware and operating system updates, incorporating crucial security improvements that fortify devices against evolving cyber threats.

Continuous monitoring in mobile computing refers to the observation of several aspects of a device's security posture, network activities, and performance in real-time. Being preventive allows irregularities or dangers to safety to be quickly discovered, and regular surveillance comprises...

- Network Gridlock Analysis: Observing the flow of both inbound and outbound network data for any signs of irregular or suspicious activities is a proactive measure aimed at detecting potential security breaches or unauthorized access. This monitoring process involves scrutinizing the data exchanges within a network to identify any patterns or behaviors that deviate from the norm. By doing so, organizations can swiftly pinpoint anomalies, enabling a prompt response to mitigate potential security threats and ensure the integrity of their network environment.
- System Health Monitoring: Consistently assessing the device's well-being, encompassing aspects like battery status, storage utilization, and overall performance, is essential to maintain optimal functionality.
- Behavioral Analyst: Analysing user behavior and patterns of application usage is instrumental in detecting abnormal activities that could signal potential security threats, such as the presence of malware or unauthorized access.
- Security Event catalog: Maintaining comprehensive logs of security events is valuable for post-incident analysis and can be instrumental in identifying patterns or trends that might signify a potential security issue.
- Vulnerability Scanning: Consistently scanning the device to pinpoint known vulnerabilities and weaknesses is essential for taking proactive measures to address potential security risks before they can be exploited.
- Security Patches: Frequent updates typically incorporate patches designed to fix recently identified vulnerabilities, thereby safeguarding the device from potential security threats.

- Bug Fixes: Updates tackle software bugs and glitches, enhancing the general stability and performance of the system (Babate A et al., 2015; Barth S et al., 2019).

Upcoming Patterns and New Technology

New trends and developing technologies that seek to address current issues and present fresh opportunities impact the direction of privacy and security in mobile computing. The landscape as a whole is anticipated to be significantly shaped by several important trends and technologies... Such as:

- Zero-Trust Structure:

It's conceivable that more people will use zero-trust security models. This methodology is predicated on the idea that no party, inside or external to the company, should be taken at face value right away. Strong access controls combined with ongoing user identity and device integrity verification improve mobile computing security.

- Entity-Level Encryption:

With the use of homomorphic encryption, a sophisticated cryptographic method, encrypted data can be computed without needing to be first decrypted. Because it allows for secure cloud data processing without disclosing sensitive information, this technology has the potential to greatly improve privacy in mobile computing.

- Utilizing Edge Computing:

Instead of going through information far away from its source, edge computing made utilize of adjacent computational resources. Since less sensitive data needs to be transmitted over networks, this trend improves privacy. Users may have more control over their data when edge computing is included in mobile devices (Hou Y et al., 2020).

- Distributed Ledger Technology (DLT) to Manage Identity:

Secure, decentralized identity management is possible with distributed ledger technologies like blockchain. By using DLT, mobile devices can lessen their dependency on centralized identity providers and provide more secure and private user authentication (Josang A, 2014).

- 5G Security Upgrades:

Security improvements tailored for 5G networks will be essential as they proliferate. A more robust and secure mobile communication infrastructure is the goal of features like network slicing and enhanced encryption techniques.

- Progress in Biometrics:

The usage of traditional passwords for authentication can be decreased with the use of biometric technologies that are constantly evolving. Examples of these technologies include vein pattern recognition, gait analysis, and behavioral biometrics (Yang W et al., 2018).

- Safeguarding Privacy with Machine Learning:

Collaborative model training is made possible by privacy-preserving machine learning methods like differential privacy and federated learning, which protect user privacy by not disclosing specific user information. This is especially important for mobile apps that use machine learning to deliver customized user experiences.

- Cryptography at Quantum Safe:

The demand for quantum-safe cryptography is increasing with the introduction of quantum computers. To overcome possible risks posed by quantum computers, mobile devices, and communication protocols will need to implement encryption methods that are resistant to quantum emulation (Noor T et al., 2018).

- Changes in Regulation:

A movement toward mobile computing environments that are more private, secure, and robust is indicated by these upcoming trends and developing technologies. To remain ahead of developing risks and maintain consumers' trust in the digital ecosystem, mobile security policies must be proactive in incorporating technological breakthroughs as they become available.

The future may be shaped by evolving security and privacy laws like GDPR. Sustained endeavors to institute and implement stringent data protection legislation may impact the advancement and implementation of solutions that give precedence to user privacy in mobile computing (Hou Y et al., 2020; Edmondson J et al., 2014).

Evolving Threat Landscape

The escalating risks to privacy and security in mobile computing are a significant concern, given the widespread use of mobile devices that have expanded the potential for cyber threats. Key security challenges include phishing attacks, malicious apps, ransomware, mobile malware, and a range of network-level threats. The integration of mobile devices into the modern workforce necessitates the development of robust security policies to mitigate these risks. As user expectations change and the mobile threat landscape grows exponentially, organizations must reassess their security strategies. This involves addressing dynamic challenges and adopting measures that align with evolving security requirements. Because they can efficiently detect and respond to a variety of threats, enterprise mobile security and mobile threat defense solutions are becoming more and more popular. Organizations must adopt security procedures and guidelines that guarantee the protection of company data to meet these issues head-on. This involves safeguarding the confidentiality, maintaining data integrity, protecting user identities, and ensuring non-repudiation. Mobile malware, including spyware, ransomware, and trojans, poses a particularly prominent threat. These malicious entities exploit vulnerabilities in both operating systems and applications, emphasizing the need for proactive and comprehensive security measures. By staying ahead of the curve with robust security policies, leveraging advanced security solutions, and being alert to new dangers, companies can safeguard confidential information and maintain the principles of identification, confidentiality, integrity, and non-repudiation in the context of mobile computing. The use of social engineering tactics to trick people into disclosing personal information has made phishing attacks more advanced. Since mobile devices have smaller screens and consumers tend to click links without giving them careful thought, they are especially vulnerable to these attacks. Financial cyber dangers have increased with the rise in the use of mobile payment systems. Attackers seek to exploit weaknesses in payment apps and banking platforms, posing a direct risk to users' financial data and transactions. Additionally, the increasing use of mobile devices in enterprise settings has given rise to targeted attacks on corporate networks through mobile endpoints, aiming to compromise sensitive business information (Kohlenberg T et al., 2010).

The security vulnerabilities inherent in public Wi-Fi networks present an ongoing risk, particularly due to the potential for man-in-the-middle attacks. Through data interceptions, these attacks can compromise login passwords, private messages, and sensitive data exchanged over such networks. The development of Internet of Things (IoT) devices, which adds new threats to the landscape, further complicates this already complex situation. Cybercriminals now have more ways to take advantage of weaknesses and obtain unwanted access to private and sensitive data thanks to these networked devices, which are frequently controlled by mobile apps. Furthermore, further privacy and security issues are brought about by the development of mobile computing ecosystems toward the integration of cutting-edge technologies like augmented reality, 5G, and AI. Massive volumes of data are created and shared inside these contexts as a result of the broad use of these technologies, creating more potential for abuse and illegal access. In essence, the insecure nature of public Wi-Fi networks Brings forth a multifaceted challenge for privacy and security. It requires a proactive and comprehensive approach to address these evolving threats and safeguard user data in an increasingly interconnected and technologically advanced landscape (Anisetti M et al., 2020; Babate A et al., 2015).

Innovations in Safeguarding of Data

In the constantly changing realm of mobile computing, prioritizing innovations in privacy and security has become essential to effectively tackle the growing challenges of protecting user data and upholding the integrity of mobile devices. One noteworthy advancement is the widespread adoption of biometric authentication, exemplified by fingerprint recognition and facial scanning. This method has proven to be both secure and user-friendly, surpassing conventional password-based approaches. The integration of advanced encryption techniques, such as end-to-end encryption and file-level encryption, into mobile applications and communication platforms has significantly strengthened data protection measures, ensuring heightened levels of confidentiality and security. Users now have increased control over their data through privacy features like detailed app permissions and privacy dashboards. Meanwhile, blockchain technology is making significant advancements in decentralized identity management, offering a secure and transparent framework for authenticating users. This ensures a robust and trustworthy authentication process.

Mobile devices are now integrating secure enclaves and hardware-based security elements, establishing secure zones for storing sensitive information that are resilient against external threats. This development enhances the overall security of mobile devices. Additionally, mobile threat defense (MTD) solutions, such as security apps, play an active role in combating various cybersecurity threats unique to mobile platforms. These solutions work to detect and mitigate issues like malware and phishing attacks, providing an additional layer of protection for mobile users. Privacy-focused operating systems, exemplified by custom ROMs for Android, prioritize user privacy and offer heightened control over data. Additionally, adherence to privacy regulations such as GDPR and CCPA has become a driving force, compelling organizations to adopt stringent measures to ensure compliance and user data protection.

Embracing the zero-trust security model signifies a departure from traditional perimeter-based security approaches. This modern model emphasizes continuous authentication, requiring constant verification of both user identity and device integrity. In the ever-evolving landscape of mobile computing, these innovations collectively pave the way for a more secure and privacy-focused ecosystem (Edmondson J et al., 2014).

Conclusion

To sum up, the surroundings of privacy and security in mobile computing have witnessed transformative changes to address the increasing challenges in our interconnected society. These include the widespread adoption of biometric authentication and advanced encryption, the emergence of privacy-centric operating systems, and a commitment to fortify the protection of user data. Continuous monitoring and timely updates have become crucial, providing real-time threat detection to ensure devices remain resilient against evolving cyber threats. Decentralized identity management on the blockchain, along with the integration of secure enclaves and hardware-based security, reflects a comprehensive approach to safeguarding sensitive information. Privacy controls, including detailed app permissions and privacy dashboards, empower users with increased authority over their data.

References

Ahmad, A., Malik, A. W., Alreshidi, A., Khan, W. and Sajjad, M., 2019. Adaptive security for self-protection of mobile computing devices. *Mobile Networks and Applications*, pp. 1-20.

Anisetti, M., Ardagna, C., Cremonini, M., Damiani, E., Sessa, J. and Costa, L., 2020. Security Threat Landscape. *White Paper Security Threats*.

Babate, A., Musa, M., Kida, A. and Saidu, M., 2015. State of cyber security: emerging threats landscape. *International Journal of Advanced Research in Computer Science & Technology*, *3*(1), pp. 113-119.

Barth, S., de Jong, M. D., Junger, M., Hartel, P. H. and Roppelt, J. C., 2019. Putting the privacy paradox to the test: Online privacy and security behaviors among users with technical knowledge, privacy awareness, and financial resources. *Telematics and informatics*, *41*, pp. 55-69.

Bilogrevic, I., Jadliwala, M., Kalkan, K., Hubaux, J. P. and Aad, I., 2011. Privacy in mobile computing for location-sharing-based services. In *Privacy Enhancing Technologies: 11th International Symposium, PETS 2011, Waterloo, ON, Canada, July 27-29, 2011. Proceedings 11* (pp. 77-96). Springer Berlin Heidelberg.

Edmondson, J., Anderson, W., Gray, J., Loyall, J. P., Schmid, K. and White, J., 2014. Next generation mobile computing. *IEEE Software*, *31*(2), pp. 44-47.

Fife, E. and Orjuela, J., 2012. The privacy calculus: Mobile apps and user perceptions of privacy and security. *International Journal of Engineering Business Management*, *4*, p. 11.

Fahrmair, M., Sitou, W. and Spanfelner, B., 2005, September. Security and privacy rights management for mobile and ubiquitous computing. In *Workshop on UbiComp Privacy* (Vol. 40).

Ghadi, S. A., 2021, April. Overview And Challenges of Security Schemes in Mobile Computing. In *Multi-Disciplinary Inter-Collegiate Online Student Resea Rch Convention 2021 Cha Ongoing Dyna Mics of Covid Er A: New Nor Ma L In Society and Industry* (P. 473).

Goundar, Sam, J. Avanija, Gurram Sunitha, K. Reddy Madhavi, and S. Bharath Bhushan, eds. Innovations in the industrial Internet of Things (IIoT) and smart factory. IGI Global, 2021.

Gupta, B. B., Yamaguchi, S. and Agrawal, D. P., 2018. Advances in security and privacy of multimedia big data in mobile and cloud computing. *Multimedia Tools and Applications*, *77*, pp. 9203-9208.

Hammouri, Q., Abu-Shanab, E. and Manasrah, A., 2016. Examining the Impact of Privacy, Security and Law on Trust in Mobile Computing. *Saba Journal of Information Technology and Networking (SJITN)-ISSN: 2312-4989*, *4*(1).

Haris, M., Haddadi, H. and Hui, P., 2014. Privacy leakage in mobile computing: Tools, methods, and characteristics. *arXiv preprint arXiv:1410.4978*.

Hou, Y., Garg, S., Hui, L., Jayakody, D. N. K., Jin, R. and Hossain, M. S., 2020. A data security-enhancedaccess control mechanism in mobile edge computing. *IEEE Access*, *8*, pp. 136119-136130.

Imielinski, T. and Korth, H. F., 1996. Introduction to mobile computing. In *Mobile computing* (pp. 1-43). Boston, MA: Springer US.

Josang, A., 2014. Identity management and trusted interaction in Internet and mobile computing. *IET Information Security*, *8*(2), pp. 67-79.

Khan, J., Abbas, H. and Al-Muhtadi, J., 2015. Survey on mobile user's data privacy threats and defense mechanisms. *Procedia Computer Science*, *56*, pp. 376-383.

Khera, G. B., Mobile Computing: Challenges and Reliability. *Recent Trends in Decision Sciences and Their Implications for Business*, p. 70.

Koyuncu, M. and Pusatli, T., 2019. Security awareness level of smartphone users: An exploratory case study. *Mobile Information Systems, 2019*.

Kohlenberg, T., Ben-Shalom, O., Principal Engineer, I. I. and Dunlop, J., 2010. Evaluating thin-client security in a changing threat landscape. *IT@ Intel White Paper*, p. 8.

Mavridis, I. and Pangalos, G., 1997. Security issues in a mobile computing paradigm. *Communications and Multimedia Security: Volume 3*, pp. 61-76.

Mollah, M. B., Azad, M. A. K. and Vasilakos, A., 2017. Security and privacy challenges in mobile cloud computing: Survey and way ahead. *Journal of Network and Computer Applications*, *84*, pp. 38-54.

Noor, T. H., Zeadally, S., Alfazi, A. and Sheng, Q. Z., 2018. Mobile cloud computing: Challenges and future research directions. *Journal of Network and Computer Applications*, *115*, pp. 70-85.

Weichbroth, P. and Łysik, Ł., 2020. Mobile security: Threats and best practices. *Mobile Information Systems*, *2020*, pp. 1-15.

Xi, K., Ahmad, T., Han, F. and Hu, J., 2011. A fingerprint-based bio-cryptographic security protocol designed for client/server authentication in a mobile computing environment. *Security and Communication Networks*, *4*(5), pp. 487-499.

Yang, W., Hu, J., Wang, S. and Wu, Q., 2018. Biometrics-based privacy-preserving authentication and mobile template protection. *Wireless communications and mobile computing, 2018*.

Chapter 12

Shaping Perspectives: Navigating Augmented Reality and Virtual Reality in Modern Mobile Computing Environments

M. Bharathi[1]
N. Ashok Kumar[1]
K. Praveena[1,*]
V. Kalpana[1]
V. Vijaya Kishore[1]
and J. Avanija[2]
[1]Department of ECE, School of Engineering, Mohan Babu University, Tirupati, A.P, India
[2]Department of AI and ML, School of Computing, Mohan Babu University, Tirupati, A.P, India

Abstract

Within the dynamic realms of augmented reality (AR) and virtual reality (VR), we e tremendous shifts in our understanding of the universe as a result of the constant evolution of modern technology. This chapter breaks down the technical jargon associated with AR and VR, highlighting their unique contributions to the transformation of our digital lives. Due to their increasing prevalence in a wide range of technological applications, it is imperative that one understands the precise differences between these terminologies. This chapter is primarily concerned with the impact that augmented reality can have.

* Corresponding Author's Email: kakarlapraveenasvec@gmail.com.

In: The Future of Mobile Computing
Editors: Sam Goundar, J. Avanija and K. Reddy Madhavi
ISBN: 979-8-89113-715-8

This discussion not only investigates into the technical intricacies of augmented reality and virtual reality, but also defines the variety of immersive experiences these technologies enable, clarifying the classification and complexity of mixed reality. This chapter gives considerable space to the interface between mobile computing and augmented reality technologies. This chapter will guide through an exploration of various augmented technologies in the field of modern mobile computing environments. Also delivers valuable understanding into the use of smartphones, whether Android or iOS, as a gateway to the fascinating field of augmented reality. Users of all skill levels can take part in an immersive experience in the world of reconstruction. This chapter explores the possible uses of AR and VR in various industries (F. Spinelli et al., 2021), including healthcare, entertainment, education, and many more. Empirical evidence highlights the significant influence of these technologies and their potential impact on professional practice, user engagement, and learning environments.

To sum up, this chapter covers the integration of virtual reality and augmented reality technologies into contemporary mobile computing settings and offers a comprehensive understanding of their intricacies. Along with that educational vocabulary, it gives students the skills and information they need to easily use augmented reality (AR) on their smartphone augmented reality (AR) on their smartphones with ease, bringing them into a realm where perception is altered as well as reality is enhanced.

Keywords: augmented reality (AR), virtual reality (VR), mobile computing, mixed reality, smartphone exploration, technology perception, digital experiences, industry applications

Introduction

In today's world, there are sophisticated interactions between virtual reality (VR) and augmented reality (AR), which can be connected to mobile computers to carry out real-time applications (Tao Zhan et al., 2020). The primary focus is on how these immersive technologies are transforming today's mobile world through observation and provision of interactions. The talk delves deeply into the complex issues surrounding the seamless integration of VR and AR technologies with mobile computing technology. It provides a comprehensive analysis of the recommendations for a wide range of clients, developers, and stakeholders. It also discusses the advantages and disadvantages that could result from this integration. The research looks into the broader effects of AR and VR on mobile apps (C. Xu et al., 2022) and user interfaces as well as the whole computing environment.

- Technical Terminology: Breaking A thorough grasp of the technical jargon associated with virtual reality (VR) and augmented reality (AR) (Y. Chen et al., 2020) can be gained from Technical Language Struggle. This subsection commences with a concise synopsis of every notion, followed by an in-depth explanation of terms like haptic feedback, gesture detection (S. Jiang et al., 2018), spatial computing, and immersive environments. The content is made more accessible by combining real-world examples and scenarios to show how these ideas are obvious in the framework of contemporary mobile computation. Using assessments and correspondences, the description creates meaningful links between formal jargon and everyday English to enhance comprehension. Figures and infographics are examples of visual aids that are purposefully used to provide as visual references and explain difficult concepts. To guarantee a complete study of complex functionality, sophisticated methods are accompanied by detailed instructions. The person speaking is straightforward and stays away from superfluous technical jargon throughout the conversation. Interactive features like augmented reality presentations and QR codes are incorporated to enhance the reading experience by giving readers a first-hand look at the subject matter. For readers with different levels of technical expertise, a supplement or a section with frequently asked questions at the end is a helpful resource. The main objective of "Technical Language" is to provide readers with a high degree of comprehension so they may confidently explore the rapidly expanding world of AR and VR in stylish mobile computing environments.
- Dissimilarities between AR and VR: Cutting edge technologies such as augmented reality (AR) and virtual reality (VR) are transforming social interactions and the way individuals see their environment. Despite the fact that they both offer immersive experiences, their approaches and the interactions they offer differ greatly.

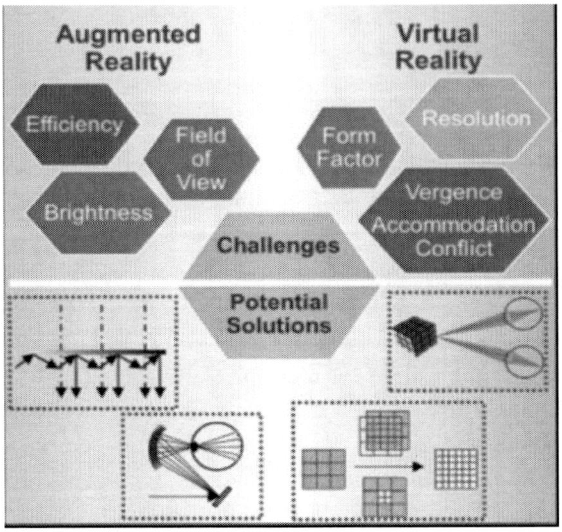

Figure 1. Distinctions between AR And VR.

Here, we list the precise distinctions between AR and VR as shown in Figure 1:

- Definition: Augmented reality (AR) is the overlaying of digital data over the real environment to improve user experience by seamlessly integrating virtual and physical aspects. Conversely, virtual reality, or VR, obscures users' physical surroundings and submerges them in a computer-generated reality, so eclipsing the real world entirely.
- User Background: With augmented reality (AR), users can benefit from digital augmentation while maintaining a strong sense of realism. Here, digital content is overlayed onto the existing environment to allow for the simultaneous manipulation of virtual and physical elements. Virtual reality, on the other hand, immerses users in a virtual environment that completely replaces the real world with a computer-generated setting in order to create a closed and immersive experience.
- Hardware & Devices: In order to access AR experiences, users commonly use tablets, smartphones, AR glasses, and heads-up displays, among other devices. Conversely, specialised gear, like virtual reality headsets, is typically needed for virtual reality, which gives a large viewing field and isolates users from the outside world.

- Collaboration: Augmented reality users can relate to both virtual and physical objects with ease thanks to voice instructions, touch gestures on devices, and real-world movements. Users interact with virtual reality primarily using motion controllers or gestures within the scene to ensure they are completely submerged in it.
- Entanglement: Unlike virtual reality, which achieves total isolation from the actual world, augmented reality (AR) maintains a symbiotic relationship with it, making for a less immersive experience. Because it immerses users completely, virtual reality (VR) gives them a strong sense of presence in the virtual environment.
- Use cases: Real-time data conception, gaming edges, and navigation apps are all areas where augmented reality is commonly employed to enhance in-person experiences. On the other hand, virtual reality is widely used in training scenarios, games, simulations, and virtual tours since these settings benefit from a completely immersive and skilful environment.
- Immersion: Augmented reality (AR) provides a less immersive experience since it maintains an interdependent connection with the real world, unlike virtual reality (VR), which achieves complete separation from the physical creation (H. Adams et al., 2022). Virtual reality (VR) provides users with a powerful sense of presence in the virtual world due to its ability to totally immerse them.

In conclusion, the degree of immersion and the manner in which each technology integrates with the outside world are what set AR apart from VR. Virtual reality (VR) immerses viewers in a meticulously designed virtual environment, providing an entirely immersive experience, whereas augmented reality (AR) skillfully blends virtual aspects into the actual world. The particular use case, the expected degree of immersion, and the amount of user interaction will determine which mix of these technologies works best.

Augmented Reality Outcomes

Viewpoints on augmented reality as a revolutionary force that is changing how digital technology is used in a variety of businesses and sectors. User commitment is significantly impacted by AR, as is the deft integration of virtual and physical elements. As a result, integration is accomplished through engaging audiences in novel ways with interactive promotions, gaming linkages, and immersive narrative.

By bringing dynamic and interactive learning experiences, augmented reality (AR) is starting a paradigm change in academia. This is made possible by the integration of 3D models, simulations, and improved opportuneness, which is a major divergence from the methods used in the literature. Augmented reality (AR) bridges the gap between online and offline shopping by enabling virtual try-ons, interactive displays, and guided in-store navigation, revolutionising the commercial sector (A. K. Chaudhary et al., 2022). Healthcare is witnessing innovation that lowers risks and raises accuracy thanks to augmented reality's improved diagnosis, operation simulations, and medical training. AR extends its reach to improve production and maintenance processes and increase efficiency through guided direction. Augmented reality (AR) brings people together by bringing shared augmented realities into the social sphere through cooperative social media projects, gaming experiences, and dynamic filters. Augmented Reality (AR) is a technological force that cuts beyond boundaries and permeates everyday life. It's expected that as technology develops, it will push the boundaries of immersive experiences, promote creativity, and alter how people engage with it in a variety of settings and industries.

Mixed Reality: Exposing Differences and Examining Intricacies

Mixed reality (MR) is the state-of-the-art immersive technology that offers a unique blend of the real and virtual worlds. Through an exploration of its many categories and minute nuances, this examination of MR reveals the different feelings it gives.

- Augmented reality (AR) and virtual reality (VR) Continuum: Mixed reality is part of a continuum that lies between virtual and augmented reality. Like augmented reality, it combines digital elements with the real world, but it also completely immerses users in a virtual environment, much like virtual reality. This continuum allows users to engage with the digital and real worlds in different ways and provides a variety of experiences.

- Augmented Reality Experiences: In the subject of mixed reality, digital overlays enhance the real world (augmented reality). This category includes applications like interactive holograms, virtual information displays, and real-time data visualisations (X. Xia et al., 2019). Users are fully submerged in an improved reality where virtual items harmoniously integrate with their surroundings.
- Virtual Reality Immersions: The term Mixed Reality falls under the same umbrella as Virtual Reality. In some cases, customers find themselves momentarily cut off from the outside world and fully engrossed in a virtual environment generated by computers (R. S. Kothari et al., 2021). This category includes interactive environments, simulations, and virtual reality tours that all contribute to improving the sense of presence and teamwork.
- Immediate Teamwork and Communication: The ability of mixed reality to facilitate real-time communication and cooperation is one of its challenges. Without being physically present, users can collaborate in the same space, engage with shared virtual items, and create mixed reality experiences. To sum up, investigating the different elements and developments of Mixed Reality offers a wide range of experiences that seamlessly combine the virtual and real worlds. As a relatively new and developing discipline, mixed reality has the power to drastically alter how we see and interact with the environment. It integrates fully immersive virtual environments with augmented interfaces that enhance the real world.
- Spatial Computing and Interaction: The goal of mixed reality is to realise the idea of spatial computing, in which a system receives inputs and reacts instantly to the outside environment. Accurate mapping of the environment becomes essential to allow digital objects to react dynamically to changes in the physical world. The same techniques that are used to interact with real-world items can also be used to interact and manipulate virtual ones.
- Wearable Technology and Headsets: Wearable technology and helmets with sensors and cameras are frequently used in mixed reality applications. Using these gadgets allows users to smoothly move between the actual and virtual worlds, which in turn makes mixed reality interactions more immersive (Goundar et al., 2021). Microsoft Hollowness and Magic Leap are two of the best examples in this field.

- Holographic Computers: The incorporation of holographic computing is a significant feature of mixed reality. In the actual world, holograms—three-dimensional virtual objects—can be created, modified, and obtained. Mixed Reality encounters are greatly enhanced by holographic computing's realism and promise.

Uncovering the Potential of Augmented Reality in Contemporary Mobile Computing: A Comprehensive Examination

The introduction of augmented reality has ushered in a revolutionary era for modern mobile computing (C. Wang et al., 2023), essentially changing how we communicate with one another through cellphones and the outside world. This chapter examines augmented reality (AR) in further detail as it relates to mobile computing, emphasising its relevance for real-time applications and providing insightful information to smartphone users.

- Integration of Mobile computing and augmented reality: Examining the ways in which augmented reality and mobile computing may coexist peacefully, emphasising the advantages of evolving AR capabilities and the dynamic qualities of modern smartphones. Examine how combining AR with other technologies improves user experiences and opens up new appointment opportunities.
- Practical Smartphone Augmented Reality Applications: Give examples of several practical uses for augmented reality that make a discernible difference in people's lives. These can include augmented reality-powered navigation, real-time language translation, interactive gaming, and apps that superimpose data on areas of interest captured by smartphone cameras.
- Using Augmented Reality in Everyday Tasks: Showcase the integration of augmented reality into people's daily lives. Talk about apps that facilitate virtual try-ons, shopping, and interior design, demonstrating how augmented reality (AR) skillfully combines digital and physical data through smartphone interfaces.
- Enhancing Social Media Interactions: Highlight how social media platforms are being impacted by augmented reality (AR), as interactive elements, filters, and effects enhance the production of

visual content. Discuss how augmented reality (AR) has evolved into a tool for creativity that enables people to communicate with and exprss themselves to their social networks.

- The AR Gaming Revolution: Examine how augmented reality has changed the gaming industry, focusing on how immersive smartphone experiences are. Talk about well-known augmented reality games and how they make use of smartphone characteristics to produce fun and interesting gaming.
- Materials and Interfaces for Augmented Reality Development: Give developers a brief overview of the platforms and technologies that they can use to create mobile augmented reality apps. Talk about how AR development kits, frameworks, and languages have evolved to allow for more ecosystem participation.
- Challenges and Future Trends: Address the problems that are keeping cellphones from being widely utilised for augmented reality, such as privacy concerns and technological limitations. Discuss potential solutions and enumerate forthcoming innovations, such as improved user interfaces, fresh augmented reality gear, and the integration of AR into everyday activities.
- Instructions and User Manuals: Provide tips and guidance to smartphone users on maximising the use of augmented reality apps. This industry can include recommended apps related to augmented reality and guidance on arranging smartphone environments for AR content, and solutions for public matters.
- Industry Integration and Commercial Applications: Look at the various applications of augmented reality in mobile strategies across various industries. Discuss the commercial applications of augmented reality (AR), such as enhanced shopping experiences, virtual product demos, and the usage of augmented reality by businesses to contact clients on mobile platforms.

In conclusion, emphasise the connection between augmented reality and contemporary mobile computing. The cutting-edge possibilities that users will have at their disposal, encouraging them to investigate and incorporate augmented reality (AR) into their smartphone experiences and, in the process, change their perceptions of and interactions with the real and virtual worlds.

An Informative Manual for Generating Augmented Reality Portals on Smartphones

In the rapidly changing world of technology, cellphones are becoming more than just instruments for completing daily tasks; they are increasingly potent entrance points into the fascinating field of augmented reality (AR) (S. Castelo et al., 2024). This entire book chapter offers helpful advice on how to maximise cellphones as entry points into the fascinating realm of augmented reality, catering to users of both Android and iOS devices. The course starts with an overview of the basic ideas of augmented reality, then moves on to discuss the underlying technologies that allow AR experiences on smartphones and goes over some important terminology. Consequently, you are led through the fundamental specifications for both software and hardware. This guarantees compatibility for the best possible experience with augmented reality (AR). Users of this research have access to a wide range of augmented reality platforms and applications in a number of industries, such as gaming, productivity, education, and navigation. Customers may quickly adjust settings and turn on augmented reality (AR) elements for an immersive overview of these interactive worlds by following comprehensive setup instructions tailored to particular smartphone models. As users embark on their adventure, this tour introduces them to the basics of augmented reality (AR) and demonstrates how to engage with virtual items and play basic AR games. Beyond the fundamentals, users are exposed to ever more advanced augmented reality features and functionalities, like markerless tracking, spatial workouts, and AR-Kit/AR-Core capabilities. Anticipating certain obstacles, the guide also provides troubleshooting tips and methods to enhance AR experiences on smartphones by utilising expert counsel and strategies, such as hidden shortcuts features. This chapter is important because it explains how permissions are managed and personal information is kept current to guarantee a secure AR experience. It emphasises how crucial user privacy and safety are when interacting with AR and VR apps.

A progressive viewpoint describes possible future developments in smartphone augmented reality in the last section. Customers are encouraged to keep up with new developments and features. In the end, this chapter highlights mobile phones as effective entry points into an immersive augmented reality world, in addition to being communication tools. This research transforms everyday smartphone interactions into remarkable and enhanced experiences by enabling people to grasp, investigate, and play with the endless potential of augmented reality.

AR and VR Technologies: Radical Impact on Work, Education, and User Experiences

This essay explores how augmented reality (AR) and virtual reality (VR) technology (F. Weidner et al., 2023) affect user experiences, the workplace, and academia in significant and apparent ways. The immersive qualities of VR and AR have completely changed how people utilise technology.

- Redefining User Interactions: As technology advances, user commitment with consumers is being altered by AR and VR technologies, which allow users to interact with the digital environment through unusual means including online buying, cooperative game-based software, and immersive narratives. To demonstrate how these technologies have changed user interactions, a few cases will be looked at.
- Pedagogical Adaptations in Education: Virtual and augmented reality are becoming ubiquitous instruments in education, changing the dynamics of the classroom. This study will investigate how augmented reality (AR) enhances and influences virtual field excursions and incorporates digital content into textbooks to establish dynamic learning environments in academic settings. In a similar vein, virtual reality immerses students in the study of skills such as knowledge enhancement, simulations, and acquisition revolutionization.
- Effect on Workplace Procedures: This article will provide actual instances of how AR and VR are changing workplace policies in different businesses and sectors. Technologies like group virtual reality systems that facilitate distant collaborating and virtual training simulations for academic experts in hazardous fields have the potential to drastically alter how work is done and skills are learned.

- Better Education and Talent Acquisition: AR and VR are useful instruments for professional training and skill development, enabling them to practice in real-world settings. This research will investigate how these technologies will support the development of skills and confidence in sectors such as manufacturing, healthcare, and aviation.
- Inclusion and Accessibility: By removing geographical obstacles and allowing for the accommodation of different learning styles or physical constraints, AR and VR contribute to better inclusion and accessibility. The study will go over how these innovations in technology foster more inclusive workplaces and educational settings.
- Effects on Thought and Memory: A thorough investigation of the psychological and cognitive effects of AR and VR will be carried out. Through an investigation of these technologies' effects on levels of engagement, cognitive processes, and affective responses in various virtual settings, this study seeks to enhance the potential benefits and downsides of these technologies.
- Industry Case Studies: To show how business successfully integrates AR and VR to boost yield, real-world case studies from a variety of sectors will be presented. The practical advantages—which range from increased manufacturing to more efficient healthcare—will be highlighted.
- Ethical Issues and Challenges: Data misuse, privacy, and the digital divide are just a few of the ethical issues and obstacles that need to be addressed in order for AR and VR to become widely accepted. The objective of the essay is to present an objective assessment of how these cutting-edge technologies are affecting society. To sum up, this chapter delves deeply into the revolutionary claims made about AR and VR technologies, emphasising how they affect user experiences, professional practices, and educational techniques. Because AR and VR are changing the way people interact with digital content and navigate learning and work environments, it is important to carefully consider the ethical implications of these technologies and the issues associated with integrating them into the real world.

Conclusion: Connecting the Gaps in Virtual and Augmented Reality Technologies with Current Mobile Computing Circumstances

The first portion of the chapter offers a precise definition and a discussion of the differences between AR and VR. It demonstrates how AR alters the physical world by overlaying virtual features on top of it, whereas VR fully submerges people in a computer-generated virtual reality. This creates the foundation for a thorough examination of the key distinctions between these two technologies. It leads the user through a range of AR and VR-shaped scenarios. Through the seamless blending of virtual and real-world elements, users of augmented reality coexist peacefully with their surroundings. Virtual reality (VR), on the other hand, submerges users entirely in a virtual environment. To demonstrate the range of user experiences, the chapter goes into detail on the various hardware requirements, which include AR glasses and smartphones. The conversation now includes how AR and VR encourage interaction. Users can utilise speech, touch, and gesture commands to interact with virtual and physical objects in augmented reality (AR). On the other hand, motion controllers are largely used by users of virtual reality (VR) to interact with the completely immersive experience. The level of immersion that each technology provides is a key distinction between AR and VR. While augmented reality (AR) provides a less intense experience while maintaining a connection to reality, virtual reality (VR) offers an entirely immersive virtual environment. The chapter looks at several use cases to show the variety of applications that these technologies can be used for. Along with AR gaming overlays and navigation apps, these include virtual reality games, virtual tours, and simulations. The chapter concludes with a synopsis of the particular distinctions between AR and VR, emphasising the variations in their approaches and how they relate to the actual world. It underlines how important it is to make informed decisions in order to integrate this ground-breaking technology.

References

Adams, Haley, Jeanine Stefanucci, Sarah Creem-Regehr, Grant Pointon, William Thompson, and Bobby Bodenheimer. "Shedding light on cast shadows: An investigation of perceived ground contact in ar and vr." *IEEE transactions on visualization and computer graphics* 28, no. 12 (2021): 4624-4639.

Castelo, Sonia, Joao Rulff, Erin McGowan, Bea Steers, Guande Wu, Shaoyu Chen, Iran Roman et al., "ARGUS: Visualization of AI-Assisted Task Guidance in AR." *IEEE Transactions on Visualization and Computer Graphics* (2023).

Chen, Yuanfeng, Hyunho Kim, Jiseob Lee, Suhui Lee, Youngbin Do, Munsu Choi, and Jin Jang. "An 18.6-μm-pitch gate driver using a-IGZO TFTs for ultrahigh-definition AR/VR displays." *IEEE Transactions on Electron Devices* 67, no. 11 (2020): 4929-4933.

Chaudhary, Aayush K., Nitinraj Nair, Reynold J. Bailey, Jeff B. Pelz, Sachin S. Talathi, and Gabriel J. Diaz. "Temporal RIT-Eyes: From real infrared eye-images to synthetic sequences of gaze behavior." *IEEE Transactions on Visualization and Computer Graphics* 28, no. 11 (2022): 3948-3958.

Goundar, Sam, J. Avanija, Gurram Sunitha, K. Reddy Madhavi, and S. Bharath Bhushan, eds. Innovations in the industrial Internet of Things (IIoT) and smart factory. *IGI Global*, 2021.

Jiang, Shuo, Bo Lv, Weichao Guo, Chao Zhang, Haitao Wang, Xinjun Sheng, and Peter B. Shull. "Feasibility of wrist-worn, real-time hand, and surface gesture recognition via sEMG and IMU sensing." *IEEE Transactions on Industrial Informatics* 14, no. 8 (2017): 3376-3385.

Kothari, Rakshit S., Aayush K. Chaudhary, Reynold J. Bailey, Jeff B. Pelz, and Gabriel J. Diaz. "Ellseg: An ellipse segmentation framework for robust gaze tracking." *IEEE Transactions on Visualization and Computer Graphics* 27, no. 5 (2021): 2757-2767.

Spinelli, Francesco, and Vincenzo Mancuso. "Toward enabled industrial verticals in 5G: A survey on MEC-based approaches to provisioning and flexibility." *IEEE Communications Surveys & Tutorials* 23, no. 1 (2020): 596-630.

Wang, Chaowei, Xiaofei Yu, Lexi Xu, and Weidong Wang. "Energy efficient task scheduling based on traffic mapping in heterogeneous mobile edge computing: A green IoT perspective." *IEEE Transactions on Green Communications and Networking* (2022).

Weidner, Florian, Gerd Boettcher, Stephanie Arevalo Arboleda, Chenyao Diao, Luljeta Sinani, Christian Kunert, Christoph Gerhardt, Wolfgang Broll, and Alexander Raake. "A Systematic Review on the Visualization of Avatars and Agents in AR & VR displayed using Head-Mounted Displays." *IEEE Transactions on Visualization and Computer Graphics* (2023).

Xia, Xinxing, Yunqing Guan, Andrei State, Praneeth Chakravarthula, Kishore Rathinavel, Tat-Jen Cham, and Henry Fuchs. "Towards a switchable AR/VR near-eye display with accommodation-vergence and eyeglass prescription support." *IEEE transactions on visualization and computer graphics* 25, no. 11 (2019): 3114-3124.

Xu, Changqiao, Jiuren Qin, Ping Zhang, Kai Gao, and Luigi Alfredo Grieco. "Reinforcement learning-based mobile AR/VR multipath transmission with streaming power spectrum density analysis." *IEEE Transactions on Mobile Computing* 21, no. 12 (2021): 4529-4540.

Zhan, Tao, Kun Yin, Jianghao Xiong, Ziqian He, and Shin-Tson Wu. "Augmented reality and virtual reality displays: perspectives and challenges." *Iscience* 23, no. 8 (2020).

Chapter 13

Multimodal AI-Embedded Blockchain Security Approach for Smart Student Monitoring

Ch. Chandra Sekhar
Naresh Tangudu*
Vineesh Pydisetti
Pramila Payli
Amitha Narindi
and Chinnikrishna Enni
Department of IT, Aditya Institute of Technology and Management Engineering College, Tekkali, Andhra Pradesh, India

Abstract

In the modern era online learning is an essential aspect of the educational environment. Maintaining academic integrity and enhancing student performance in distant settings, on the other hand, present substantial obstacles. This study offers a practicable Multi-Model Student Online Monitoring System (MONITORING SYSTEM) that makes use of a variety of monitoring strategies. Monitoring system integrates standard proctoring services, automated plagiarism detection, LMS analytics, and behavior analytics with cutting-edge technologies including facial expression analysis, sentiment analysis in discussions, eye-tracking, and natural language processing. This comprehensive method offers a balanced and privacy-conscious monitoring system that allows for real-time assessment of student involvement, emotions, focus, and material quality. It aims to promote academic integrity in the digital education

* Corresponding Author's Email: itsajs@gmail.com.

In: The Future of Mobile Computing
Editors: Sam Goundar, J. Avanija and K. Reddy Madhavi
ISBN: 979-8-89113-715-8

space, thereby fostering a more conducive learning environment. By doing so, it not only improves the quality of online learning but also enhances the freedom in education, thereby making it more accessible and inclusive. It provides a balanced, privacy-conscious, and effective approach to monitoring student engagement and learning quality, thereby enhancing the overall educational experience. This research proposes for the efficient application of Monitoring system to improve online learning activities and enhance freedom in education academic integrity.

Keywords: data security, learning management system (LMS), biometric authentication, IP tracking, attendance monitoring, assessment and grading, real-time dashboards, automated proctoring, live proctoring

Introduction

Online education has grown in popularity as a result of technological developments and increasing internet accessibility. There has been a significant increase in the use of virtual classrooms as a result of the flexibility and convenience it offers to a variety of learners (Barbara B. Lockee. et al., 2016). But along with this growth have come difficulties regarding student participation and academic honesty. To address these problems, a multi-model student online monitoring system has arisen. These systems enable secure and reliable online learning, promoting an environment favorable to academic success, by integrating capabilities like facial recognition, keystroke analysis, and eye-tracking. This personalized approach to learning can significantly enhance the overall educational experience (Shivangi Dhawan et al., 2019).

Background and Motivation

Online education has experienced significant growth over the past two decades, fueled by advancements in technology and the internet's widespread accessibility. However, this shift to virtual learning environments has also raised concerns about academic integrity, student engagement, and performance monitoring. As the number of online learners continues to increase, there is a pressing need for effective monitoring systems that ensure a secure and productive learning experience, track student progress, and detect potential issues like cheating and disengagement in real-time (Muthu prasad et al., 2019) figure.

Contributing to the Rise of Online Education

- Advancements in Technology: The rapid advancements in technology, especially the internet and digital devices, have made online education accessible to a global audience. With the proliferation of smartphones, tablets, and laptops, learners can access educational content from anywhere, at any time.
- Flexibility and Convenience: Online education offers unparalleled flexibility to learners, allowing them to study at their own pace and fit learning into their busy schedules. This convenience has attracted working professionals, students with family commitments, and individuals seeking to enhance their skills (Alexis D. Souchet et al., 2020).

Research Objective

The research objective of the Multi-model Student Online Monitoring System is to develop and analyses an innovative solution that comprehensively tracks and assesses students' online activities, interactions, and performance in educational settings. The study aims to explore the system's architecture, features, and potential benefits, providing educational institutions with real-time insights to ensure a safe and productive virtual learning environment.

Scope and Limitations

The research approach for the Multi-model Student Online Monitoring System will involve a combination of qualitative and quantitative methods. It will include a comprehensive literature review to understand the existing monitoring systems, technologies, and ethical considerations related to student online monitoring. Additionally, it will incorporate a survey or interviews with educators, administrators, and students to gather their insights and perspectives (Li Fang et al., 2022).

Data Collection Methods

The data collection methods will include gathering data from various sources such as online learning platforms, student interactions, performance metrics, and system logs.

Analysis Techniques

The research will employ various analysis techniques, including ML algorithms for anomaly detection, predictive analytics for student performance evaluation, and sentiment analysis to assess students.

Literature Review

The evolution of online education has been a transformative journey that has revolutionized the way students access and engage with educational content. Over the years, advancements in technology have played a crucial role in shaping the landscape of online learning, leading to the development of the Multi-Model Student Online Monitoring System. This section explores the key milestones in the evolution of online education, highlighting the need and scope for a comprehensive monitoring system (Andrea L Schaffer et al., 2018). Researchers have explored the integration of various modalities, such as text analysis, video tracking, and biometric data, to create comprehensive monitoring systems. These systems not only provide real-time feedback on student engagement, but they also enable personalized learning experiences through adaptive content delivery. However, ethical concerns, including privacy issues and algorithmic biases, require careful consideration in the design and implementation of such systems. Furthermore, the integration of multimodal data streams poses technical challenges in terms of data arranged in Table 1.

Challenges of Online learning

The Multi-model Student Online Monitoring System brings numerous advantages to online learning environments. However, it also comes with its fair share of challenges. Some of the key challenges of implementing such a system are:

Privacy Concerns

Monitoring students' online activities raises privacy concerns. Balancing the need for monitoring with protecting students' privacy and data security is crucial. Institutions must ensure that data is handled ethically and transparently.

Ethical Considerations

There are ethical questions about the extent of surveillance and the potential impact on students' psychological well-being and academic performance. Striking a balance between monitoring and respecting students' autonomy is a significant challenge.

Data Management and Storage

The system generates vast amounts of data that need to be processed, stored, and analyzed in real-time. Managing and securing this data can be complex and require robust infrastructure and data management practices.

Technical Challenges

Implementing a multi-model monitoring system involves integrating different technologies and platforms. Ensuring seamless interoperability and overcoming technical glitches can be a significant hurdle.

Table 1. Online proctoring software's functionalities

Functions	Proctor track	Mercex mettl	Talview prove	Proctor exam	Proctor Edu	Top hat	Promet ric	Maple lms	Paper shala
Identity verification	YES	YES	NO	NO	NO	YES	NO	YES	YES
Live monitoring	YES	NO	NO	YES	YES	YES	YES	NO	YES
Performance Analysis	YES	YES	YES	NO	YES	YES	YES	YES	YES
Recording	YES	YES	NO	YES	NO	YES	YES	NO	YES
Browser lockdown	YES	NO	YES	YES	YES	YES	YES	NO	NO
A1 analysis	YES	NO	NO	NO	YES	NO	YES	NO	YES
Screen capture	NO	YES	NO	YES	NO	YES	NO	NO	NO
Alerts & Flags	YES	NO	YES	NO	NO	NO	YES	NO	NO
Environment Check	NO	YES	NO	YES	NO	YES	YES	YES	NO
Data security	NO	YES	YES	YES	YES	YES	YES	NO	YES
Attendance Tracking	YES	YES	YES	YES	YES	YES	NO	NO	YES
Time tracking	YES	YES	YES	YES	YES	NO	NO	YES	NO
Screen sharing	YES	YES	YES	NO	YES	YES	YES	YES	YES
Accessibility feature	YES	YES	YES	YES	NO	YES	YES	YES	YES
Plagiarism detection	YES	YES	YES	YES	YES	NO	NO	YES	NO
Mobile device detection	YES	YES	YES	YES	YES	YES	NO	NO	NO
Robustness	YES	YES	YES	YES	NO	YES	YES	YES	YES
Polling	NO	NO	YES	NO	NO	YES	YES	YES	YES
Chat/chat bot	YES	YES	YES	YES	NO	YES	NO	YES	NO
Authenticity & validity	TES	YES	YES	YES	NO	YES	YES	YES	YES
Quizzes	YES	YES	NO	NO	YES	YES	YES	NO	YES
LMS Integration	YES	NO	NO	YES	YES	YES	NO	YES	YES
Assignment Tracking	YES	YES	NO	YES	YES	YES	YES	YES	YES

Functions	Proctor track	Mercex mettl	Talview prove	Proctor exam	Proctor Edu	Top hat	Prometric	Maple lms	Paper shala
Location Tracking	YES	NO	NO	NO	YES	YES	NO	YES	NO
Con's	Limited feedback	No proctoring, cost	Lack of customer support	Cost & limited access	Technical issues, data breaches	Cost, poor management	Slow software	Require IT & more complexity	Lack of storage, high cost
Deployment	Web	Web, windows	Web, Android	Web, Android	web	web	web	Web, windows	Windows, web

Table 2. System based online exam proctoring features

Functions	Proctor track	Mercex mettl	Talview prove	Proctor exam	Proctor Edu	Top hat	Promet ric	Maple lms	Paper shala
Access control									
Security feature	Strong	Strong	Strong	Strong	Strong	Weak	Weak	Weak	Weak
Access control	No	No	Yes	Yes	No	No	Yes	Yes	No
Username and password process	Yes	Yes	Yes	Yes	Yes	Yes	Yes	Yes	No
Multiple device login disabled	No	No	No	Yes	Yes	Yes	No	No	No
Multiple platform login disabled	Yes	Yes	No	Yes	No	Yes	Yes	No	Yes
Ip home access	No	Yes	Yes	Yes	Yes	Yes	No	Yes	Yes
Mac access	Yes	Yes	Yes	Yes	Yes	No	Yes	Yes	No
Content security feature	Strong	Weak	Weak	Weak	Weak	Weak	Strong	Weak	Weak
Content security features									
Screen capture disabled	Yes	Yes	No	No	Yes	Yes	Yes	No	No
Screenshot disabled	Yes	No	No	Yes	Yes	Yes	Yes	Yes	Yes
User id flashing on screen	Yes	Yes	No	Yes	No	No	Yes	No	No
Limited access to demo practices	Yes	Yes	No	Yes	Yes	Yes	No	No	Yes
Secure connection enabled	Yes	Yes	Yes	Yes	Yes	Yes	Yes	No	Yes
Printing disabled	Yes	Yes	Yes	Yes	Yes	No	Yes	No	No
Exam proctoring feature	Strong	Strong	Strong	Strong	Strong	Weak	Strong	Weak	Strong
Exam proctoring features									
Airplane mode enabled	No	No	No	No	No	No	Yes	No	No
Wi-fi disabled	Yes	Yes	No	Yes	Yes	Yes	Yes	No	Yes
Encrypted question paper	Yes	Yes	Yes	Yes	No	Yes	Yes	No	Yes
Question shuffling	No	Yes	Yes	Yes	No	Yes	Yes	No	Yes
Change device during test disabled	Yes	Yes	Yes	Yes	No	Yes	Yes	Yes	Yes
Right click disabled	Yes	Yes	No	Yes	Yes	Yes	No	No	No

Functions	Proctor track	Mercex mettl	Talview prove	Proctor exam	Proctor Edu	Top hat	Promet ric	Maple lms	Paper shala
Copy-paste Disable	Yes	Yes	Yes	Yes	No	Yes	No	No	Yes
External keystroke disabled	Yes	Yes	Yes	Yes	Yes	No	Yes	Yes	Yes
Minimize window disabled	Yes	Yes	Yes	Yes	Yes	Yes	Yes	No	Yes
Open calculator, word, excel disabled	Yes	No	No	Yes	Yes	Yes	Yes	Yes	Yes
Photo capture enabled	No	No	No	No	No	No	No	No	No

Heterogeneity

Combining models from diverse frameworks and languages creates challenges in data exchange, format conversion, and ensuring compatibility across the entire pipeline.

Resource Optimization

Efficiently allocating resources for multiple models with varying computational demands requires balancing performance and cost.

Absence of Prompt Conversation

In a face-to-face setting, communication occurs quickly and makes it easier for students to get answers and clarify confusing concepts. In an e-learning environment, communication is often asynchronous, which means there is a gap between teachers and students. In these spaces, misunderstandings can easily arise; Sometimes problems can be shelved before we can solve them.

Responses Not Received in Timely Manner

Providing feedback is one of the most important and valuable ways for teachers to interact with students. When feedback is delayed or delayed for weeks because of the online format, students may feel confused or uncertain about your expectations, their progress, and their performance in the classroom.

Contextual Understanding

The system needs to consider the context and nuances of online learning. Certain behaviors or interactions may seem suspicious but could be legitimate in an online educational setting. Overcoming these challenges requires a thoughtful approach, involving collaboration between educators, students, technologists, and policymakers. Open communication and transparency are vital in gaining stakeholders' trust and ensuring the system's successful integration into online learning environments. Clearly communicating the system's capabilities, limitations, and ethical considerations is crucial. Openness builds trust, mitigates concerns, and allows for ongoing evaluation and refinement of the AI-based detection tools. Clearly communicating the system's capabilities, limitations, and ethical considerations is crucial. Openness builds trust, mitigates concerns, and allows for ongoing evaluation and refinement of the AI-based detection tools. Some of the challenges are followed by several software's list out of them with all set of features listed in Table 2.

The systems typically incorporated various features and technologies to track students' online activities, interactions, and performance (M. Atherton et al., 2020). Here are some examples specified in Table 3.

Table 3. System components and importance

Systems	Importance
LMS Monitoring Platform	LMS platforms, like Moodle, Canvas, and Blackboard, tools for course management, content delivery, and student assessment. Hey often provide track and reporting features, allowing educators to monitor student's engagement and progress.
Online Assessment proctoring	Proctoring solutions, such proctoral, Examity, and Proctor are used during online assessments to prevent academic dishonesty. Hey often employ various monitoring methods like video recording, screensharing, and AI based Behavior analysis.
Learning Analytics System	These systems, such as Brightspace Analytics, offer data driven insights into student performance and engagement. They use analytics and data visualization techniques to identify patterns and trends in student Behavior (E. R. Kahu et al., 2019).
Hybrid Manage Learning Tools	Tools like Go Guardian and Lan School focus on managing student's devices during online classes. Educators can monitor students' screen, restrict access to certain websites, and control device usage (9. B. Lorenz et al., 2021).
Attendance Monitoring system	Some LMS platforms and school management systems include attendance tracking features to monitor students' participation in classes. It's a very smart system for monitoring people.
Video Conferencing platform	Platforms like Zoom and Microsoft Teams allow educators to conduct online classes. While they may not have dedicated features, they offer engagement metrics and attendance tracking.

It is important to note that while these systems focus on specific aspects of student monitoring, a comprehensive "multi-model student online monitoring system" might integrate elements from various existing systems to provide a holistic view of students' online activities, performance, and well-being. Here, we will provide an example to demonstrate how a proctoring service works in real-time while working with software. It is as follows:

Case Study 1

In the landscape of online education, maintaining exam integrity remains a crucial challenge. This document delves into the fascinating intersection of technology and trust, where AI-powered proctoring software aims to safeguard academic honesty. It presents a treasure trove of data on user behavior during online exams, offering invaluable insights into how examinees interact with the monitoring system. By analyzing the frequency of head movements, lip motions, and screen deviations, we embark on a data-driven journey as specified in Figure 1.

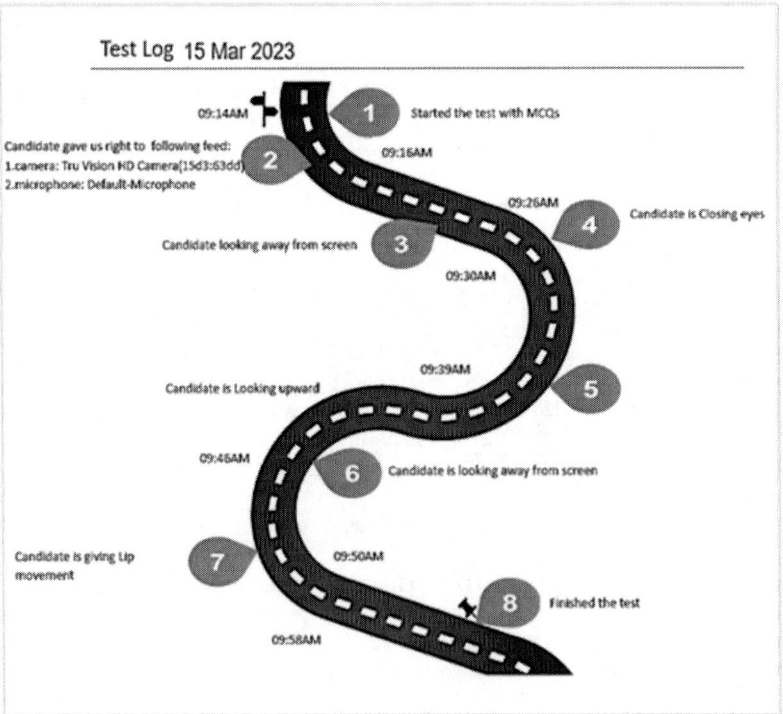

Figure 1. Real-time monitoring g system software.

Working Process

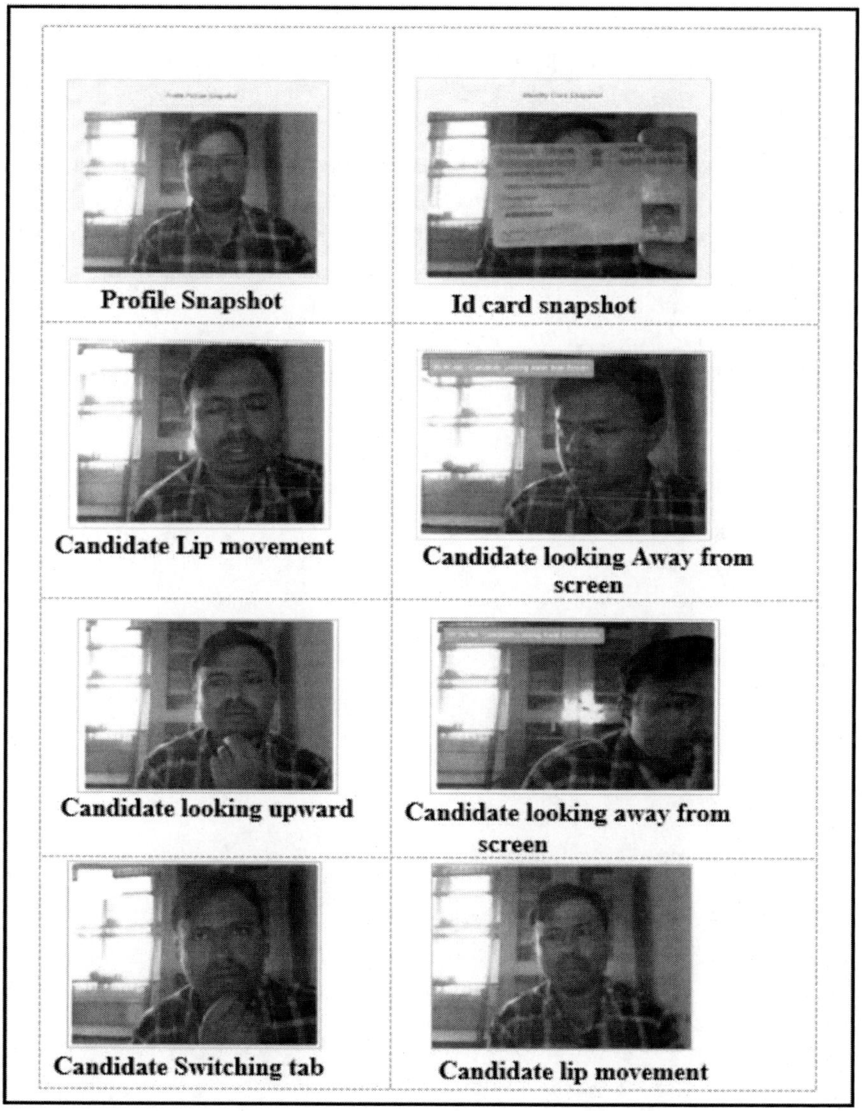

Figure 2. Real-time Monitoring Snapshots.

Before taking an exam, a person must take a photo of themselves and present a photo of their ID card. If the user deviates from the screen or exhibits suspicious behavior, such as glancing up or moving their lips, the software gives alerts. The alerts can be set to notify the user when they are looking away from the screen, turning their head or gazing up, or moving their lips, among other things. This document provides data on the frequency of head movements, instances of lip motions, and instances of looking away from the screen as specified in Figure 2. Also, an overall test summary view is provided in Figure 3.

The report also includes important exam performance characteristics such as the number of questions answered, the number of correct responses, and the number of incorrect answers. This detailed report provides an important summary of the individual's exam performance, and results as found in below Figure 4.

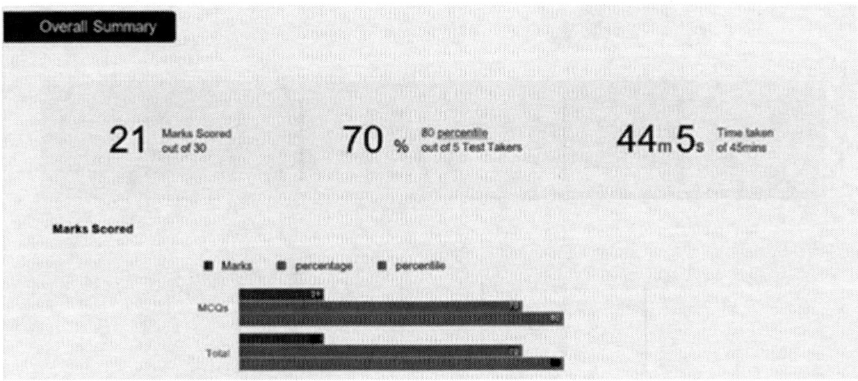

Figure 3. Overall test summary view.

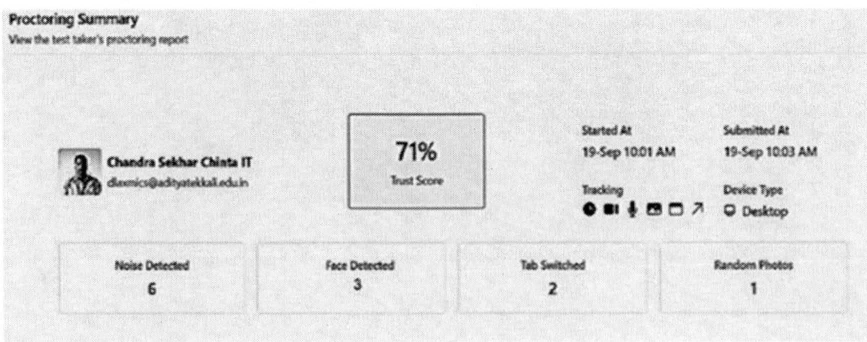

Figure 4. Overall proctoring analysis.

Case Study 2

Evidence type	Occurred at	Captured
Noise detected	19/09/23 9:10AM	
Noise detected	19/09/23 9:13 AM	
Random Face detected	19/09/23 9:17 AM	
Multiple Faces detected	19/09/23 9:25AM	
Noise Detected	19/09/23 9:27 AM	
Multiple Faces Detected	19/09/23 9:33 AM	
Noise Detected	19/09/23 9:40 Am	
Switched to different sites for 7seconds	19/09/23 9:47 AM	--------
Multiple Faces Detected	19/09/23 9:55 AM	
Full screen Exited	19/09/23 9:58 AM	--------
The face is away from the screen	19/09/23 10:03 AM	

Figure 5. Evidence reports for Test summary.

In a world where education increasingly transcends physical boundaries, ensuring exam integrity poses unique challenges. Enter the virtual proctor—an AI-powered sentinel designed to uphold academic honesty in online testing environments. This case study explores the capabilities and impact of virtual proctoring, delving into its potential to transform the landscape of remote assessments which can br observed in below Figure 5.

Working Process

This activity checks test environment is safe and secure. It is just like a person who is watching you take the test like a teacher or invigilator. This service monitors the camera and mic during the test. When the test loads it grants auto proctor access to both, else person cannot take the test. If it cannot detect the face at the beginning of the test, then the test will not load once the person's face is detected it will capture the first photo throughout the test and ensure the camera can see the face. This will take a photo and store it for later, calls these events violations let's look at how it can avoid other violations. some of them are:

- Do not take the test in a dark room.
- Background shouldn't have too many objects or a bright light.
- If any noise is detected it will be recorded during the test.
- Do not switch to a different tab or application, you must always be on the screen.

Case Study 3

- Admin View: Admin has gone to the examination data of the users who have joined and writing the exam and Suspecting the Suspicious activities.
- Suspicious Activity: In one of the questions, the candidate exhibited behavior that was deemed suspicious. Their actions during the test Warranted further investigation.
- Plagiarism Detection: During the assessment, the examiner flagged a candidate for potential plagiarism. The candidate responses raised suspicious regarding authenticity of their work.

- High Percentage Match: Upon closer examination, it was discovered that the candidate's answers bore a striking similarity to those of another candidate, with a significant percentage of matching content. Based on the investigation, decide whether the match constitutes clear evidence of cheating or requires further clarification. If cheating is confirmed, outline the penalties or disciplinary actions according to institutional policies.
- Low Score: Despite the similarities in answers, the candidate's performance only yielded a score of 25 percent certainty. This low score indicated a potential lack of originality and understanding of the subject matter.

Multi-Model Approach in Education

In the realm of education, the advent of digital technology has paved the way for innovative approaches to teaching and learning. The multi-model approach is founded on the principle that learners possess distinct learning styles, preferences, and strengths. The Monitoring System embodies the essence of the multi-model approach by combining various monitoring techniques to capture a comprehensive view of students' online learning behaviors. Each monitoring technique corresponds to a distinct facet of student engagement within the virtual learning environment (Ngoc Anh, B et al., 2019).

Case Study 4

By using blockchain technology, educational institutions can address the unique cybersecurity challenges of AI-embedded platforms. This can promote a more secure, transparent, and trustworthy learning environment for students and educators alike. Some of the use cases which are useful for online monitoring systems:

- Diploma and Transcript Verification: Blockchain's immutable ledger can securely store student diplomas and transcripts, preventing fraud and facilitating easy verification by employers or other institutions as shown in Figure 6.

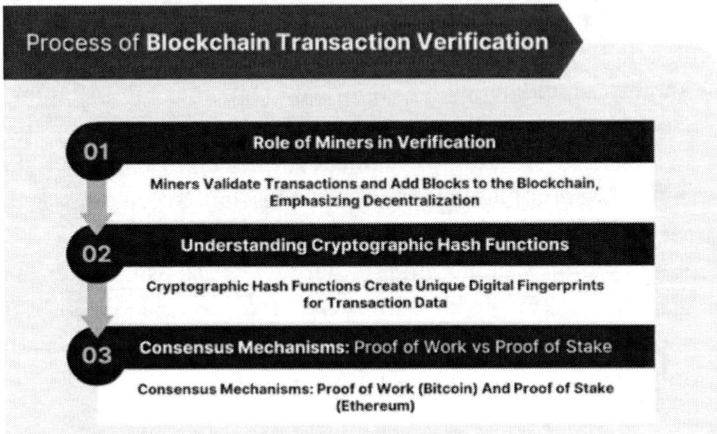

Figure 6. Blockchain Transaction Verification.

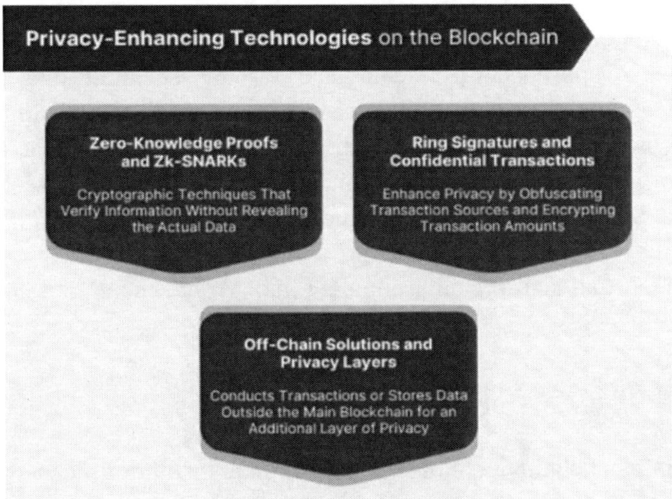

Figure 7. Privacy- Enhancing Technology.

- Secure Data Sharing: Sensitive student data like attendance records and grades can be encrypted and shared securely among authorized parties (e.g., teachers, administrators) on a blockchain platform, preventing unauthorized access or manipulation and rest of all privacy concerns are clearly mentioned in below diagram i.e., Figure 7.

- Plagiarism Detection: AI-powered plagiarism detection tools can be combined with blockchain to create a decentralized database of unique student work, enhancing accuracy and making it harder for students to copy existing content.
- Secure Credential Issuance: Blockchain can be used to issue tamper-proof digital credentials like badges or certificates for completed courses or skills acquired. This can improve transparency and facilitate learner mobility which can be shown in Figure 8 below.
- Secure Communication Platform: Integrating blockchain into online learning platforms can create a secure communication channel for students and teachers, ensuring message integrity and preventing unauthorized access.

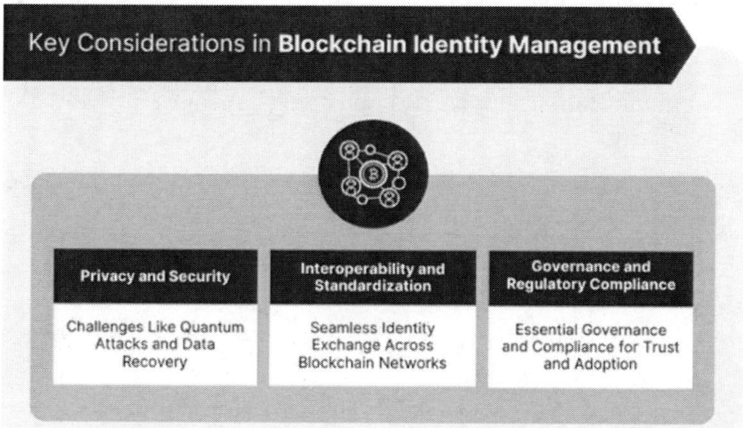

Figure 8. Key Identity Management.

Methodology

System Architecture and Components

- Collection Layer: The is the core Layer, responsible for gathering diverse data streams that reflect students' interactions and behaviors during online learning. This layer incorporates multiple monitoring techniques, including real-time video analysis, keystroke dynamics, mouse movement analysis, and sentiment analysis (Sun. B et al., 2021).

- Data Processing Layer: The Data Processing Layer receives and preprocesses the raw data collected from various sources. This layer involves data cleans informalization, and transformation to ensure consistency and accuracy. Additionally, data fusion techniques may be applied to merge the disparate data streams into a cohesive student profile.
- Analysis and Modelling Layer: In the Analysis and Modelling Layer, machine learning algorithms come into play These algorithms analyses the pre-processed data to extract meaningful insights about student Behavior, engagement patterns, and learning.
- Dashboard and Visualization Layer: The insights generated by the analysis layer are presented to educators through a user-admin interconnection-based dashboard. This dashboard provides visualizations, metrics, and real-time reports that facilitate educators' understanding of students' progress, engagement, course progress, communication support and potential challenges.

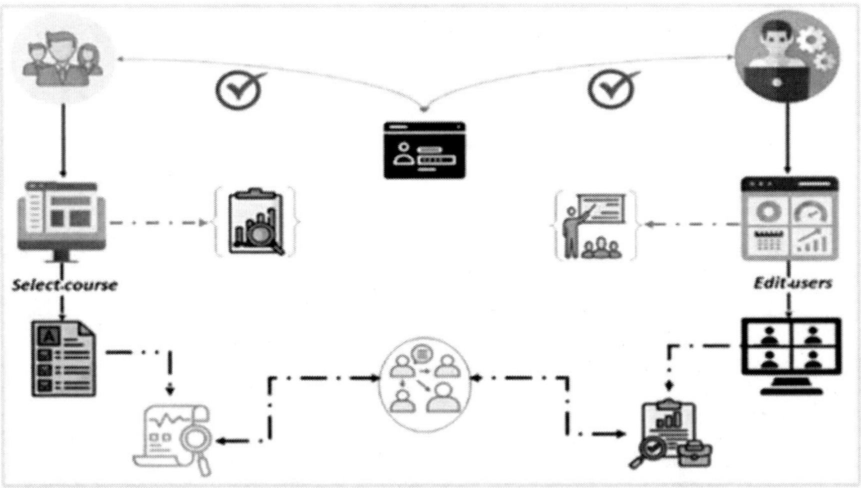

Figure 9. Relationship among Admin and User.

- Integration Layer: The Integration Layer ensures smooth communication between the Monitoring System and existing Learning Management Systems (LMS). It enables data exchange, synchronization, and integration of monitoring capabilities seamlessly into the online learning environment as shown in Figure 9.

- Security and Privacy Layer: With a focus on safeguarding student data and privacy, the Security and Privacy Layer implements encryption, access controls, and data anonymization techniques.

Proposed Solution for Monitoring System

In the Multi-model Student Online Monitoring System (Monitoring System), we envision an integration of various monitoring techniques:

- Recording System: Utilizing passive video and audio recording to capture the entire online learning session for later review, promoting transparency and accountability.
- AI Proctoring System: Implementing AI-driven tools to monitor for suspicious behaviors, plagiarism, and engagement levels, offering real-time alerts and data-driven insights.
- Human Proctoring System: Combining AI with human proctors for a balanced approach, allowing for immediate intervention in cases where AI alone might lack context or judgment.

Data Collection Techniques

- Real Time Video Analysis: This component captures students' facial expressions, gaze direction, and posture during online sessions. Computer vision algorithms analyses these visual cues to infer attention levels, emotions, and engagement.
- Keystroke Dynamics Component: Monitoring students' typing patterns, this component detects variations in typing speed, keystroke intervals, and error rates. It provides insights into students' cognitive load and potential distractions.
- Mouse Movement Analysis Component: Tracking mouse movement and click patterns, this component gauges students' interactions with course materials and platforms. Anomalies in movement may indicate disengagement or confusion.

- Sentiment Analysis Component: Utilizing natural language processing, this component analyses written communication (chat messages, forum posts) for sentiment and emotional tone. It helps identify students' emotional states and overall satisfaction (Kosheleva et al., 2018).

Data Preprocessing and Integration

Before analysis and integration, the raw data collected from different monitoring techniques undergo preprocessing to ensure consistency, accuracy, and compatibility across various data sources. Some of the key steps are Data Cleaning, Data Transformation, Normalization, Feature Extraction, Data Fusion etc... Data integration involves merging data from the Monitoring System with existing Learning Management Systems (LMS) and educational databases. This integration ensures that the monitoring system complements the broader educational ecosystem. Key aspects of data integration include API Integration, Data Mapping, Data Synchronization, Dashboard Integration etc(Hooshyar, D, et al., 2020).

Machine Learning Algorithms for Student Behavior Analysis

- Clustering Algorithms: Clustering algorithms such as K-means and hierarchical clustering are utilized to group students based on their behavioral patterns. For example, identifying a cluster of highly engaged students might lead to acknowledging their efforts, while a cluster displaying signs of disengagement could prompt proactively support (Jommanop, T et al., 2019).
- Classification Algorithms: Classification algorithms, including decision trees, random forests, and support vector machines, are employed to predict student outcomes based on Behavioral data. For instance, by analyzing keystroke dynamics and mouse movement, the system can predict the likelihood of a student completing an assignment on time.
- Time Series Analysis: Time series analysis, utilizing techniques like ARIMA (Autoregressive Integrated Moving Average) or LSTM (Long Short-Term Memory) networks, enables the system to

recognize temporal patterns in student Behavior. For instance, sudden drops in interaction time might suggest a need for additional support (Reynaldo, V et al., 2019).

- Sentiment Analysis: Natural language processing techniques are applied for sentiment analysis of text-based interactions. By analyzing the sentiment of discussion forum posts, chat messages, or written assignments, the system can gauge students' emotional states and provide insights into their attitudes towards the course content (Azevedo, R., et al., (2019).
- Reinforcement Learning for Adaptive Interventions: Reinforcement learning techniques are explored to develop adaptive interventions. For instance, if a certain type of feedback has been proven effective in increasing engagement for a specific student profile.

Dashboard Interface for Educators

The design of the dashboard interface prioritizes user-friendliness, visual clarity, and accessibility. It provides educators with an intuitive platform that allows them to navigate through different sections effortlessly while accessing a wealth of student data (Romero, C et al., 2013).

Some of the key Features are:

- Real-time monitoring Management
- Alert and Notifications
- Attendance and location tracing
- Sentimental Analysis
- Customize views
- Implementation

Implementation

Technology Stack and Tools

The multimodal online student monitoring system typically employs a combination of technologies. It commonly includes a web-based interface using HTML, CSS, and JavaScript for user interaction. The backend relies on a server framework like Django, Ruby on Rails, or Node.js. Data storage and management are achieved through database systems such as MySQL, PostgreSQL, or MongoDB.

Integration with Learning Management Systems (LMS)

Integrate our multi-model online student monitoring system seamlessly with your Learning Management System (LMS) to provide real-time insights into student engagement, performance, and Behavior. This integration will empower educators with holistic data, including video analysis, text sentiment, and activity tracking, enabling timely interventions and personalized support. Elevate the online learning experience by combining the power of our monitoring system with your LMS for enhanced student success (Hwang, W. Y., et al., 2020).

Benefits of Remote Learning

Remote learning, enabled by advancements in technology, has brought about numerous benefits and impacts on education, including:

Improving Academic Performance

Remote learning allows students to access a wide range of online resources, including video lectures, interactive simulations, and digital textbooks. This flexibility enables students to review materials at their own pace, which can cater to diverse learning styles.

Enhancing Teacher-Student Interaction

While remote learning may seem disconnected, it can facilitate more meaningful interactions between teachers and students. Digital platforms provide various channels for communication, such as discussion boards, video conferencing, and email.

Personalized Learning and Adaptive Instruction

Technology in remote learning enables the implementation of personalized learning paths. Learning platforms can analyse student data and adapt the content and pacing based on their progress. Adaptive learning technology can identify gaps in knowledge and offer targeted resources or exercises to fill those gaps, leading to a more comprehensive understanding of the subject matter (Ribeiro, D. et al., 2020).

Implementation Challenges

Technological Infrastructure

Establishing a reliable and scalable technological framework to support the student monitoring system can be a challenge. This involves ensuring the availability of necessary hardware, software, and network resources, as well as maintaining data security and privacy.

Teacher Training and Acceptance

Training educators to effectively use the student monitoring system and integrating it into their teaching practices can be a hurdle. Acceptance from teachers is crucial, as they need to understand its benefits and be comfortable with the technology.

Addressing Cultural and Societal Concerns

Student monitoring systems may raise cultural and societal concerns related to privacy, data security, and ethics. Striking a balance between monitoring for educational purposes and respecting individual rights and cultural sensitivities is important (Hernández-García, Á., et al., 2019).

Results and Discussion

Effectiveness in Monitoring Student Engagement

In this section, you would discuss the extent to which the online student multimodal monitoring system effectively tracks and measures student engagement. You can present data, graphs, or any relevant metrics that demonstrate how the system is capable of monitoring various aspects of student engagement in an online learning environment.

Correlation with Academic Performance

This section would focus on exploring the potential correlation between the data gathered by the multimodal monitoring system and students' academic performance. You might analyse whether there's a relationship between engagement levels as measured by the system and students' grades or other academic achievements.

Ethical Considerations and Privacy Concerns

Here, you would delve into the ethical implications of using a monitoring system like Monitoring System. Discuss the potential privacy concerns that might arise from collecting and analyzing student data. Address how the system safeguards sensitive information and maintains compliance with relevant data protection regulations.

Faculty and Student Perspectives on Monitoring System

This section would involve presenting the opinions and feedback from both faculty and students regarding the online student multimodal monitoring system. You could include survey results, interviews, or any qualitative data that provides insights into how the system is perceived by its users. Highlight any positive or negative viewpoints and discuss potential areas for improvement.

Implications and Future Directions

Enhancing Personalized Learning Paths

The future of remote learning involves even more sophisticated algorithms and analytics that can deeply understand individual student learning patterns and preferences. This could lead to highly personalized learning paths.

Early Intervention and Student Support

Remote learning platforms could incorporate early intervention mechanisms that identify students who are struggling or falling behind in real-time. Through data analysis, educators can identify signs of difficulty and provide timely interventions, whether through additional resources or targeted exercises.

Potential for Hybrid Learning Environments

The future might see the merging of traditional classroom settings and remote learning to create hybrid learning environments. This allows for a flexible approach where students can attend some classes physically and engage in others remotely.

Incorporating Real-time Feedback Mechanism

As technology advances, the ability to provide instant, detailed feedback to students will become more refined (Pereira, A. et al., 2020).

Conclusion

Through rigorous research and testing, it was found that the student multimodal online monitoring system effectively tracks and analyses various aspects of students' online learning experiences. The system's integration of multiple data sources, such as video feeds, screen activity, and engagement metrics, provides a comprehensive view of student engagement and performance. This holistic approach enables educators to identify patterns, assess the effectiveness of instructional strategies, and offer timely interventions to enhance student learning outcomes.

Contributions to Education and Technology

The implementation of the student multimodal online monitoring system brings several notable contributions:

- Enhanced Pedagogical Insights: The system provides educators with real-time insights into students' learning behaviors, enabling them to adapt teaching methods and content to better suit individual needs.
- Personalized Learning: By analysing student's interactions with learning materials, the system recommends personalized resources and activities, fostering a more tailored learning experience.
- Data-Driven Decision-Making: Educators and administrators can make informed decisions about curriculum design, instructional strategies, and resource allocation based on the comprehensive data collected by the system.

Call for Further Research and Development

While the student multimodal online monitoring system shows great promise, there are areas that warrant further research and development.

- Ethical Considerations: As with any technology that involves data collection and analysis, ethical concerns must be addressed. Research should explore the privacy implications of collecting sensitive student data and develop safeguards to protect student privacy.
- Validation Studies: Conducting larger-scale studies in diverse educational settings will validate the system's effectiveness across various contexts and age groups.
- User Experience: Continued development should focus on improving the user interface, ensuring that educators find the system user-friendly and easily integrated into their teaching practices.
- AI and Predictive Analytics: Exploring the potential of artificial intelligence and predictive analytics to anticipate student challenges and offer proactive interventions could further enhance the system's capabilities. Long-Term Impact: Research should investigate the long-term effects of using such a system on student motivation,

engagement, and learning outcomes, as well as the potential for unintended consequences.

References

Alwahaby, H., Cukurova, M., Papamitsiou, Z., & Giannakos, M. (2022). The evidence of impact and ethical considerations of Multimodal Learning Analytics: A Systematic Literature Review. *The Multimodal Learning Analytics Handbook*, 289-325.

Atherton, M., Shah, M., Vazquez, J., Griffiths, Z., Jackson, B., & Burgess, C. (2017). Using learning analytics to assess student engagement and academic outcomes in open access enabling programmers. *Open Learning: The Journal of Open, Distance and e-Learning*, *32*(2), 119-136.

Dhawan, S. (2020). Online learning: A panacea in the time of COVID-19 crisis. *Journal of educational technology systems*, *49*(1), 5-22.

Fu, X., Shimada, A., Ogata, H., Taniguchi, Y., & Suehiro, D. (2017, March). Real-time learning analytics for C programming language courses. In *Proceedings of the seventh international learning analytics & knowledge conference* (pp. 280-288).

Hooshyar, D., Yang, Y., Predate, M., Huang, Y. M., *Clustering Algorithms in an Educational Context: An Automatic Comparative Approach*. IEEE Access 2020, 8, 146994–147014.

Iglesias-Pradas, S., Hernández-García, Á., Chaparro-Peláez, J., & Prieto, J. L. (2021). Emergency remote teaching and students' academic performance in higher education during the COVID-19 pandemic: A case study. *Computers in human behavior, 119*, 106713.

Kahu, E. R., & Nelson, K. (2018). Student engagement in the educational interface: Understanding the mechanisms of student success. *Higher education research & development*, *37*(1), 58-71.

Kosheleva, O., & Villaverde, K. (2018). How Interval and Fuzzy Techniques Can Improve Teaching. *Switzerland: Springer Verlag*.

Li, Fang, Ding Yi, Que Huimin*On the evolution and future development of online education*, Publisher: IEEE.

Lockee, B. B. (2021). Online education in the post-COVID era. *Nature Electronics*, *4*(1), 5-6.

Lorenz, B., Sousa, S., & Tomberg, V. (2013). Privacy awareness of students and its impact on online learning participation–a case study. In *Open and Social Technologies for Networked Learning: IFIP WG 3.4 International Conference, OST 2012, Tallinn, Estonia, July 30–August 3, 2012, Revised Selected Papers* (pp. 189-192). Springer Berlin Heidelberg.

Mangaroska, K., Sharma, K., Gaševic, D., & Giannakos, M. (2020). Multimodal Learning Analytics to Inform Learning Design: Lessons Learned from Computing Education. *Journal of Learning Analytics*, *7*(3), 79-97.

Muthu prasad, T., Aiswarya, S., Aditya, K. S., & Jha, G. K. (2021). Students' perception and preference for online education in India during COVID-19 pandemic. *Social sciences & humanities open*, *3*(1), 100101.

Ngoc Anh, B., Tung Son, N., Truong Lam, P., Phuong Chi, L., Huu Tuan, N., Cong Dat, N., ... & Van Dinh, T. (2019). A computer-vision based application for student behavior monitoring in classroom. *Applied Sciences*, *9*(22), 4729.

Philippe, S., Souchet, A. D., Lameras, P., Petridis, P., Caporal, J., Coldeboeuf, G., & Duzan, H. (2020). Multimodal teaching, learning and training in virtual reality: a review and case study. *Virtual Reality & Intelligent Hardware*, *2*(5), 421-442.

Reynaldo, V., Wicaksana, A., & Hansun, S. (2019). Brotli data compression on moodle-based E-learning server. *ICIC Express Lett. Part B Appl*, *10*, 963-970.

Ribeiro, D., & Pereira, A. (2020). Data privacy in educational technologies: *A survey from the student perspective. Computers & Security*, 90, 101714.

Romero, C., & Ventura, S. (2013). *Educational data mining: A survey from 1995 to 2005. Expert Systems with Applications*, 40(1), 135-146.

Sáiz-Manzanares, M. C., Rodríguez-Díez, J. J., Díez-Pastor, J. F., Rodríguez-Arribas, S., Marticorena-Sánchez, R., & Ji, Y. P. (2021). Monitoring of student learning in learning management systems: An application of educational data mining techniques. *Applied Sciences*, *11*(6), 2677.

Schaffer, A. L., Dobbins, T. A., & Pearson, S. A. (2021). Interrupted time series analysis using autoregressive integrated moving average (ARIMA) models: a guide for evaluating large-scale health interventions. *BMC medical research methodology*, *21*(1), 1-12.

Sun, B., Wu, Y., Zhao, K., He, J., Yu, L., Yan, H., & Luo, A. (2021). Student Class Behavior Dataset: a video dataset for recognizing, detecting, and captioning students' behaviors in classroom scenes. *Neural Computing and Applications*, *33*, 8335-8354.

Chapter 14

EmoLex-Enhanced Computational Analysis of Anxiety and Sadness: A Mobile Computing Approach at the Intersection of Mental Health

M. Bharathi[1,*]
N. Ashok Kumar[1]
G. Sandhya Kumari[2]
V. Madhurima[3]
Saleha Tabassum[4]
and G Srihari[5]
[1]Department of ECE, School of Engineering, Mohan Babu University, Tirupati, Andhra Pradesh, India
[2]Department of ECE, Siddartha Institute of Science and Technology, Puttur, Andhra Pradesh, India
[3]Department of ECE, S V College of Engineering, Tirupati, Andhra Pradesh, India
[4]Department of EEE, KSRMCE, Kadapa, Andhra Pradesh, India
[5]Department of ECE, School of Technology, The Apollo University Chittoor, Andhra Pradesh, India

Abstract

The importance of digital communication has made it essential to understand and handle both mental and health issues. In this research, computational semantics and mental health has been discussed to provide an innovative method for analyzing the text data to diagnose depressive and anxious emotions. This work highlights the prominence of

---

* Corresponding Author's Email: bharathi891@gmail.com.

In: The Future of Mobile Computing
Editors: Sam Goundar, J. Avanija and K. Reddy Madhavi
ISBN: 979-8-89113-715-8

identifying expressive indications to identify and treat the mental health disorders early on, using a Flask-based WebApp and the EmoLex emotion vocabulary. Not only specifically formulated for anxiety but also for unhappiness, the EmoLex vocabulary is essential in understanding the various emotional variations between these illnesses. This section highlights the need for computational diagnostic methodology to use text normalization and tokenization to carefully pre-process data before extracting emotions from it. The EmoLex lexicon offers an ample information of the emotional components of text and enlarges the degree of categorization of sentiments. By using an EmoLex-based web application that is Flask-style and gives instant feedback on emotive emotions, the solution endorses better emotional management and to enhance self-awareness. A comprehensive examination demonstrates the methodology's facility to recognize the depressive and anxious symptoms across a various text. Emotionally charged content is preserved with care, and ethical considerations of user privacy or data security are considered. This research totally gives the first-ever fusion of computational linguistics and mental health analysis, which is made probable by the EmoLex vocabulary. Flask-based WebApp agreements an emotional journey with dynamic ecology. The new method presents intelligible and user-centered perspectives on emotional health, aligning with future of mobile computing and location the stage for innovative approaches in mental health and human emotions.

Keywords: anxiety analysis, computational analysis, mobile computing, EmoLex, depression analysis, emotional expression, mental health, early detection, emotion lexicon

Introduction

Overview of NLP and Mental Health

A person's mental health affects every part of their life and is essential to their general wellbeing and quality of life. Still, it's a complex and multifaceted issue that affects millions of individuals worldwide with diseases including depression and anxiety (L. Minkowski et al., 2021). Thanks in part to technology improvements, the field of Natural Language Processing (NLP) has made enormous strides in identifying and comprehending mental health issues. This section establishes the framework for the rest of the chapter by highlighting the vital significance of treating mental health issues and how NLP has evolved into an effective tool for analysis and assistance.

The importance of addressing mental health concerns: The necessity of addressing mental health concerns on both an individual and societal level has gained more recognition in recent years. Anxiety (Z. Chen et al., 2021), depression, other mental health issues can have an equally disadvantageous effect on a person's day today's life, general quality of life and relationships as physical disorders (A. Al-Ezzi et al., 2022). As more people understand the importance of mental health as well physical health, the stigma associated with mental health problems is gradually disappearing. The exacerbation of these illnesses can be avoided in large part by early detection (A. Puli et al., 2020) and taking necessary action. This work highlights the prominent benefits of addressing mental health issues and stresses the need of initial identification and assistance, who are depressed and anxious.

The Function of Natural Language Processing (NLP) in the Analysis of Mental Health

The artificial intelligence subfield of natural language processing (NLP) has become a game-changer in the field of mental health analysis. NLP is primarily interested in how computers and human language interact. NLP provides a special talent in the context of mental health: the capacity to examine and comprehend the subtleties of human expression as it is expressed in text. People frequently use words to communicate their emotional states, especially those linked to anxiety and depression—whether in private chats, online forums, or social media posts (S. C. Yeh et al., 2018).

These textual signals can be interpreted using NLP techniques and tools, which can reveal information on emotional health. This chapter explores how NLP can be used to recognise and assist people who are depressed or anxious, emphasising the possibility of early intervention and the development of a society that is more sympathetic and caring.

It is crucial to understand that, as we set out on this adventure at the nexus of emotional analysis, mental health, and computational linguistics, our methodology is both profoundly human-centric and technologically new. The sections that follow in this chapter will go into further depth on the methods and strategies that support this forward-thinking method of mental health analysis, with the ultimate goal of enhancing the wellbeing of those who encounter these difficulties.

Text-Based Emotional Expression

Textual emotional expression is a complicated and multidimensional process. It acts as a potent conduit for people to express their deepest emotions, especially those related to anxiety (D. Hawes et al., 2023) and sadness. In this section, we explore how people communicate these feelings through language and discuss the difficulties in identifying the frequently subtle and nuanced emotional nuances hidden in textual data.

How People Communicate Their Feelings about Depression and Anxiety in Text

It is essential to comprehend these textual clues in order to promptly support and intervene on behalf of those who are suffering from sadness and anxiety. By identifying possible mental health problems, it makes it possible for support networks and specialists to get in touch and provide help when it's required. However, computational analysis faces substantial problems due to the complexities in text-based emotional expression.

The Difficulties of Interpreting Textual Data for Subtle Emotional Nuances

In the realm of Natural Language Processing (NLP), identifying and effectively interpreting subtle emotional nuances in text data is a challenging task. A few major obstacles are as follows:

- Ambiguity: Depending on the situation, words can have a variety of emotional meanings. As one example, the term "down" can denote both physical orientation and melancholy or a poor mood.
- Polysemy: Many words can have more than one meaning, some of which may be strongly emotive while others may be emotionally neutral. This uncertainty might cause problems for sentiment analysis models.
- Irony and Sarcasm: Irony and sarcasm are frequently hidden in text, which might cause sentiment analysis algorithms to perceive them incorrectly and produce false findings.

- Cultural and Contextual Differences: Different cultures express emotions in different ways, and within a culture, subgroups may display emotions differently as well. Furthermore, different settings might elicit distinct emotions from the same words.
- Mixed Emotions: People frequently experience a range of emotions, making precise analysis difficult. Sentiment analysis becomes more difficult when someone expresses hope and concern in the same statement.

NLP Library for Anxiety, Stress and Depression Analysis

To do sentiment analysis and emotional analysis—which are important for comprehending emotions like tension, anxiety, and sadness in textual data—a number of general-purpose NLP libraries and tools can be used. Consider the following libraries and resources:

Text Blob is a flexible natural language processing (NLP) package that offers simple-to-use tools for typical NLP tasks, such as sentiment analysis. It may not be specifically designed for the study of anxiety, stress, or sadness, but it can still be helpful for general sentiment analysis tasks including emotional states.

VADER, or the Valence Aware Dictionary and Sentiment Reasoner, is a rule-based sentiment analysis tool and lexicon that is intended to capture both positive and negative emotions as well as sentiment intensity. It could be helpful in locating emotional material associated with stress, despair, and anxiety.

The potent transformer-based approach known as BERT (Bidirectional Encoder Representations from Transformers) can be adjusted for a variety of natural language processing applications, such as sentiment analysis. Its capacity to comprehend textual context and subtleties can be useful for identifying intricate emotional expressions linked to mental health.

EmoLex is an emotion lexicon with words labelled with various feelings. You can use it with your analysis pipeline, even though it's not a full-fledged library, to give text emotional labels that include feelings like stress, worry, and despair.

LIWC (Linguistic Inquiry and Word Count): This software looks for psychological and emotional elements in text by applying pre-established linguistic categories. It can be helpful in recognising particular language patterns linked to depression, (A. Oduntan et al., 2022) stress, and anxiety (R. K. Tripathy et al., 2023).

Recall that interpreting textual emotions connected to mental health is a challenging endeavour that may need for a blend of lexical analysis, machine learning models, and domain-specific expertise. Moreover, as NLP and mental health analysis are fields that are fast developing, after my September 2021 update, there might be newer tools and libraries available. For the most recent information, make sure you always refer to the most recent studies and resources available in this field.

EmoLex: A Lexicon of Emotions

A core resource in the field of Natural Language Processing (NLP), EmoLex, short for "Emotion Lexicon," is essential for comprehending and evaluating the emotional content contained in textual data. This section introduces the EmoLex emotion lexicon, explains how it assigns words to different emotional dimensions, and discusses its significance for sentiment analysis and natural language processing.

The EmoLex Emotion Lexicon Overview

A carefully selected list of words and phrases with meticulously documented emotional labels makes up the EmoLex emotion lexicon. From positive feelings like happiness and love to negative ones like rage and fear, these categories depict the whole range of human emotions. The lexicon is an invaluable tool for learning how words and phrases are connected to particular emotions because it is intended to capture the emotional aspects of language.

EmoLex is a popular tool for analysing and quantifying emotional expression in text, with applications ranging from computational linguistics to psychology and linguistics. Its use is not limited to sentiment analysis; it may be found in domains such as social sciences, marketing, and—most importantly for this chapter—mental health analysis.

How Words Are Classified by EmoLex into Emotional Dimensions

EmoLex uses lexical analysis and manual annotation to classify words and phrases into emotional dimensions. Every word or phrase in the lexicon has an emotional label that is carefully assigned by lexicographers and linguistic experts based on the term's associations and connotations with particular emotions. Words that are frequently linked to a specific feeling, like "joy" for happiness or "anger" for impatience, are labelled appropriately.

These affective descriptors usually fit into a few categories, such as:

- Joy, love, and happiness are positive feelings.
- Negative feelings include dread, grief, and anger.
- Words that don't strongly express anyone feeling are considered neutral.

EmoLex utilises this methodical classification to offer an organised depiction of the affective significance of vocabulary in written communication, facilitating the numerical evaluation of affective manifestations.

The Function of Sentiment Analysis and NLP's Emotion Lexicons

In the field of NLP, emotion lexicons such as EmoLex are crucial, especially when it comes to sentiment and emotional analysis. These lexicons allow text to be categorised into different emotional dimensions by acting as useful references for sentiment analysis models and algorithms.

The following succinctly describes the function of emotion lexicons in NLP:

Sentiment analysis models with labelled emotional features are made possible by emotion lexicons. Sentiment analysis algorithms can classify text as positive, negative, or neutral by assigning sentiment scores based on word matches in the text to the emotional labels in the lexicon.

- Emotion Detection: Beyond sentiment, emotion lexicons enable the identification of certain emotions conveyed in text, for as identifying depressive or fearful sentiments in conversations about mental health.

- Contextual Understanding: EmoLex and other lexicons help to grasp the text's emotional context, which improves the accuracy of emotional analysis and increases NLP models' ability to capture the nuances of human emotions.

The capacity of EmoLex to classify words according to emotional characteristics makes it very useful in the area of mental health study. It facilitates a deeper comprehension of the emotional foundations of textual content, helps identify emotional signs associated with anxiety and depression, (F. Hao, 2019) and allows for prompt intervention and support. In this chapter, the role of EmoLex as an emotion lexicon is examined, providing a basis for computational emotional analysis in the field of mental health, in the analysis of anxiety (Z. Li et al., 2022) and depression in textual data.

Emotional Analysis and Computational Linguistics

Theoretical Underpinnings of Computational Linguistics' Emotion Analysis:

The foundation of computational linguistics' emotion analysis is the hypothesis that our emotional states are reflected in the language we use. The theoretical underpinnings of the study of emotions in computational linguistics are examined in this section.

- Emotion as Linguistic Cues: According to linguistic theory, linguistic cues are frequently used to convey emotions. Certain words, phrases, sentence patterns, and even punctuation might serve as these indications. To interpret these clues, lexicons and dictionaries that link words to emotional categories have been produced by researchers.
- Emotions can be classified into two categories: valence, which can be either good or negative, and arousal, which can be either intense or quiet. When evaluating the emotional content of text, computational models take these characteristics into account.
- Context & Co-Occurrence: It is uncommon for emotions to be expressed alone. They frequently co-occur with other emotions and are seen in context. Accurate emotion analysis requires an understanding of the relationship between word combinations and linguistic patterns and emotional content.

Sentiment vs. Emotion Analysis: A key idea in this subject is the distinction between sentiment analysis, which concentrates on positive, negative, or neutral sentiment, and emotion analysis, which explores particular emotional categories like joy, rage, or sadness. It is necessary to create computational models that can distinguish between the two.

The Connection between Emotional Content and Linguistic Patterns

The complex link between language patterns and emotional content is explored in this section. It highlights how particular words, grammatical constructions, and language usage context can disclose subtle emotional undertones.

- Emotion-Specific Vocabulary: Certain vocabulary is linked to particular emotions. Examples of terms that convey fear are "anxious," "terrified," and "panic," whereas terms that convey happiness are "joy," "delight," and "euphoria."
- Contextual Cues: Context frequently has an impact on emotions. For computational models to effectively judge emotions, the text's overall context must be taken into account. For example, based on the situation, saying "I'm so tired" could convey feelings of despair or tiredness.
- Metaphor and Figurative Language: Metaphor and figurative language are additional tools for communicating emotions. For example, "the weight of the world on my shoulders" is a stress- and burden-related metaphor.
- Syntactic and Semantic Structures: Emotional expression is influenced by the way sentences are put together and the semantic connections between words. Sentences in the active voice, as opposed to those in the passive voice, may have a higher emotional tone.

Preparing Data for Emotional Examination

Lowercasing: To maintain uniformity in word representations, all text should be converted to lowercase. By doing this, the model is unable to distinguish between a word in uppercase and lowercase.

Words like "the," "and" and "is," which have no emotional resonance, should be eliminated. This is known as stop word removal. Eliminating these terms lowers analytical noise. Eliminating punctuation from text in order to prevent it from interfering with sentiment analysis systems. In general, punctuation has little bearing on emotional significance.

The Function of Tokenization in Dividing Text into Useful Units

Tokenization is the process of dividing a text into discrete words or tokens. This procedure is essential for evaluating emotional content since it enables algorithms to operate on single words or sentences.

N-grams: Tokenization can produce n-grams, which are collections of n tokens, in addition to single words. A bigram, for instance, might interpret "feel good" as a single word, maintaining the context in between.

Word Lemmatization and Stemming: To help the algorithm identify variants of the same word, tokenization sometimes involves reducing words to their root forms by lemmatization or stemming (e.g., "running" and "ran" reduced to "run").

These data pretreatment methods ensure that the text is suitably formatted, free of superfluous parts, and amenable to efficient sentiment analysis algorithms, which paves the way for successful emotional analysis in computer linguistics (A. Kushki et al., 2015).

How Sentiment Analysis is Integrated with EmoLex

To extract emotional insights from textual data, it is imperative to include EmoLex into the sentiment analysis process. The smooth integration of EmoLex with sentiment analysis is examined in this section:

- Emotion Lexicon Lookup: EmoLex is a reference used by sentiment analysis models and algorithms. Every word in the input is searched for related emotional labels in the lexicon during the text analysis process. Words that coincide with lexical items are assigned labels or emotional scores.
- Aggregation of Emotional Scores: An overall emotional score for the entire text is created by adding together the emotional labels or scores given to each individual word. This score may indicate a text's major emotional dimension, which may be neutral, negative, or positive.
- Contextual Analysis: The analysis of the emotional context is made possible by the integration of EmoLex. Sentiment analysis models can provide a more sophisticated emotional assessment by taking into account the surrounding words and sentence structure in order to determine how emotions change within the text.

Using EmoLex to Assign Text Words Emotional Labels

Using EmoLex, the process of giving text phrases emotional labels follows a methodical process:

- Word Selection: Text terms are chosen for emotional analysis during sentiment analysis. Words with the greatest emotional weight are usually substance words, such adjectives, verbs, and nouns.
- Lexicon Lookup: Every word that is chosen is compared to the EmoLex entries. The word is given the corresponding emotional label or score if there is a match. For instance, the word "happy" is given a positive emotional classification if it is discovered. Scoring and Categorization: The words are categorised into emotional dimensions, such as positive, negative, or neutral, using the emotional labels or scores that have been assigned. This classification adds to the text's overall emotional evaluation.

Creation of the Flask-Powered Web Application into a Mobile Computing Application

The user interface, input management (N. B. Oğur et al., 2022), and output display must all be modified to make the Flask-based web application mentioned above suitable for mobile devices. The following is how you should go about each stage of a mobile app:

- Mobile User Interface Design: Create a user interface that is responsive to different screen sizes and orientations. Put ease of use and simplicity first when it comes to touch-based interactions. Make use of mobile-friendly navigation and user interface elements. Maintain accessibility guidelines and make sure the content is readable on smaller displays.
- Mobile Data Input: Make the input forms as touch- and mobile-friendly as possible. Give consumers the option to enter text using a mobile-friendly interface. Incorporate functionalities like audio input and photo uploading, keeping in mind mobile accessibility. A key element in the real-time analysis of emotional content is the creation of a Flask-based WebApp. The main phases in developing the WebApp are described in this section:
- EmoLex Mobile Integration: Modify EmoLex integration so that it functions flawlessly in a mobile setting. Enhance sentiment analysis in real time for mobile devices. Make sure that data processing is done quickly and without delaying user engagement.
- Display of the Output on a Mobile Device: Create clear, eye-catching displays (X. Zhang et al., 2022) for mobile screens. Present the results of your emotional analysis using graphs, charts, or other visual aids that are optimized for mobile devices. Make written comments easier to read on mobile devices. Make sure the materials and advice are displayed in a way that is compatible with mobile devices.
- Mobile-Specific Points to Remember: Use capabilities on your device, including push notifications, to provide suggestions or feedback. For users who are in places with spotty internet, take into account offline functioning. Optimize taking into account platform-specific design requirements for both the iOS and Android platforms.

Test extensively across a range of mobile devices and screen sizes.

Examine how well the app performs, particularly with regard to managing real-time analysis on mobile devices. Make that the app abides with privacy and security regulations for mobile devices.

Tools for development: Select suitable mobile development frameworks, such as native development for iOS and Android, Flutter, or React Native. Provide a mobile-friendly integration for the EmoLex library or API.

- Implementation: Release the mobile application in the appropriate app stores (App Store for Apple, Play Store for Google).

Update the app frequently to incorporate security patches, enhancements, and new features.

These instructions will help you modify the Flask-based web application to run in a mobile computing environment and give consumers a smooth and user-friendly mobile experience.

- The WebApp's User Interface and Experience: An important factor in the design of the Flask-based WebApp is the user experience:
- Intuitivity: The WebApp's interface is made to be user-friendly, making it simple for people to engage with it. It should be very easy to use with little guidance.
- Feedback Mechanism: The WebApp analyses users' input emotionally and gives them fast, unambiguous feedback on it. It is possible to offer the feedback in a way that gives users the ability to recognize and deal with their emotional states. Assessment and Validation Techniques and Measurements Applied to Verify Emotional Analysis's Accuracy. Ensuring the reliability of the methodology requires a high level of validation of the accuracy of the emotional analysis. The techniques and measurements used for validation are covered in this section:
- Ground Truth Data: To assess how well the emotional analysis method is working, a dataset containing annotated emotional labels or scores is utilised as ground truth. This ground truth data makes quantitative evaluation possible.
- Metrics: The efficacy of the emotional analysis model is assessed using metrics including accuracy, recall, F1-score, and precision. These metrics evaluate how well the model can identify emotional content in textual content.

Case Studies and Illustrative Cases of the Approach in Use

The practical use of the emotional analysis methodology is demonstrated through the presentation of case studies and real-world situations.

- Use Cases: Case studies illustrate situations where the approach has been used, such as evaluating the emotional content of online support forums or searching social media for insights on mental health.
- Findings and Implications: The emotional analysis's findings are examined in relation to how they may be used to comprehend the emotional states associated with anxiety and depression (V. Borba de Souza et al., 2022). Case studies aid in illustrating the methodology's practical application. Through the combination of EmoLex and the Flask-based WebApp, these case studies and examples serve to evaluate the efficacy of the emotional analysis process and offer concrete evidence of its utility in mental health analysis.

Discussion and Future Directions: Conclusion Drawn from the Study

Particularly in relation to mental health, anxiety, and depression, the research discussed in this chapter has shed important light on the field of computational emotional analysis:

- Improved Emotional knowledge: By combining EmoLex with sentiment analysis methods, it is now possible to gain a deeper knowledge of how people express and deal with their emotions in textual data. It has illuminated the affective aspects of sadness and anxiety.
- Real-Time Analysis: The Flask-based WebApp's development has demonstrated the possibility of real-time emotional analysis. Through user interaction, users can receive real-time feedback on their emotional states, which can lead to early intervention.
- Privacy and Ethical Issues: When handling emotional content in digital settings, privacy and ethical issues have been emphasised by the research. To ensure the proper use of technology in mental health analysis, several factors are essential.

Prospects for the Future and Progress in Computational Emotional Analysis

Computational emotional analysis is still in its early stages of development. The knowledge gathered from this study opens doors for new opportunities and developments in the future.

- Multimodal Analysis: Computerised emotional analysis may go beyond text in the future to include other modalities including audio and visual data. Multimodal analysis provides an even more thorough understanding of emotions.
- Cross-Cultural Analysis: Researching how different languages and cultures communicate emotions differently is a promising field. Creating models that are sensitive to cultural quirks is essential for international use.
- Personalised Mental Health care: According to the research, real-time emotional analysis may be used to provide personalised mental health care. Future systems may offer advice and resources that are specifically designed for those who require them.
- More Complex Machine Learning Models: By incorporating more complex machine learning models (E. W. McGinnis et al., 2019), such as deep learning and neural networks, it may be possible to improve the precision of emotional analysis and provide a more thorough comprehension of emotional states.

Conclusion and Significance

In final, this chapter marks a substantial advancement in the fields of emotional comprehension, mental health care, and computational linguistic analysis. The implications of this study are extensive:

- Increasing Emotional Awareness: EmoLex's integration with the Flask-based WebApp enables people to become more conscious of their emotions, especially those connected to anxiety and depression.
- Early Intervention: The WebApp's real-time functionality offers a platform for early intervention, enabling people to quickly seek out resources and support. Technological Approaches to Mental Health:

This study highlights how technology is helping to advance the analysis and treatment of mental health issues. It serves as an example of how sentiment analysis and natural language processing can be used in novel ways to improve emotional well-being. This research has wider ramifications that go beyond the scope of this chapter. It envisions a time where technology acts as a kind companion, helping people make their way across the complex terrain of emotional health. In the future, the combination of mental health assistance and computational emotional analysis may lead to more inclusive, proactive, and compassionate solutions in the field of mental health. The possibilities uncovered by this research provide light on the path that is still being travelled.

References

Al-Ezzi, Abdulhakim, Amal A. Al-Shargabi, Fares Al-Shargie, and Ammar T. Zahary. "Complexity analysis of EEG in patients with social anxiety disorder using fuzzy entropy and machine learning techniques." *IEEE Access* 10 (2022): 39926-39938.

Chen, Zheyuan. "Information Statistical Analysis on the Effect of Anxiety Level on College Procrastinators and Non-procrastinators on Academic Grades." In *2021 2nd International Conference on Information Science and Education (ICISE-IE)*, pp. 574-577. IEEE, 2021.

de Souza, Vanessa Borba, Jeferson Campos Nobre, and Karin Becker. "Dac stacking: A deep learning ensemble to classify anxiety, depression, and their comorbidity from reddit texts." *IEEE Journal of Biomedical and Health Informatics* 26, no. 7 (2022): 3303-3311.

Hawes, Dan, and Ali Arya. "Technology solutions to reduce anxiety and increase cognitive availability in students." *IEEE Transactions on Learning Technologies* 16, no. 2 (2023): 278-291.

Hao, Fei, Guangyao Pang, Yulei Wu, Zhongling Pi, Lirong Xia, and Geyong Min. "Providing appropriate social support to prevention of depression for highly anxious sufferers." *IEEE Transactions on Computational Social Systems* 6, no. 5 (2019): 879-887.

Kushki, Azadeh, Ajmal Khan, Jessica Brian, and Evdokia Anagnostou. "A Kalman filtering framework for physiological detection of anxiety-related arousal in children with autism spectrum disorder." *IEEE Transactions on Biomedical Engineering* 62, no. 3 (2014): 990-1000.

Li, Ziyu, Xia Wu, Xueyuan Xu, Hailing Wang, Zhenghao Guo, Zhichao Zhan, and Li Yao. "The recognition of multiple anxiety levels based on electroencephalograph." *IEEE Transactions on Affective Computing* 13, no. 1 (2019): 519-529.

McGinnis, Ellen W., Steven P. Anderau, Jessica Hruschak, Reed D. Gurchiek, Nestor L. Lopez-Duran, Kate Fitzgerald, Katherine L. Rosenblum, Maria Muzik, and Ryan S. McGinnis. "Giving voice to vulnerable children: machine learning analysis of speech detects anxiety and depression in early childhood." *IEEE journal of biomedical and health informatics* 23, no. 6 (2019): 2294-2301.

Minkowski, Laura, Kristiina Valter Mai, and Dharmendra Gurve. "Feature extraction to identify depression and anxiety based on EEG." In *2021 43rd Annual International Conference of the IEEE Engineering in Medicine & Biology Society* (EMBC), pp. 6322-6325. IEEE, 2021.

Oduntan, Adenrele, Oladapo Oyebode, Amelia Hernandez Beltran, Jonathon Fowles, Darren Steeves, and Rita Orji. ""I Let Depression and Anxiety Drown Me…": Identifying Factors Associated with Resilience Based on Journaling Using Machine Learning and Thematic Analysis." *IEEE journal of biomedical and health informatics* 26, no. 7 (2022): 3397-3408.

Oğur, Nur Banu, Celal Çeken, Yavuz Selİm Oğur, Hİlal Uslu Yuvaci, Ahmet Bülent Yazici, and Esra Yazici. "Development of an artificial intelligence-supported hybrid data management platform for monitoring depression and anxiety symptoms in the perinatal period: Pilot-scale study." *IEEE Access* 11 (2023): 31456-31466.

Puli, Akshay, and Azadeh Kushki. "Toward automatic anxiety detection in autism: A real-time algorithm for detecting physiological arousal in the presence of motion." *IEEE Transactions on Biomedical Engineering* 67, no. 3 (2019): 646-657.

Tripathy, Rajesh Kumar, Dinesh Kumar Dash, Samit Kumar Ghosh, and Ram Bilas Pachori. "Detection of Different Stages of Anxiety from Single channel Wearable ECG Senor Signal using Fourier-Bessel Domain Adaptive Wavelet Transform." *IEEE Sensors Letters* (2023).

Yeh, Shih-Ching, Yuan-Yuan Li, Chu Zhou, Pin-Hua Chiu, and Jun-Wei Chen. "Effects of virtual reality and augmented reality on induced anxiety." *IEEE Transactions on Neural Systems and Rehabilitation Engineering* 26, no. 7 (2018): 1345-1352.

Zhang, Xiaowei, Jing Pan, Jian Shen, Zia Ud Din, Junlei Li, Dawei Lu, Manxi Wu, and Bin Hu. "Fusing of electroencephalogram and eye movement with group sparse canonical correlation analysis for anxiety detection." *IEEE Transactions on Affective Computing* 13, no. 2 (2020): 958-971.

Chapter 15

Navigating the Innovation Frontier: A Comprehensive Exploration of Transformative Technologies and Their Integration with Mobile Computing

M. Bharathi[1,*]
N. Ashok Kumar[1]
G. Sandhya Kumari[2]
V. Madhurima[3]
J. Avanija[4]
and K. Reddy Madhavi[4]
[1]Department of ECE, School of Engineering, Mohan Babu University, Tirupati, Andhra Pradesh, India
[2]Department of ECE Siddartha Institute of Science and Technology, Puttur, Andhra Pradesh, India
[3]Department of ECE, S V College of Engineering, Tirupati, Andhra Pradesh, India
[4]School of Computing, Mohan Babu University, Tirupati, Andhra Pradesh, India

Abstract

Our book chapter, "Navigating the Innovation Frontier," delves into the essential elements of innovation, offering readers a comprehensive synopsis and practical guidance on utilising cutting-edge technologies. The complexities of innovation dynamics are explored in this chapter along with the critical role those transformative technologies like

---

* Corresponding Author's Email: bharathi891@gmail.com.

In: The Future of Mobile Computing
Editors: Sam Goundar, J. Avanija and K. Reddy Madhavi
ISBN: 979-8-89113-715-8

connectivity, robotics, data analytics, augmented reality (AR), virtual reality (VR), mixed reality (MR), Internet of Things (IoT), and artificial intelligence (AI) play. The critical role that innovation plays and how new technologies serve as catalysts to advance and enhance the innovation process will become abundantly clear to readers. An in-depth examination of the difficulties associated with quality, problem-solving, and opportunity identification opens the investigation. The story emphasises the value of efficacy and efficiency and presents invention as a major force behind ongoing development. Moving on, the chapter deconstructs key technology enablers to fully submerge readers in the world of future manufacturing. A thorough analysis is conducted on connectivity, AR/VR/MR, IoT, robotics, and other revolutionary technologies. With the exploration of cutting-edge ideas like Additive Manufacturing (3D printing), Cloud Computing, Data Mesh, Blockchain, Advanced Analytics, and Big Data, a comprehensive picture of the technological environment influencing the future is offered. This research's connection to mobile computing is a key component. The way these revolutionary technologies blend in with mobile computing to create an innovative interface will be explored by readers. The chapter helps readers understand how these technologies and mobile computing work together, encouraging a comprehensive approach to innovation that can be used in a variety of organisational settings. In summary, "Navigating the Innovation Frontier" equips readers with the information and resources they need to successfully negotiate the rapidly changing terrain of transformational technologies. Through the chapter, people can apply innovation effectively in their organisations by connecting these advancements to mobile computing. This will usher in a future where data-driven decision-making, immersive experiences, and connectivity come together to create unprecedented advancements across a variety of industries.

Keywords: innovation frontier, transformative technologies, connectivity mobile computing integration, future manufacturing, emerging technologies, data-driven decision-making, holistic innovation approach

Introduction

The fundamentals of innovation: In today's fast-paced world, innovation is not just a catchphrase; it is essential to advancement and development. Innovation is fundamentally the act of introducing novel, creative concepts, procedures, or technology that result in a notable improvement in the world. We investigate the essential elements that make innovation a potent force propelling evolution in our investigation of the dynamics of innovation.

Innovation can take many different forms, ranging from small-scale advancements to game-changing discoveries. It entails not just coming up with original solutions but also successfully putting them into practice to solve problems or meet demands that already exist. The complexity of invention is examined in this chapter, taking into account not just the final result but also the procedures, frames of mind, and surroundings that support and encourage creative thought. We look at how innovation encompasses enhancements to services, procedures, and organisational structures in addition to product development. Readers will obtain a sophisticated view on innovation's revolutionary potential by comprehending its many elements.

Emphasising Innovation's Crucial Role in Continuing Development

Innovation is essential to sustainable development—it is not a luxury. This section highlights the critical role that innovation plays in directing the course of continuous development in a variety of industries. Whether in technology, business, healthcare, or any other sector, innovation (Wang et al., 2022) is what keeps things moving forward and enables them to stay ahead of the curve and adjust to changing environments. The chapter emphasises the close relationship between growth and competitiveness and innovation. Businesses that embrace innovation are better able to overcome obstacles, grasp opportunities, and establish a unique brand in the global marketplace. We demonstrate how innovation has been a driving force behind success by offering case studies and real-world examples. We also highlight the impact that innovation has had on societal advancement, economic growth, and personal empowerment. Readers will learn why it is so important for organisations and communities to develop an innovative culture through a thorough analysis of the crucial role that innovation plays. This prepares us for the investigation of innovation dynamics that follows, in which we examine the intricacies, difficulties, and revolutionary technologies reshaping the frontier of innovation.

Investigating Cutting-Edge Technology

We will take a thorough look at the disruptive technologies that are changing the face of innovation in this area. These innovative technologies all contribute in a different and significant way to expanding the realm of the possible and ushering in a new era of options and possibilities (Huang et al., 2021).

Interaction:

- Definition and Importance: The capacity of systems, devices, and people to easily share and transmit information is known as connectivity. It provides real-time interaction, data exchange, and collaboration by laying the groundwork for a connected society.
- Applications: Examine how developments in industries like smart cities, healthcare, and manufacturing are being fueled by connectivity. Talk about how 5G technology can improve connectivity and open up new opportunities.

Automation:

- Robotics is the design, development, and application of intelligent machines that can work independently or in conjunction with people to carry out tasks. Industries are revolutionised by robotics since it increases human skills and automates procedures.
- Applications: Examine particular application cases, such as the integration of robots in logistics and services, industrial robotics, and medical robotics. Talk about the effects of robotics on productivity, accuracy, and security.

Analytics of Data:

- Data analytics is the process of analysing large datasets in order to identify important trends, patterns, and insights. It is a vital component of strategic planning and well-informed decision-making.
- Applications: Examine the applications of data analytics in a variety of fields, such as marketing, finance, business intelligence, and healthcare. Emphasise how machine learning and predictive analytics help to extract useful information from data.

AR, or augmented reality:

- Augmented Reality (AR) is a technology that superimposes digital data on the physical world to improve the user's perception and interaction with it. Through the blending of the actual and virtual worlds, immersive experiences are produced.
- Applications: Talk about the real-world uses of augmented reality in industries like gaming, education, healthcare, and maintenance. Examine how augmented reality is improving user engagement and training programmes.

Virtual Reality (VR):

- Virtual reality (VR) generates an immersive, simulated environment that users may engage with through specialised equipment. People can go to virtual worlds using it, providing them with experiences that are not limited by the physical world.
- Applications: Look at how VR is used in education, gaming, professional training, and healthcare (virtual surgery and therapy). Talk about how VR may improve learning results and produce realistic simulations.

Mixed Reality (MR):

- Mixed reality (MR) is a concept that smoothly blends virtual and actual worlds by incorporating aspects of both AR and VR as shown in Figure1. It lets users interact with real-world and digital items at the same time.
- Applications: Examine the many uses of MR, including immersive storytelling, remote collaboration, and interactive design. Talk about the ways that mixed reality is dismantling the conventional divide between the virtual and real worlds.

IoT, or the Internet of Things:

- The Internet of Things (IoT) is a network of linked objects that are equipped with sensors and actuators, allowing them to exchange and gather data. It serves as the foundation of an intelligent, networked ecosystem.

- Applications: Examine how the Internet of Things is changing sectors such as industry, healthcare, smart homes, and agriculture. Talk about the potential and problems brought about by the growth of IoT devices.

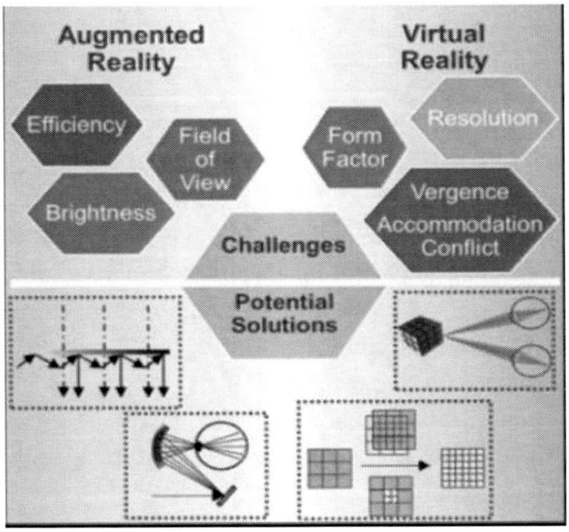

Figure 1. AR And VR.

Intelligent artificial systems (AI):

- Artificial intelligence (AI) is the process of creating systems and algorithms that simulate human intelligence, allowing robots to carry out cognitive activities. It serves as the impetus for intelligent decision-making, predictive analysis, and automation.
- Applications: Examine the various ways artificial intelligence is being used in computer vision, driverless vehicles, natural language processing, and healthcare. Talk about the ethical issues raised by AI and its possible effects on society.
- The comprehensive examination of every disruptive technology offers readers a sophisticated comprehension of their importance, prospective effects on innovation dynamics, and applications. It prepares us for a closer examination of how these technologies

interact and work together to propel previously unheard-of breakthroughs across a range of industries.

Analysing Innovation Dynamics' Complexities

The process of innovation is complex and dynamic, with several interrelated phases that each provide unique opportunities and problems. Comprehending the intricacies of innovation dynamics is imperative for enterprises aiming to cultivate an environment of perpetual enhancement and maintain a competitive edge in swiftly changing marketplaces (Bauer et al., 2020).

Finding the Opportunities;

- Challenges: It takes sharp observation and a thorough grasp of consumer demands and industry trends to identify chances for innovation. Understanding growing demands and latent opportunities is an issue that organisations frequently encounter.
- Strategies: Investigate approaches that help identify opportunities, such as market research, design thinking, and customer feedback systems. Stress the value of creating an environment where staff members are encouraged to find and suggest novel ideas.

Idea Generation and Conceptualization:

- Challenges: One of the most frequent obstacles in the innovation process is coming up with original, workable concepts. It might be difficult to overcome resistance to change and make sure a variety of viewpoints are included in the idea development process.
- Techniques: Talk about idea management platforms, brainstorming sessions, and cross-functional collaboration as methods to foster creativity. Stress how crucial it is to have a welcoming atmosphere that promotes experimenting and taking risks.

Analysis of Feasibility:

- Challenges: Technical, financial, and operational elements must be evaluated in order to determine whether suggested concepts are feasible. The issue of balancing innovation with real-world limits is substantial.

- Techniques: Emphasise the importance of prototype development, R&D and business team collaboration, and feasibility studies. Talk about the efficient resource allocation strategies that companies can use to assist with innovation activities.

Prototyping & Development:

- Challenges: Converting ideas into physical prototypes necessitates resolving resource shortages, establishing alignment with organisational objectives, and overcoming technical obstacles.
- Techniques: Examine quick prototyping, cross-functional teams, and agile development approaches as ways to optimise the development process. Stress the value of ongoing feedback loops for iteratively improving prototypes.

The Effect of Connectivity on Upcoming Manufacturing

Networking via Wire: Examples of wired connections, such as Ethernet and Industrial Ethernet, are defined. Benefits of reliable data flow, stability, and dependability in manufacturing settings (Long et al., 2018).

Use scenarios (such as vital control systems) where wired connections are preferred.

Wireless Communication: Definition and illustrations of wireless connectivity, such as Bluetooth, Wi-Fi, and Zigbee. Advantages in terms of flexibility and mobility for factory-floor linked devices. Wireless connectivity applications for mobile devices and sensor networks.

Summary of Networking and the Internet's Function in Manufacturing: The Internet of Manufacturing:

- integration of the wider internet with production operations.
- utilising cloud computing to handle, store, and retrieve data.
- An overview of the Industrial Internet of Things concept (IIoT).

Industrial Networking: An explanation of LANs (local area networks) in an industrial setting.

Global wide area networks, or WANs, link several production locations. Network infrastructure is essential for facilitating real-time communication and teamwork.

Smart Factories' Connectivity: The definition and features of intelligent manufacturing.

An essential component of creating smart factories is connectivity. Facilitating easy data interchange and system and device compatibility.

- IIoT's role: Deployment of actuators and sensors to gather data. Manufacturing data analysis and visualization through the use of IIoT platforms. Using linked devices to achieve predictive maintenance and optimisation.
- 5G Manufacturing and Technology: A description of fifth generation (5G) wireless technology.

Important characteristics include enormous device connectivity, low latency, and high data speeds. advantages of 5G for changing production procedures. Allowing for the monitoring and control of machinery in real time.

In Manufacturing, Augmented Reality (AR), Virtual Reality (VR), and Mixed Reality (MR)

The integration of Augmented Reality (AR), Virtual Reality (VR), and Mixed Reality (MR)—all of which fall under the general category of Extended Reality (XR)—stands out as a revolutionary force in the quickly changing manufacturing landscape. By superimposing visual instructions onto actual machinery, augmented reality (AR) with its hands-free applications redefines assembly processes and technician training, increasing productivity and reducing errors in complex operations. Additionally, AR develops become a potent tool for maintenance and troubleshooting, giving professionals access to context-specific, real-time information that helps them identify and fix problems.

Conversely, virtual reality (VR) is revolutionising product design and prototyping. By immersing stakeholders in virtual worlds, it simulates the functionality and performance of products, enabling iterative development and collaborative design experiences. The transition to mixed reality (MR) significantly enhances the industrial environment by allowing real-time, seamless integration of virtual and physical components. This improves real-time communication with both physical and digital entities while also transforming collaborative workspaces.

It acknowledges challenges including user uptake and technology constraints and emphasises the need for ongoing improvements and efficient training methods. Prospectively, the amalgamation of AR, VR, and MR with technologies such as IoT and Big Data is anticipated to establish a comprehensive digital ecosystem, hence inaugurating a future in which immersive and interactive experiences would not only optimise but also revolutionise manufacturing processes. The tangible benefits are emphasised by success stories and useful case studies, which open the door for widespread adoption and ongoing innovation in the manufacturing sector. Finally, the substantial effects of AR, VR, and MR9 (Xiao et al., 2023) on manufacturing represent a paradigm change that will shape a future in which digital and physical domains seamlessly merge for unprecedented efficiency and collaboration. These effects go beyond simple technological breakthroughs.

Internet of Things (IoT) Revolutionizing Manufacturing: The Internet of Things (IoT) has emerged as a revolutionary force in the dynamic manufacturing scene, radically changing how industries function and optimise their processes. Building a strong IoT infrastructure in manufacturing plants is the cornerstone of this revolution. In order to create a ubiquitous network of fluidly communicating devices, sensors and actuators must be strategically embedded into machinery. Numerous applications are made possible by this interconnection, with predictive maintenance being one of the most significant. Manufacturers can monitor the state of their equipment in real time and switch from reactive to proactive maintenance practices by utilising the Internet of Things. By predicting and preventing potential equipment failures, condition-based monitoring helps to minimise downtime and maximize operational efficiency. IoT is also essential to supply chain optimisation, since it transforms the tracking and management of both raw materials and completed goods. Manufacturers can see raw material movements in real time with the help of IoT-enabled tracking devices, which enhances supply chain efficiency and enables better decision-making. This makes it feasible to manage inventory in real-time, which lowers the possibility of stockouts or surplus inventory. Moreover, IoT makes demand forecasting easier by analysing data from several supply chain locations, allowing enterprises to react quickly to shifting market conditions.

Another area where IoT has a lasting impact on manufacturing operations is quality control. Throughout the production cycle, numerous factors are continuously monitored to guarantee that the highest standards of product quality are maintained. IoT provides real-time insights into the production environment and may be easily integrated into quality assurance processes. This promotes a more flexible and agile production system in addition to aiding in the early detection of flaws.

Essentially, the Internet of Things transforms the industrial industry by offering an all-encompassing and networked structure that encompasses everything from equipment to supply chains and quality assurance procedures. A new era of efficiency and competitiveness for manufacturers is ushered in by the predictive capabilities, real-time monitoring, and optimisation opportunities provided by IoT, which are promoting a paradigm shift in the way manufacturers approach production and resource management. With sectors still embracing the Internet of Things' revolutionary power, the manufacturing industry is poised for a technological renaissance that might bring about previously unheard-of increases in productivity and operational excellence.

The Role of Robotics in Manufacturing

Robotics is a key component of the ever-changing industrial industry, transforming production environments and bringing previously unheard-of levels of accuracy and efficiency. An overview of industrial robotics demonstrates a wide range of robot types, such as manipulators and mobile robots, each designed to perform certain tasks in a production setting. Following the development of industrial robotics over time reveals a story of technological innovation, from the first robotic arms to the present day, which is distinguished by highly developed mobility, adaptability, and control systems. One of the most revolutionary uses is seen in automated assembly lines, where robots are essential to process simplification. These mechanical counterparts do repeated activities with diligence and precision, reducing errors and costs while increasing efficiency.

The introduction of Collaborative Robots, or Cobots, which mark a paradigm change in human-robot collaboration, is a noteworthy advancement within this setting. These robots are made to cooperate with human operators in jobs requiring dexterity comparable to that of a human. Because Cobots are cooperative, people and machines may work together harmoniously to maximise strengths and achieve increased flexibility and efficiency in the industry (Huang et al., 2020).

The integration of robotics into the data-driven production ecosystem represents a significant technological convergence. In this setting, robotics blends in perfectly, taking on the roles of both physical objects and data sources for analysis and judgement. Robots produce useful data points during task execution that advance our understanding of industrial processes as a whole. Manufacturers are able to gain practical insights, streamline processes, and make well-informed decisions thanks to this data integration, which is driving the manufacturing ecosystem into a new phase of efficiency and flexibility. Essentially, robotics plays a complex function in manufacturing that goes beyond simple automation; it is a revolutionary force that not only transforms processes but also plays a crucial part in the data-driven manufacturing of the future.

Cutting-Edge Ideas Shaping the Future

Innovation with Additive Manufacturing (3D Printing)

A Brief Overview of Additive Manufacturing

3D printing, also referred to as additive manufacturing, has become a groundbreaking advancement in manufacturing techniques. By stacking materials to produce three-dimensional things, it can accomplish complicated geometries and remarkable design flexibility that may be difficult to attain with typical production methods.

- Applications and Benefits: Additive Manufacturing has applications in a wide range of industries, including aerospace (lightweight components) and healthcare (customised prosthesis). The technique lowers waste and costs associated with traditional manufacturing by enabling on-demand production in addition to facilitating rapid prototyping.
- Material Advancements: The range of applications is expanded by the continuous improvements in materials that are suitable for 3D printing, such as metals, polymers, and composites. The technology's versatility and potential to completely change the manufacturing environment are enhanced by its ability to print with a variety of materials.

- Issues and Prospects for the Future: Although additive manufacturing has received a lot of attention, issues including scalability, material constraints, and post-processing requirements still exist. Ongoing research and development aimed at surmounting these obstacles, however, portend a time when 3D printing is integrated into standard production procedures.

The Function of Cloud Computing in Upcoming Technologies

Fundamentals of Cloud Computing

The methods for processing, storing, and accessing data have all been completely transformed by cloud computing. It entails the online supply of computer services, such as software, processing power, and storage. Because it offers scalable and adaptable resources, cloud computing fosters innovation in the manufacturing sector (Mishra et al., 2022).

- Collaborative Manufacturing Platforms: Cloud-based platforms enable real-time data exchange and collaboration between scattered teams, fostering collaborative work environments. Manufacturers can use these platforms for project management, simulation, and collaborative design to promote innovation through smooth teamwork.
- Scalability and Economic Efficiency: Cloud computing's scalability enables firms to adjust their computer resources in response to demand. This adaptability guarantees that producers have access to the computing capacity required for data-intensive activities, simulations, and analytics in addition to optimising costs.
- Integration and Data Security: Cloud computing companies take strong security precautions to allay worries about data protection. Additionally, cloud computing makes it easier to integrate data from many sources, which improves decision-making and data analytics skills.

Blockchain, Data Meshes, and Their Effect on Innovation

Concept of Data Mesh

A fundamental shift in how businesses handle data architecture is represented by Data Mesh. It promotes data as a product and calls for a decentralised, domain-oriented approach to data ownership. The problems with conventional centralised data structures are intended to be addressed by this decentralised approach (Wang et al., 2019).

The decentralised and secure distributed ledger technology known as blockchain guarantees data traceability, immutability, and transparency. Blockchain can revolutionise manufacturing by improving traceability, streamlining supply chains, and enabling smart contracts, all of which can disrupt established corporate procedures.

- Integration of Blockchain and Data Mesh: A robust and scalable data infrastructure is produced by combining the concepts of Data Mesh with Blockchain technology. Through the promotion of decentralised ownership and the use of Blockchain's security characteristics, entities can guarantee data integrity, transparency, and accessibility throughout their communities.
- Impact on Collaboration and Innovation: Data Mesh and Blockchain work together to foster a more inventive and cooperative data ecosystem. They enable organisations to get important insights, make data-driven choices, and encourage innovation in a reliable and decentralised environment by facilitating safe and transparent data sharing.

Using Big Data and Advanced Analytics to Inform Decision-Making

Big Data's Place in Manufacturing

Large-scale data gathering and processing from a variety of sources, such as supply chain management systems, industrial machinery, and sensors, is known as big data in the manufacturing industry (Goundar et al., 2021). This data's diversity and volume offer important insights into supply chain dynamics, product quality, and operational effectiveness.

- Advanced Analytics Techniques: Predictive modelling and machine learning are two examples of advanced analytics that can extract useful information from big data. Advanced analytics can improve overall efficiency, minimise downtime, and optimise manufacturing processes in the areas of quality control, demand forecasting, and predictive maintenance. Real-Time Decision-Making: Manufacturers may move quickly and decisively by utilising Big Data and sophisticated analytics in real-time. This capacity, which enables quick reactions to shifting market conditions, manufacturing bottlenecks, and quality problems, is especially important in dynamic contexts.
- Continuous Improvement and Optimisation: A culture of continuous improvement is supported by the integration of big data and advanced analytics. Manufacturers can gain a competitive advantage in the market, increase productivity, and cost savings by identifying patterns, trends, and areas for optimisation.

In summary, the technology frontier influencing the future of manufacturing is composed of these innovative concepts: Advanced Analytics with Big Data, Cloud Computing, Data Mesh and Blockchain Integration, and Additive Manufacturing. Their combined effect includes encouraging creativity, teamwork, and flexibility in addition to streamlining current procedures.

Mobile Computing as an Integrative Element

Mobile computing (Gao et al., 2021) appears as a key integrative component in the quickly evolving technological landscape, blending together a number of ground-breaking technologies to change the boundaries of innovation. A dynamic synergy is created when mobile computing interacts with disruptive technologies like virtual reality (VR), augmented reality (AR), and the internet of things (IoT). In addition to serving as endpoints, mobile devices also develop into potent gateways that increase the capability and reach of these technologies. The advancement of mobile computing stimulates the development of novel interfaces that break beyond conventional barriers.

The combination of AR and VR in mobile computing creates immersive experiences that make it difficult to distinguish between the actual and virtual worlds. These experiences are facilitated by mobile devices, which provide consumers never-before-seen levels of involvement and engagement. In a similar vein, these devices become major centres for real-time data collecting, monitoring, and control when mobile computing and IoT are combined. By employing a holistic approach to innovation, mobile computing serves as the connecting element that unites disparate technical strands into a harmonious whole, providing a single platform for original problem-solving and creative thinking.

The applications of mobile computing in big data, blockchain, data mesh, cloud computing, additive manufacturing, and advanced analytics are just a few examples of how versatile it is in innovation (Gao, Mingjin et al., 2020). It serves as a channel for collaborative design processes, instantaneous decision-making, and real-time data availability. Professionals in a variety of industries find that mobile devices are an essential tool for staying up to date with the latest technological advancements, as they provide them with access to a plethora of information and resources. This all-encompassing approach to innovation, made possible by mobile computing, not only simplifies procedures but also fosters an attitude of flexibility and responsiveness to the ever-evolving technological environment.

To sum up, mobile computing is a revolutionary force that combines and magnifies the effects of cutting-edge technologies. Mobile computing serves as a means for people and organisations to traverse the complexity of the digital frontier by introducing novel interfaces and encouraging an all-encompassing approach to innovation. In this mobile-first paradigm, innovation is envisioned as a dynamic, linked ecosystem rather than merely a process, as it emerges as a tapestry of seamless interactions, immersive experiences, and data-driven insights.

Recognising the Interaction between Mobile Computing and Technologies

Useful Mobile Computing Applications for Innovation

The relationship between mobile computing and technology offers a natural synergy that expands both domains' capabilities and promotes innovation in other disciplines. Comprehending this synergy requires acknowledging mobile computing as the glue that binds and magnifies the effects of many technological innovations, rather than merely as a stand-alone device. With the increasing prevalence and potency of mobile devices, they serve as a conduit between emerging technologies like augmented reality (AR), data analytics, the Internet of Things (IoT), and artificial intelligence (AI) (Xia et al., 20210.

These developments smoothly merge thanks to mobile computing, which creates an ecosystem of interconnected gadgets where data is exchanged without interruption. In the context of the Internet of Things, for example, mobile smartphones take on the role of central command centres, providing real-time control and monitoring of networked objects. Whether in smart homes, healthcare, or industrial settings, this interconnection improves the effectiveness and responsiveness of Internet of Things applications.

The real-world uses of mobile computing in innovation are numerous and significant. Mobile gadgets help with remote patient monitoring in the medical field. This allows medical staff to access real-time health data and make prompt interventions. Collaborative workspaces in the commercial sector are powered by mobile computing, which enables teams to communicate and work together regardless of their actual location. Mobile augmented reality apps change the way people engage with the actual environment, whether they are in training situations, games, or navigation.

Furthermore, voice recognition, predictive analytics, and intelligent personal assistants are made possible by the combination of mobile computing and artificial intelligence. By improving user experiences, this integration makes technology more user-friendly and flexible to meet different needs. For example, mobile computing is used in production as a robotic system control interface, allowing workers to monitor and modify processes while on the go.

When mobile computing facilitates the real-world implementation of innovations, innovation flourishes. The versatility and ease of use provided by mobile devices enable people to fully use the promise of emerging technologies, whether in the fields of education, entertainment, or business. Thus, the continued convergence of innovations and mobile computing opens up new avenues and streamlines daily chores. This creates an environment where innovation is not limited to a single technology but rather consists of a collection of interconnected and empowered tools. This symbiotic relationship between mobile computing and technology is likely to continue influencing how we work, live, and develop in the future.

Future Implications and Industry Advancements

Future ramifications and industry developments brought about by the swift integration of transformational technologies depict a scene in which increased connectivity, immersive experiences, and data-driven decision-making come together to completely reshape several businesses. Looking ahead, it becomes clear that data-driven decision-making will be essential to the success of organisations. The Internet of Things (IoT) and other linked devices, sensors, and systems are generating massive amounts of data that provide businesses a never-before-seen chance to gain insights. A culture of agility and adaptability is fostered by decision-makers' ability to make well-informed decisions, optimise procedures, and forecast trends thanks to the real-time analysis of large datasets.

Concurrently, the emergence of immersive experiences is set to transform other industries. Virtual reality (VR), mixed reality (MR), and augmented reality (AR) are no longer limited to specialised applications; instead, they are evolving into indispensable tools for a variety of industries. Immersion technologies are opening up new channels for connection and engagement, from improving manufacturing training programmes and product design to revolutionising retail customer experiences. The promise for improved learning, innovative problem-solving, and customer connection becomes a driving force for innovation and competitive differentiation as sectors increasingly adopt these immersive experiences.

As the backbone of industry innovations, connectivity is essential to determining the future of the landscape. A strong networking infrastructure that facilitates the smooth integration of technologies promotes cooperation, information sharing, and operational effectiveness (Yao et al., 2015). Industry 4.0, which is defined by intelligent networking systems and equipment, is evidence of the revolutionary potential of connection. The potential for real-time monitoring, predictive maintenance, and agile reactions to market dynamics becomes more than just a theoretical concept as enterprises embrace smart manufacturing, supply chain digitization, and networked ecosystems.

In conclusion, the trinity of data-driven decision-making, immersive experiences, and connectivity is inextricably linked to the implications for the future and industrial breakthroughs. Organisations that leverage the potential of these innovations could gain a competitive edge as they traverse this disruptive landscape. The future is not just a concept of technology advancement but a real and present evolution of companies that redefine innovation and operational excellence by being driven by data insights, engaged in interactive experiences, and connected through strong connections. The path ahead calls for a dynamic interaction of these components, forming a future in which industries rise above the constraints of the present and seize the entire range of opportunities presented by the rapidly advancing technological frontier.

Conclusion

In summary, the investigation of "Navigating the Innovation Frontier" has shed light on important perspectives about the revolutionary terrain of developing technologies and their significant influence on innovation. When we summarise these observations, it is clear that the necessary components include connection, immersive experiences, data-driven decision-making, and cooperative integration of state-of-the-art technologies. This all-encompassing approach to innovation emphasises the interconnection of different technology enablers while also acknowledging the complexity of the innovation process.

One important aspect that becomes apparent is the need for practical assistance when implementing innovation in organisations. This is because adopting transformative technologies successfully calls for a strategic and flexible approach. It is recommended that organisations develop a culture that values ongoing learning, encourages experimentation, and accepts change. The creation of interdisciplinary teams that can capitalise on the synergies between various technologies should be prioritised in order to make innovation a fundamental component of an organization's culture.

A dynamic and linked world is vividly shown when one imagines a future powered by data, immersion, and connectivity. In this future, organisations will use real-time insights to gain agility and competitiveness, and data-driven decision-making will become the cornerstone of strategic choices. Immersion experiences improve learning, collaboration, and engagement by redefining how people connect with technology. This vision's ubiquitous connectivity facilitates smooth cooperation and creates smart ecosystems where people, systems, and gadgets may interact with one other with ease.

Understanding that the technology frontier is dynamic and always changing is essential as we navigate the future of innovation. This necessitates a dedication to flexibility and an attitude that welcomes the ongoing investigation of cutting-edge technologies. Immersion experiences, data-driven decision-making, and networking all come together to portend a future in which innovation crosses boundaries and weaves a web of interconnected possibilities.

Essentially, "Navigating the Innovation Frontier" gives readers the theoretical know-how as well as the real-world wisdom to navigate the intricacies of the rapidly changing technology environment. Unprecedented improvements await us in the future, and those who successfully navigate it will be those that use data, connectivity, and immersion to steer towards innovative excellence. As we set out on this journey, our goal is for organisations, driven by a holistic approach to innovation, to help shape a future that is not only cutting edge in terms of technology but also sustainable and socially meaningful.

References

Bauer, Wilhelm, and Sven Schimpf. "Back to the future: scoping dynamics in industrial innovation." *IEEE Engineering Management Review* 48, no. 2 (2020): 72-82.

Gao, Bin, Zhi Zhou, Fangming Liu, Fei Xu, and Bo Li. "An online framework for joint network selection and service placement in mobile edge computing." *IEEE Transactions on Mobile Computing* 21, no. 11 (2021): 3836-3851.

Gao, Mingjin, Rujing Shen, Jun Li, Shihao Yan, Yonghui Li, Jinglin Shi, Zhu Han, and Li Zhuo. "Computation offloading with instantaneous load billing for mobile edge computing." *IEEE Transactions on Services Computing* 15, no. 3 (2020): 1473-1485.

Goundar, Sam, J. Avanija, Gurram Sunitha, K. Reddy Madhavi, and S. Bharath Bhushan, eds. Innovations in the industrial Internet of Things (IIoT) and smart factory. IGI Global, 2021.

Huang, Zhenhua, Elias Kougianos, Xun Ge, Shuping Wang, P. Daniel Chen, and Liping Cai. "A systematic interdisciplinary engineering and technology model using cutting-edge technologies for STEM education." *IEEE Transactions on Education* 64, no. 4 (2021): 390-397.

Huang, Bo, MengChu Zhou, Abdullah Abusorrah, and Khaled Sedraoui. "Scheduling robotic cellular manufacturing systems with timed petri net, a* search, and admissible heuristic function." *IEEE Transactions on Automation Science and Engineering* 19, no. 1 (2020): 243-250.

Long, Yang, Yanan Gao, and Tao Yang. "Research on ultra-reliable and low-latency wireless communications in smart factory with finite block-length." In *2018 IEEE/CIC International Conference on Communications in China (ICCC Workshops)*, pp. 158-162. IEEE, 2018.

Mishra, Shilpi, Manish Kumar, Niharika Singh, and Stuti Dwivedi. "A survey on AWS cloud computing security challenges & solutions." In *2022 6th International Conference on Intelligent Computing and Control Systems (ICICCS)*, pp. 614-617. IEEE, 2022.

Wang, Shuai, Liwei Ouyang, Yong Yuan, Xiaochun Ni, Xuan Han, and Fei-Yue Wang. "Blockchain-enabled smart contracts: architecture, applications, and future trends." *IEEE Transactions on Systems, Man, and Cybernetics: Systems* 49, no. 11 (2019): 2266-2277.

Wang, Guihan, and Liyan Zhang. "Simulation analysis of dynamic feedback correlation between advanced manufacturing technology (AMT) and product innovation performance." *IEEE Engineering Management Review* 50, no. 1 (2022): 113-131.

Xiao, Jiakai, Yang Qian, Wei Du, Yuyang Wang, Yuanchun Jiang, and Yezheng Liu. "VR/AR/MR in the Electricity Industry: Concepts, Techniques, and Applications." In *2023 IEEE Conference on Virtual Reality and 3D User Interfaces Abstracts and Workshops (VRW)*, pp. 82-88. IEEE, 2023.

Xia, Xiaoyu, Feifei Chen, Qiang He, Guangming Cui, John Grundy, Mohamed Abdelrazek, Athman Bouguettaya, and Hai Jin. "OL-MEDC: An online approach for cost-effective data caching in mobile edge computing systems." *IEEE Transactions on Mobile Computing* (2021).

Yao, Dezhong, Chen Yu, Laurence T. Yang, and Hai Jin. "Using crowdsourcing to provide QoS for mobile cloud computing." *IEEE Transactions on Cloud Computing* 7, no. 2 (2015): 344-356.

Index

D

E

F

H

I

K

L

M

N

P

R